# ROBERTSON DAVIES
## An Appreciation

# ROBERTSON DAVIES
## An Appreciation

*edited by Elspeth Cameron*

**broadview press**       *Journal of Canadian Studies*

Cataloguing in Publication Data

Main entry under title:
  Robertson Davies: an appreciation

"A journal of Canadian studies book"
ISBN   0-921149-81-6


1.  Davies, Robertson, 1913-    . I.  Cameron, Elspeth, 1943-    .

        PS8507.A95Z75  1991     C813'.54     C91-094909-3
        PR9199.3.D3Z75  1991

broadview press              OR              broadview press
P.O. Box 1243                                269 Portage Rd.
Peterborough, Ontario                        Lewiston, NY
K9J 7H5    Canada                            14092    USA


*printed in Canada*

Cover art by Anthony Jenkins

# Contents

# Introduction

The aim of this collection of essays is to enhance an understanding of Robertson Davies' work by juxtaposing a number of different perspectives on it. The collection is arranged in three sections: first, Davies' own remarks in a 1986 interview with Elisabeth Sifton, one of his editors; second, the personal reminiscences of two long-term friends—Herbert Whittaker and Martin Hunter—and two fellow Ontarians—novelist Timothy Findley and economist John Kenneth Galbraith; and third, a selection of scholarly articles and reviews that not only mark some of the high points of Davies criticism, but also demonstrate the dramatic range of opinion on his oeuvre.

The broad outlines of Davies' long, varied and productive career can be found in more than one of the essays to follow. Elisabeth Sifton offers a concise objective synopsis, for example, whereas Whittaker and Hunter subjectively recall specific details of certain stages of Davies' professional life.

What emerges from a contemplation of this collection as a whole, however, is a conviction that there have been certain pivotal points in Davies' life and career which are not necessarily emphasized in common accounts. Though the evidence provided in a collection such as this is necessarily incomplete, it appears that the three most significant of these pivotal points were Davies' decision around the beginning of the 1950s to focus his creative efforts on novels rather than plays; the mid-life crisis about which he theorized extensively just prior to the publication of *Fifth Business* in 1970; and the effect upon him of assuming the position of first Master of Massey College, the University of Toronto's graduate college, an administrative post he held from 1963 until his retirement in 1981.

Davies' shift from playwright to novelist was evolutionary rather than revolutionary. As the subject of his first novel *Tempest-Tost* (1951) indicates and his later determination to see his second novel *Leaven of Malice* (1954) performed in a stage version suggests, Davies turned to the novel not because he was attracted to a different genre, but because he sought a more effective way to accomplish what his plays were failing to do. Even playwriting was, to some extent, a compromise, since his original ambition—one he failed to fulfil because he was not talented enough—had been to become an actor. Although, as Whittaker demonstrates, Davies made a unique contribution to the establishment of theatre in Canada at a time when there was almost no infrastructure and virtually no indigenous body of dramatic works, his own plays have not been appreciated as classics. Richard Plant posits an interesting rationale for this: that Davies so distrusted the theatrical resources at his disposal that he was too heavy-handed in his directions for actors, directors and scene-setters; and, worse, that he used the theatre to vent his spleen against the lack of cultural sophistication in Canada, thereby insulting the very audiences he needed to court if the situation were to be remedied. More than a whiff of the frustration and rage that drove him from drama to novels can be caught in the remark quoted by Plant:

> I knew that there must be some other, more effective way of grabbing the public by the windpipe and making it listen to what I had to say. So I tried my hand at writing a novel, and lo! it worked.

Certainly, as Hugo McPherson noted in his early treatment of Davies' Salterton Trilogy, Davies' first stance *vis-à-vis* his public was satiric—sometimes wittily, sometimes maliciously so. But, as McPherson also notes, behind the Marchbanks mask of the satirist stood a serious writer of romance.

That writer of romance—a writer not at all cold, calculating and condescending—was not to emerge fully until *Fifth Business* (1970). Much has been said and written about the clear shift in Davies' sensibility in that novel. He himself theorized widely about middle life, particularly about how those elements of personality which had been repressed in youth were likely to rebound with renewed force to cause a mid-life crisis that disrupted and reshaped life according to new priorities. As Gordon Roper's classic essay on *Fifth Business* reveals, this radical departure in Davies' fiction resulted largely from the fact that Davies found in C.G. Jung's theories a replacement for the Freudian dynamics on which he had based the characterizations in his earlier work.

In a pattern that seems to be typical of Davies, however, such theories concealed as much as they disclosed. Hunter's stark revelation that Davies had been diagnosed as having cancer at that time goes much further towards explaining the shift from flippant satire to a more serious soul-searching exploration of the human condition than any intellectualizing about mid-life crises or Jungian theory. Indeed, there are some, like Joyce Carol Oates, who find Davies' understanding of Jung "disappointingly simplistic," an opinion which, in the end, is irrelevant to the novel Jung's theories partly inspired.

Because *Fifth Business* incorporates human warmth and vulnerability and acknowledges how painful it is to engage with life, it is more fully a novel (and less a theatrical dramatization) than Davies' previous works of fiction. To use McPherson's terms, the writer of serious Canadian romance was unmasked, and the satirist of Canadian foibles—though far from absent—was marginalised. The resulting disclosure of heart and soul (especially as it reflected a Canadian sensibility), marked the point at which critical recognition of Davies also took on a new seriousness. After Roper's article on *Fifth Business*, a large and impressive body of scholarly work quickly began to emerge, samples of which appear in this collection. That body of critical work shows promise of deepening and broadening well into the future. One of the tasks critics undertook was a return to the third Salterton novel, *A Mixture of Frailties* (1958), which appeared, with hindsight, not to be merely a theatrical satire, but to anticipate like a butterfly half-emerged from a confining chrysalis the depth and strength of *Fifth Business*. Three essays here—Clara Thomas' textual analysis, William Keith's source study and Plant's thematic one—analyze this seminal novel.

Davies' position as Master of Massey College appears gradually to have imprinted itself on the later stages of his fiction. Both Whittaker and Hunter note the shift from what Hunter terms "the attacker of conformity to the defender and establisher of tradition." The college, established by former Governor-General Vincent Massey in frank imitation of Oxbridge, secured for Davies a tiny empire without fixed style which he was encouraged to shape. Davies treated this appointment imaginatively by developing ritual ceremonies, for example, and from this base produced the steady stream of novels—

known after the fact as the Deptford Trilogy and the Cornish Trilogy—as well as a range of other works. None of these, however, displayed the touching vulnerability of *Fifth Business*. Davies as established authority (both inside Massey College and in the larger literary world) returned to the assured stance of a sophisticated man of the world, though without the pique and peevishness of his early satire.

Critical response to any writer takes on a life of its own which may bear little connection to the author's intentions. This is true in Davies' case. That he feels frustration as a result is suggested in the deprecating term "flawyers" which he uses in his interview with Sifton to describe those academic critics who pride themselves on detecting flaws in his work. Such flippancy does not do justice to the critical debates sparked by Davies' work, which are unusually intense and complex. These debates are best considered in juxtaposition with the personal reminiscences in this collection, for, even if the subjective observations of Davies' friends and admirers and Davies' own characteristic evasiveness mean that we must remain sceptical, the corroboration and contextualization of critical discussion is sometimes elucidating.

Though other critical debates might have emerged from a different selection of essays than those which follow, the issues provoked here include these: first, whether Davies' work represents a single point of view or several points of view; second, the consequent difficulty of defining Davies' ideology; third, the significance of master/apprenticeship relationships in his work; and finally, Davies' status in the Canadian literary tradition.

Just as we all attempt to find coherence in the disorder of life, critics attempt to locate a didactic programme in literary works. Davies' writings have proved to be deeply intractable in this regard. McPherson sees a serious writer of romance behind a satiric mask. Roper sees in *Fifth Business* a work structured, fairly simply, on Jung's individuation process. But Wilfred Cude sounds a clear warning in 1972: *Caveat lector* (Let the reader beware!). His important analysis of *Fifth Business* cautions against any simple reading of Davies' text (such as Gordon Roper's), since things are presented "from more than one vantage point," an important observation, and one on which much depends. In her review of *World of Wonders* (1975), Patricia Monk struggles to accommodate a jarring juxtaposition of discourses into some single meaning by crediting Davies with the deliberate intention of "[revising]...our notions of good and evil" through magician-like narrative tricks that give an illusion of formlessness. But the question is: "Did Davies *deliberately* create formlessness, or were his novels poorly crafted?" It's still a moot point. Even Davies isn't helpful. While admitting in his interview with Sifton that his novels (and trilogies) are "unplanned," he also describes the elaborate method of note-taking by which he prepares to write them and, further, admits that a novel without tricks would not be a novel by him.

In his seminal 1977 essay, Stephen Bonnycastle unmasks Davies as an unpleasant elitist. He sees all of Davies' Deptford novels as essentially a monologue advocating a repugnant anti-rationalist hierarchy. Simultaneously, James Neufeld notes the ways in which the Deptford Trilogy confounds our "expectations of continuity and symmetry" and concludes that—despite obvious framing devices—the only thing binding the trilogy together is the "egotism" of the author. This line of thought reaches its apotheosis in Joyce Carol Oates' scathing attack on Davies' "colossal vanity" in *One Half of Robertson Davies* and in Linda Lamont-Stewart's conclusion after analyzing the Cornish Trilogy that Davies' reactionary commitment to "an aristocracy of the spirit" "trivializes serious social problems" because it frees a wealthy elite "to ignore the human suffering that supports their privileged status."

Davies' comment to Sifton on such critics suggests that there is some truth in their attacks:

> I think that civilization—life—has a different place for the intelligent people who try to pull us a little further out of the primal ooze than it has for the boobs who just trot along behind, dragging on the wheels. This sort of opinion has won me the reputation of being an elitist. Behold an elitist.

A completely different perspective on this issue surfaces in Barbara Godard's two landmark essays (1984/5 and 1987)—a condensed amalgamation of these appears here—which apply the theories of Russian critic Mikhail M. Bakhtin to Davies' novels. Arguing against Bonnycastle, Godard makes a convincing case that Davies uses fiction in ways described by Bakhtin to recontextualize European traditions and authority in Canadian terms. Such techniques as "carnivalisation," embedding, doubling, framing and juxtaposing discourses, she argues, are "purposeful incongruity," which demonstrates that Davies—far from being a monologist—remains "uncommitted to a single value system." This is the line of thought also pursued by Ian Munro in his recent essay on the Cornish Trilogy. Munro sees the complexity detected by Cude (and the formlessness identified by Monk) as a deliberate and subtle deconstruction of texts by Davies which "makes us question the conventions of narrative" and, ultimately, "concerns the intelligibility of life." If Godard and Munro are right, detailed source studies such as Keith's examination of the interplay between *The First Violin* and *A Mixture of Frailties* (which alludes to it) will become increasingly necessary to understand Davies' works.

The two views—one maintaining Davies is a monologist with fixed hierarchical values and the other maintaining Davies is a dialogist pitting one authority against others without reaching fixed conclusions—are radically opposed. And our understanding of Davies' ideology depends entirely on which of the two we endorse. If he is a monologist, it follows that his world view is elitist. But, if he is a sophisticated deconstructionist, deliberately using post-modern techniques in a Bakhtinian way, he displays an ideology that recognizes the relativity, and possibly the irrationality, of life.

Central to Davies' view of life—no matter how we are inclined to view his techniques and his ideology—is the relationship between master and apprentice. Throughout his work, such relationships abound. There is evidence, too, that Davies' own life evolved through master/apprentice relationships. Hunter, for one, thought it an important enough theme to structure his reminiscence of Davies. He reports on Davies' three most important mentors: his father, Senator Rupert Davies, a self-made newspaperman; Tyrone Guthrie, the British director who first influenced Davies when he aspired to become an actor at the Old Vic in London, and later worked closely with Davies (who was "resident pedant" for him) when Guthrie came to Stratford trailing clouds of British actors to direct the first seasons of the new Shakespearean Festival in the early 1950s; and Vincent Massey, who was influential when Davies became Master of Massey College.

Professionally speaking, it was probably Guthrie who most influenced Davies with his love of theatre, his grand vision and his predilection for comedy. Massey, according to Hunter, imparted cynicism and manipulative skills. But as Hunter also suggests, Davies' career smacks more than a little of the pattern his father established. Those whose reminiscences appear here agree in one fundamental view: that Davies never really abandoned his original ambition to become an actor, that he turned his own life into a dramatic presentation by creating for himself a series of "roles" or "performances." In that sense, he, like his father, has been a self-made man.

Master/apprentice relationships are founded on inequality: the master has power, the apprentice none, though he keenly anticipates the day when he will be the master and someone else the apprentice. Lamont-Stewart maintains, further, that in such relationships as Davies depicts them "violence is implicit." Ultimately, she argues, by manipulating the narrative voice, Davies adopts the role of the master, expecting his readers to become his apprentices, a position he abuses, in her opinion, to preach profoundly anti-modern values such as anti-feminism, racism, homophobia and elitism. Others, such as Thomas, however, see Davies' portrayal of masters and apprentices as venues through which to probe questions of guilt and responsibility, which lead him to conclusions that are not judgmental in any exclusive way. None the less, there is something both chilling and compelling about Godard's description of the way in which Davies draws on the writers of the past: "he is engaged in an originating act of parricide, both killing them off, to make way for something new, and enthroning the figure of authority."

Finally, there is much dispute about Davies' position in Canadian letters. The two extremes can be found here in Galbraith's hearty endorsement of the validity of Davies' treatment of the rural Ontario milieu in which he and Davies both grew up. Without qualification he concludes that Davies' novels "will be recognized with the very best work of this century. And they will last." Oates, on the other hand, accords Davies only "modest though agreeable gifts" and deplores most of his views (she appears to see him as a monologist), as well as his "windy rhetorical conventions." She concludes, "It is grossly misleading to bill Davies as Canada's 'leading man of letters,' and he should certainly not be taken, by non-Canadians, as a 'great' Canadian writer." Others in this collection fall somewhere in between.

No matter where our opinions fall along this spectrum, Davies has emerged by general agreement as a consummate story-teller.

Almost all the contributors represented here bear witness to Davies' skills of enchantment. Perhaps Galbraith puts it best:

> Davies deals with matters far beyond the experiences of his readers; yet, you find yourself taking his word for it, according him full faith and credit. Even if he invents the way a magician practices his art, you have to believe that the invention is at least the equal of the original.

That, after all, was what he sought through acting in the first place: the power to create a reality other than ordinary reality and make other people believe in it. He failed to achieve this through acting and through his plays, but he has most surely achieved it in his novels, which descend directly from those of his own favourite author, Charles Dickens. To his critics, or admirers, or friends, Davies seems variously a Prospero, a Magus, a Wizard of Oz, a Wizard of the North, an Emperor with imaginary clothes—always a magician whose crafty tricks may be benign or sinister, but whose ability to create and sustain illusion on a grand scale is formidable.

Elspeth Cameron
University of Toronto
July 1991

# The Art of Fiction:
# Robertson Davies

*Elisabeth Sifton*

*W*hen we met in the autumn of 1986 to conduct this interview in front of an audience at the 92nd Street YMHA in New York, Robertson Davies was already famous not only as a novelist, critic, and man of letters but also as a compelling performer of literature: his readings and lectures were always given to sold-out houses. The robust presence of this "wizard of the North" (characteristically he was as gratified to inherit this title from Walter Scott as he was amused that few people any longer knew where it came from) came as no surprise: a filled out broad-chested figure, clad in slightly old-fashioned clothes (that evening he wore his signature leather waistcoat, all the better looking for age, beneath a well-cut jacket), with an easy, erect carriage, a deep, skilfully-modulated voice, fine straight nose, luxuriant white beard and hair.

"The introducer has approached me by what may be called the biographical path," Davies once wrote. "He begins by telling that I was born, and when, and where. As soon as he mentions the date of my birth I can see the audience doing a little sum in their heads, after which they look at me with renewed interest to see how I am carrying the burden of my years. He is kindness; he romps through the public details of my life, but under the circumstances I cannot laugh or weep."

*Voilà.* Mr. Davies was born in 1913 in Ontario and educated in Canada and at Balliol College, Oxford. He worked at the Old Vic as writer, teacher of drama history, and actor; it was there that he worked with Tyrone Guthrie, and there that he met his wife, whom he married in 1940. Upon his return to Canada, Davies embarked on a career as a kind of one-man Canadian cultural centre, embassy, and gadfly; apparently he had little difficulty doing several full-time jobs at once, as well as writing plays and novels, stories, lectures, and critical essays. In 1942 he became editorial writer for the Peterborough Examiner; he was the paper's editor and publisher from 1946 until 1963. He also wrote a column under the pseudonym of Samuel Marchbanks, as well as other reviews and criticism.

During the 1950s, Davies' first novels — the three that are now called the Salterton Trilogy — were published; he became literary editor of Saturday Night, for which he wrote book reviews; he was elected to the board of governors of the Stratford Shakespeare Festival, a position he held until 1971; and with Guthrie he documented, in three books, the festival's activities in its initial years. In 1959 he began another newspaper column, "Writers Diary," in the Toronto Daily Star.

In 1963, Davies moved to Massey College at the University of Toronto as Master, a position that kept him at the centre of Canadian academic life until his retirement in 1981. Meanwhile, he composed the novels of the Deptford Trilogy (Fifth Business, The Manticore and World of Wonders) and the first book of the Cornish Trilogy, Rebel Angels. Since his retirement, the best-selling What's Bred in the Bone and The Lyre of Orpheus have completed this threesome.

Throughout these years, in countless lectures, articles, and public appearances, Mr. Davies continually urged upon his sometimes unwilling, unready, or unable countrymen the delights, rewards, and indispensable glories of art. "What does Canada expect from her writers?" he asked. "Canada expects nothing from her writers. But what may Canada expect from her writers? She may reasonably expect what other countries get from a national literature. First, a sense of national character. Second, vigilance on behalf of intellectual freedom and moral vigour. Last, we may expect a true depiction of the essence of what our life in Canada is." And what kind of literature is that? "Works with completely irrefutable power to convince," he continued, "works that cause the reader to be visited, dimly, briefly, by revelations such as cannot be produced by rational thinking. Works in which you can see not yourself but, for one second, the Inaccessible. Ah, but to have glimpsed the Inaccessible is, *however imperfectly, to have gained access to it. That is what your writers can give you, if you want it, and let them know that you want it. The decision rests with you. "*

### INTERVIEWER

You've just returned from a triumphant trip to Scandinavia and also to London. In the past you've remarked that the British view of "colonial" writers was not as generous as it might be. How was it this time?

### ROBERTSON DAVIES

Well, it was a mingled greeting. A great many people were extremely kind and friendly, and of course the more informed British—that is roughly ten percent of the population—no longer regard Canadians as colonials. But some do, and one or two quite influential reviewers made it very, very clear that they expect little from Canada. One of the strangest experiences that I've had as an author was some years ago when a novel of mine was reviewed in the *Times* of London, and reviewed very favourably. But the review began with these chilling words: "To speak of a good novel from a Canadian writer sounds like the beginning of a bad joke." With friends like that, who needs enemies?

### INTERVIEWER

This travel must be gratifying, but surely it takes time and energy away from your writing, and you've told me that life has been very hectic since you retired from Massey College in 1981. How do you manage all these public engagements?

### DAVIES

It's difficult to manage public engagements particularly when you're retired. When people ask me what I'm doing, I have to tell them that I'm doing very much what I did before I retired, except that now I have secretarial assistance only one day a week. People deluge me with things to be done and when I say I am busy, they fall into extravagant mirth and shout "You can't be busy, you're *retired*!" I have been wasting my time doing things which seem to be imperative without being in the least important. I think you know that it is very unfortunate for a writer to spend too much time jaunting about talking, for although that is flattering, and it is delightful to appear before audiences and to meet people directly in this way, you really ought to be home working at your desk. Quite honestly, if you wanted to, you could as a writer spend twelve months of the year at conferences, pep groups and ginger sessions, talking to students and doing all kinds of things except your proper work. You just simply have to get down to it. Meanwhile, I have sat in a sort of pen at the Booksellers' Fair, autographing copies of bound proofs for supposedly eager booksellers, and otherwise making myself a motley to the view, as Shakespeare, who knew all about it, says. My publishers are anxious that I should rush about and talk to people but I have laid down a few ground rules: I *will not* drive wildly fifty miles at dawn in order to breakfast with fourteen librarians in a cellar somewhere, nor will I speak to schools. My agent is anxious that I should be on something called *The Today Show*, which is apparently big magic, but I daren't tell him I have never heard of it. I recall once being "cased" by one of Dick Cavett's underlings to see if I would be any good on his show, but I was found unworthy. Ah, if all this brouhaha had happened thirty years ago, when I had energy and appetite for it! As I once said of George Bernard Shaw, he bloomed at twenty, but nobody smelled him till he was forty. My scent has been even later in catching the breeze. The BBC also wanted a film about me for its *Authors and Places* series, so I had to hie me to the beautiful old city of Kingston where I grew up—a very beautiful Loyalist place, full of domes and towers and looking altogether more like Bath than a place on this continent—and revive my childhood and youth for the camera. Great fun; we had horses, and soldiers, and all sorts of gaudy delights. And the weather was good to us.

**INTERVIEWER**

What are you working on now? Or do you resist being asked this?

## DAVIES

No, no. I am at the moment winding up to write another novel, and when I say "winding up" I mean I am making notes and plans and perpetually building up what I will eventually write: that is the way I work. I make very, very careful plans and a great many notes—so many notes indeed that sometimes they are as long or longer than the eventual book. And sketches of characters and suggestions and references to things that will be useful. All that takes a long time. Getting to work on a new novel is a dismal business, for the beginnings never seem to get any easier with the passing of time. I toil like a swimmer who feels himself about to sink beneath the waves at any moment. Like all my novels, this one began with quite a simple idea, but as I work on it a mass of complexities assert themselves, and I have to struggle to keep from being overwhelmed by extraneous detail. But then—at least the way I work—when you begin to write, you can write quite briskly because you have done all the preparatory work beforehand. I hope it turns out well. But with novels, like cakes, you never know. Even when I finish a book, I'm never sure whether it is good or rubbish. This new one has a few characters of marked oddity, some explorations of realms of knowledge not visited by everybody, and a view of life and people that is decidedly unsentimental, though not wanting in pity. My books come in threes, and though not really trilogies or series, they are linked by characters and a point of view. But they are tedious about chronology: *What's Bred in the Bone* leaps backward in time from *Rebel Angels*, and this third book—its name is *The Lyre of Orpheus*—moves forward in time. If I *planned* them, this would not happen, but I don't; they just occur.

## INTERVIEWER

What gets you started? Do you start with the characters, with a situation, with a dramatic kernel of something? In the actual drafting of the text, do you start at the beginning and go right to the end?

## DAVIES

The kernel is something that recurs to me over and over and over again, that will not be escaped and that I realize finally is demanding to be written about. It may be either a picture in my mind of something happening, or an idea of something that might conceivably come about. If it is appreciably insistent, I eventually know that it must take the form of a novel and I must get busy on it. The book forces itself into my mind when I am lugging furniture or pulling weeds, and I have hopes of it. I often read, with amazement, of people who suffer from writer's block; I might enjoy a wee block, just to have time to catch my breath. I find in the initial, discovery stage that a great deal of other matter which is supportive to the kernel idea has also been building up. That's when the note-taking begins, and it moves quite rapidly. For instance I did not write *Fifth Business* until ten years had passed since I first became aware of the idea that lay behind it: it was simply a scene that kept occurring in my mind, which was of two boys on a village street on a winter night—I knew from the look of the atmosphere that it must be just around Christmastime—and one boy threw a snowball at the other boy. Well, that was all there was to it, but it came so often and was so insistent that I had to ask myself, Why is that boy doing that and what is behind this and what is going on? Then the story emerged quite rapidly.

### INTERVIEWER

When you saw those boys on the snowy street, was it a generalized Canadian street or was it a specific locale?

### DAVIES

It was the street on which I was born in a Canadian village, and it was right outside my own house. But you see, it was not anything directly associated with my own childhood because the boys were ten, eleven, twelve years old and I left that village when I was five.

### INTERVIEWER

Is it in the note-taking or in the actual writing that the characters take on their own life, or does this occur earlier?

### DAVIES

Well, you see, I hesitate to talk about this, because it sounds mystical and perhaps rather absurd, but I assure you it is not: the minute I recognized that the picture meant something I should pay attention to, the whole thing began to come to life, and I knew who the boys were and I knew what the situation was and I quickly became aware of what lay behind it. Some of it had to be invented, some of it had to be fetched up and rejected—a great deal is rejected in the course of such work—but it was all there as soon as I began to work. And when I began writing, I wrote from the beginning to the end as I always do. I know that many writers—Joyce Cary for instance—compose the principal scenes of a novel before putting the connective work around it; other people work backward and do all sort of interesting things, but I don't. I just go from start to finish, and that's the first draft.

INTERVIEWER

A number of writers who similarly go from start to finish find that their novels change enormously as they are written, surprising their creators. Have you had that experience?

DAVIES

I do know the story when I begin, but I don't know how it's going to end. I know about two-thirds of it, and then the end emerges as I go on. I shrink from saying this, but I've agreed to come here and talk about it, and it's true: I hear the story, I am told the story, I record the story. I don't pretend that some remarkable person somewhere else is whispering in my ear, or that a beautiful lady in a diaphanous garment is telling me what I should write. It is just a part of my own creative process which I am not immediately in touch with and certainly not in full control of and so the story emerges. There can be no two ways about how it's going to end. It just ends the way it's going to end. I don't think that is very mysterious, for if the story is any good, it must have an inevitability, although some critics dispute that. They say they're full of coincidence and this, that or the other; but the fact is that my life seems to be much fuller of coincidence and curious happenings than the lives of critics. What I mean is, the kind of mind which makes a critic is analytical, cool, an infinitely, unenviable, cautious mind. A recent piece of professorial criticism of *What's Bred in the Bone* was very severe with me for my attraction to arcane lore and weird belief—no use explaining that to me the arcane lore isn't arcane at all, and makes wonderful sense, and that almost all belief is strange, if you catch it with the light falling on it in a certain way. I wish professorial critics, who often write so dully, would give me the credit for a minimum of wits, and stop elevating themselves as the standard by which all belief and understanding should be measured! What sort of books would Balzac and Dickens have written if they had listened to such stuff?

INTERVIEWER

You once wrote, "All the critics in this town are the bastard children of Scotch parents."

DAVIES

Yes, critics have this nanny quality, but they vary enormously. Some are friendly and kindly, and are interested in your work and take it seriously, but the ones who get under my skin are the academic critics whose whole training is to detect faults. They call them "flaws." I call them "flawyers," which they do not like. I one time nailed one of these people and said, "Tell me of a novel that you know that is free from flaw. Now how about *War and Peace*?" "Oh, infinitely flawed." "What about *Remembrance of Things Past*, Proust's great novel?" "Oh, a mass of flaws." I think it would be splendid if we could get a committee of these wonderful people to write a flawless novel, but they won't do it and I question whether it would reach publication. The opposite sin is the creation of meaning or intent where none was planned. A Ph.D. candidate wrote of *World of Wonders* that its hero was christened Paul, and that his life story exactly parallelled that of Saint Paul! I said mildly that this had not occurred to me. He replied, with an indulgent smile, that many things appear to the critical reader of a book which have eluded the attention of the author, and that this gave the book "resonance"—for me, the resonance of a dull thud. It is extremely disagreeable to be treated as a sort of *idiot savant* who must be explained to himself and to his readers.

### INTERVIEWER

Now, the requisite *Paris Review* question: How do you write your novels? In your instance, this is a more interesting question than usual because you have an extraordinarily beautiful italic hand. Do you write the first draft of your novel longhand or do you type?

### DAVIES

I type because writing by hand I find to be a very great betrayer. If you write carefully and try to write legibly, as I do, you finish a page and think, that's a handsome page. This is absolutely wrong. Also, you can only write so long with a pen before your hand becomes tired, and then your invention begins to tire. If you type, which I do because I had my earliest training as a newspaperman and learned to use the typewriter readily, you have what you've written there before you cold and bare. Then you can go over it, and it is as though someone else had written it and you can edit it with great severity. I am a terrible fidget about *form*, and the first typed draft is often pitifully ragged and messy. But then after it goes to my secretary, who makes a clean copy, I revise extensively. The heavy work is done, but I like revising. As for editing, though I try to be stringent, you will recall that I resist your editor-like zeal for total clarity—all the lights blazing and not a dark corner to be found. I am a writer much given to light and shade, and I firmly believe that to know all is to despise all.

### INTERVIEWER

I want to ask about your early newspaper experience. Your father owned and edited a newspaper, and you became well acquainted not only with the typewriter but with the entire printing process—the linotype machines, the presses, the distribution network. How has your knowledge of the way a work of art is mechanically reproduced and distributed to the public influenced your sense of your own writing?

## DAVIES

It's influenced my writing immeasurably more than I could possibly define. When I was a boy, my father was a newspaperman, my two brothers were newspapermen, my mother was intensely interested in newspaper work, and I heard newspaper talk at every meal. In a newspaper family you learn not only all the news that's fit to print, but all the news that is *not* fit to print and you acquire an insight into human nature and the essence of a community which is very hard to acquire, I think, in any other way. I was the editor of a newspaper for twenty years. During that time I had to deal with not only the recorded news, but the news I knew about which might be supportive of the recorded news but some of which could not possibly be printed because it was so extraordinarily damaging and often wounding. You find out what people are like, and how they live, and what they're up to at night, and what goes on behind the lace curtains. The world you report is rarely more than half the world you know.

## INTERVIEWER

Presumably you also learn something about people's interest in these matters and how they respond to news.

## DAVIES

Yes, and how disagreeably they gloat over the misfortunes of their neighbours, and how they wince and scream when some folly of their own has to be reported in the paper. Oh, you can find out a lot about people running a newspaper.

## INTERVIEWER

Are these responses which you anticipate or play upon in your work as a novelist?

## DAVIES

Yes. As a newspaper editor you have to sit there in your office and listen to the knock on the door and know that some angry, offended person is going to come in and tell you about something which you never thought would have offended an angel in heaven.

### INTERVIEWER

You have combined novel-writing not only with newspaper work but also with academic work. You just spoke rather scathingly about academics. Those run-of-the-mill academics you were talking about can't have been entirely happy when you showed up in the halls of Massey College at the University of Toronto. You must have been a rather exotic bird compared to many of them. How did it go?

### DAVIES

It went extremely well. When I speak harshly of academics, I am speaking about less than fifty percent of them. Most of my academic friends are marvellous people, and it was a great pleasure to work with them and to talk with them and to hear their opinions about everything. So it was wonderful to join them, and I greatly enjoyed teaching. I liked the association with students and I liked the association with my colleagues. Not all of my colleagues, of course, took the same view I did of the kind of work I did. A few of them felt that I was a blackleg because I should have been criticizing, and I was writing.

### INTERVIEWER

What is a blackleg?

### DAVIES

A blackleg? A blackleg is a scab. It's an old term and perhaps one not familiar in the United States, but it's a common English expression. I should explain to your audiences by the way, that I am not English, whatever appearances there may be to the contrary. I am the usual Canadian cocktail—Welsh, Scots, quite a bit of Dutch, a dash of Red Indian, but no English. And all, of course, dominated by the old Empire Loyalist bias.

## INTERVIEWER

Do I hear a rumble of Canadian nationalism?

## DAVIES

Canadian nationalism is a very hot topic at present, and nationalism always brings a lot of idiots into prominence who cannot see beyond the ends of their noses. Of course we Canadians don't want to be eaten by the USA, but anybody with any wits knows the small countries—and we are small in population—must be linked with somebody, and the United States is the obvious link for us, in economic matters; as for art and literature, we are nationalist when we feel these to be in peril. I think myself lucky that in my lifetime Canadian writers have ceased to be asked by publishers in New York to change the venue of their stories to somewhere south of the border. That certainly happened to me in connection with several plays. Our independence is a dicey affair and can never be complete; who is completely independent? We just don't want to be chewed down to a nubbin.

## INTERVIEWER

Hear, hear. Now what about Marchbanks, your alter ego in the newspaper column you wrote for so many years, whom you have comment that becoming a professor "would ruin one for comprehensible writing of any kind." It didn't seem to ruin you. On the contrary, your novels got better and better while you were running Massey College. Was there some kind of synergistic interplay and feedback between your work at Massey and your novel writing?

## DAVIES

No, it wasn't precisely that. When I'd been a newspaper editor, I had been engaged chiefly in writing plays. For a variety of reasons which any playwright will understand, I decided that wasn't satisfactory and I was going to try my hand at writing novels, and I did and liked it much better.

## INTERVIEWER

What did you prefer about novel-writing?

## DAVIES

Anybody who has been a playwright, unless he's a playwright of well-established reputation, knows that his position in the theatre is a very weak one, and that the wish of the director or some important actor infinitely outweighs his; and the opinions of the money people, who always want something that's already happened to happen again, are very important. You're perpetually subjected to governance by people who haven't written the play and are trying to make it as much like some previous success as possible. That's very tedious and you get sick of it. When you're a novelist, you're writing a play but you're acting all the parts, you're controlling the lights and the scenery and the whole business, and it's your show. When it's done, one turns it over to the editors and they are delightfully kind about it and away you go.

## INTERVIEWER

You worked for many years with Tyrone Guthrie. Do you feel that the work you did with him, or with other actors and directors—indeed your theatrical work in general—has affected your novels in any way?

## DAVIES

Yes, it's affected them very strongly. I'm not in any way a devotee of realism, and the theatre is never realistic, even when it's pretending to be intensely so. It is selective, the dialogue is selective, and the dialogue in the kind of plays I like best is *immensely* selective— finely polished, and arranged to convey the greatest possible amount of meaning with the least use of words. That is what I think really good dialogue ought to be. It is not a phonographic reproduction of the way people actually talk. It's the way they would talk if they had time to get down to it and refine what they wanted to say. Working with Tyrone Guthrie was interesting because he was a man of extraordinary capacity in his dealings with comedy. He had a remarkable sense of comedy, and you couldn't work with him without being infected by it. He had not, however—I don't say this in a derogatory way, because he was a dear friend of both myself and my wife—he had not a great deal of compassion and had a weak understanding of tragedy, and you need those things if you're going to be a novelist. So that had to come from somewhere else.

### INTERVIEWER

Then compassion and a sense of tragedy go together, perhaps?

### DAVIES

Yes. True compassion—not just what Mark Twain called "leaky water works." And tragedy as purgation and exaltation.

### INTERVIEWER

Many of your readers and reviewers are dazzled by how much you know about everything, by how much they can learn about so many things in your novels—some of it quite arcane and special, some of it information that perhaps we all should know but don't. Mary McCarthy once argued eloquently that the novel is among other things a conveyor of a huge amount of social and cultural, as well as psychological and philosophical, information and truth. You can learn to make strawberry jam by reading *Anna Karenina*, as she said. Do you like the idea of instructing your readers on all that lore about gypsies or cellos or art forgery or Houdini, to name a few subjects quite randomly?

### DAVIES

Well, you see, the actual fact is that I don't. I say a few things, I provide a few details, but if I may be permitted to say so, I work on the Shakespearean plan. Everybody says, "Oh, Shakespeare must have been a sailor. Do you notice how in the beginning of *The Tempest* people cry, 'Man the bowsprit,' or 'Split the binnacle,' or whatever it is. He must have been a sailor." Others say, "No, no, he must have been a lawyer. Remember in *The Merchant of Venice* he has a scene in a law court that is quite like a law court." "No, no, no, Shakespeare must have been a soldier because he has a place where Henry V cries, 'Follow your spirits and upon this charge,/ Cry God, for Harry, England and Saint George'." It's all hooey. Shakespeare had a few telling details which he injected into his plays that made them seem realistic, and I have the same in my novels. I don't know a very great deal about anything. Indeed, the areas of my ignorance are fantastic in their scope. But you know, I have one reminiscence which has a bearing on this. When I wrote *Fifth Business*, there were some scenes in it which took place in the First World War, the experiences of a Canadian soldier. I say virtually nothing about the war except that there was a great deal of mud, that there were a lot of horses who might panic, and that most of the time it was infinitely boring. That is all. But you know, one man said to me, "Where were you during the war?" and I said, "Well, frankly, after I got here I was in the cradle." But he had fought in France and he said that it was just like that. He asked, "How did you know it was like that?" If you have the kind of imagination a novelist needs, you have a notion of why it was like that. You do not need to write endlessly about what kind of sidearms somebody takes when he goes on a night raid and that kind of thing. That creates boredom.

### INTERVIEWER

I see that, and indeed your novels are filled with the suggestive, essential detail and not the unnecessary supporting material. But they're also filled with details that I suspect you may make up. For example, in *Rebel Angels*, packing the cellos in a special poultice of horse manure to "cure" them. Do tell us....

### DAVIES

Well now, I'm not going to answer your question technically. I'll just put it to you: If you were going to bring a sick cello back to its full voice, how would you do it?

### INTERVIEWER

That's the way I'd do it. Absolutely!

### DAVIES

You ask yourself those questions and the answer asserts itself unequivocally…. Still, there must be a few tricky bits in my books or they wouldn't be books by me.

### INTERVIEWER

There are two subjects you surely know a great deal about. One is children.

### DAVIES

Children?

### INTERVIEWER

Children. Your first book was about Shakespeare's boy actors, you've written operas for children, you've taught them how to do stage work, and the childhood scenes in your novels are especially powerful. You've also said that you think great novels have a kind of "enchanter" quality. What are your notions about this kind of spellbinding magic, which, of course, children attach immediately to art?

### DAVIES

My family background was Welsh, and the Welsh are very, very fond of storytelling and tend to be rather good at it. They're also fond of children, but they are not in the modern way infinitely tolerant of children. They think children need to be *taught* and they *teach* them. They teach them very often through stories. I feel that this quality of storytelling is basic to the novelist's art. Sometimes I am asked to talk to groups of students about writing, and the poor souls are filled to the brim with all the complex business about theories and types of narrative and this, that and the other. What I say to them is, "If you're a writer, a real writer, you're a descendant of those medieval storytellers who used to go into the square of a town and spread a little mat on the ground and sit on it and beat on a bowl and say, 'If you give me a copper coin I will tell you a golden tale.' If the storyteller had what it took, he collected a little group and told them a golden tale until it got to the most exciting point and then he passed the bowl again. That was the way he made his living, and if he failed to hold his audience, he was through and had to take up some other line of work. Now this is what a writer must do." I get so sick of writers who make tedious demands on their readers and expect them to bear with them through infinitely refined analyses of meaning and this, that and the other. You really must have a story and you must tell it, or people will just put the book down and they will find it to be one of those books, unlike the ones you sometimes read about in book reviews, that once put down is impossible to take up again.

### INTERVIEWER

On the other hand, in your own book reviews you are insistent on recommending certain writers whose work is rather difficult, maybe even tiresome in patches, but well worth the effort. Surely you're not advocating merely simple stories, for after all you admire greatly some very complex and demanding writers.

### DAVIES

Yes, I do, and I admire writers who are sometimes enviably self-indulgent, like Victor Hugo. Last summer, I was rereading *Les Misérables*, and really that book has sometimes as much as ninety pages about something which just happens to interest him, a political or religious matter or something of the sort. And you think, When is he ever going to get on with the story? But the story is so good that you put up with these digressions, and also he writes so fascinatingly about his odds and ends that you can't stop.

### INTERVIEWER

He's a special favourite of yours.

### DAVIES

I'm very fond of Victor Hugo, and a book which I read when I was eleven years old and have reread many times through my life and admired enormously is *Notre Dame de Paris*. I wish that the people who see those many movies called *The Hunchback of Notre Dame* would read the novel. It's worth any of those movies twenty times over. Or a great nineteenth-century novelist like Balzac—infinitely enchanting. You cannot put him down. Even when he is telling you the details of rural newspaper publishing. Well, of course, that is very interesting. It absolutely grips you. You cannot stop reading Balzac. You cannot stop reading any of the great Russians. The great English writers: Dickens more than Thackeray, but Thackeray is much finer than some people are prepared to admit. Trollope is endlessly gripping, though it's rather crunchy granola: you chomp your way resolutely through it, and it's worth it because the story is so good. It's the storyteller's quality that they have. Nabokov said that he thought that the most important element in a novelist's armoury was what he called by a Russian word, *shamanstvo*. It means the enchanter-quality. The word *shaman* is familiar to everyone. The enchanter-quality, the ability to keep people wanting more, is not something which can be taught, and often it is associated with what critics call a "bad literary style," but it is irresistible. Dickens had it. Nobody praises Dickens' style, but who can resist his enchantment? Only professors, and only some of those.

### INTERVIEWER

These are all nineteenth-century writers. Are there twentieth-century writers who have this enchanter-quality?

### DAVIES

Yes, Evelyn Waugh, for instance. I think that Graham Greene has it also. A substantial number of the modern writers who have this ability tend to be either continental or American. I think that English writing at the moment is somewhat in a trough. There aren't the writers who grip you and hold you quite as much as there were. For instance, when Evelyn Waugh was still alive. J.B. Priestley, whom so many critics put aside, had extraordinary *shamanstvo*.

## INTERVIEWER

The writers whom you love or who impress you form one category; the writers whom you feel have influenced you form another. Bruce Chatwin once remarked that there were two ways of reading, reading for love and reading for plunder, in other words, reading to learn how writers accomplished certain effects, solved certain technical problems or just in general went about doing their work. That's a legitimate means of being influenced. Who are the writers who have influenced you? Did you become acquainted with them in your childhood or adolescence, or later on when you began writing?

## DAVIES

Well, I don't know. I'm quite often asked about influences and I don't know of influences. I can't recognize them, and if I could recognize them I would be terrified that I was copying someone else and they are inimitable. The narrative energy of Dickens and Balzac, the many-layered irony of Thomas Mann—wondrous to admire and dangerous to imitate. The only influence I can think of is...well, there are two, and they were both encountered when I was a child. One everybody knows, and that was Daniel Defoe. I used to tell young reporters that if they wanted to learn to write magnificent newspaper English they should learn to write like Daniel Defoe. None of them did. The other writer who immensely influenced me as a child, just because I loved the story rather than the style—it was a translation—is a writer named Johann Wyss who wrote *The Swiss Family Robinson*. It is a tale of infinite enchantment, and I thought, This is the way to do it, you know. He just keeps the marvels coming and coming and coming.

## INTERVIEWER

Another influence on your work that I know you've been asked a great deal about is that of Jung. Before you read Jung, you read Freud, and there are critics who say that your early work is influenced by Freud, that you can see the influence of him in the pages. Tell us about Freud first and then we'll get to Jung. How did you go from one to the other?

## DAVIES

Ah, you see, when I first went to university in Canada, we had a very fine professor of psychology. He was very keen on Freud and knew very little of Jung, and he lectured us about Freud and encouraged us to read Freud, and I did. I found Freud extraordinarily fascinating and refreshing because he seemed to find answers to questions which I had asked, and to confirm things which I had dimly suspected. In that way he was enormously helpful and enlarging to a very young man. But as time went on, I discovered that Freud's attitude toward life was what is called in the lingo of psychoanalysis "reductive." Everything is brought down to something quite small. It is as though we were all still children, whatever age we might have reached: children weeping in the darkness for some fancied trouble of the past, or some denial in love, or misery of some sort. You can get enough of that. As I read Freud and about Freud, I discovered that there were very few people who discussed Freud without taking a fearful swipe at somebody called C.G. Jung. And I wondered, why do they hate Jung so much? I must have a look. And so I began to read Jung and immediately became enchanted by him. I discovered that Jung was a man with whom I had far more basic sympathy than with Freud. Jung had, like myself, a country childhood. He grew up among country people, and farms, and farm animals, and quite simple people who worked on the land—instead of very cultivated Viennese neurotics. So his outlook on life was much more like the one to which I had been accustomed. Of course, there was the basic fact that Freud was Jewish, and the Viennese Jewish culture gave his thought a cast which I could understand and sympathize with but not enter into. Jung was Swiss and Protestant, and I could understand his sort of world-view, and the ethical background of his thinking, more readily. Also, his disposition to regard myth and legend as feeding life and springing from life, as well as being a constant source of reference and refreshment in the living of life, seemed to me to be wonderfully enriching. I became a great devotee of Jung without ever rejecting or pooh-poohing Sigmund Freud, who is one of the great liberators of the human mind.

INTERVIEWER

And without in fact undergoing any analysis?

DAVIES

Oh, no, no, no. I didn't because of the advice Dr. Jung himself gave to Laurens van der Post who went to him and said that he wished to be analyzed. Jung said "Why do you want to be analyzed?" and van der Post said, "Well, because it is one of the great experiences of our culture in our time, and I wish to share it." Jung said, "Oh my friend, don't talk like that. When something in your life becomes wholly intolerable, come to me and I perhaps will analyze you. But don't undergo this experience simply to find out what it is like. It is too demanding, too exhausting." And though he didn't say it, it is also too hard on the bystanders. This is true. I'm sure that there are people in this audience who have been associated with someone undergoing analysis. It's rough on the standers-by. So Jung simply talked with van der Post most productively and enrichingly. That is why I would never undergo a Jungian analysis. Nothing is killing me, though I am not utterly free of neurosis and foolishness.

INTERVIEWER

What do analysts say about the analysis in *The Manticore*?

DAVIES

Ah well, that has been a source of enormous pride to me. I wrote that book with a good deal of misgiving because what I had to do, or what I was attempting to do, was to collapse a Jungian analysis—the first part of it, the Anamnesis—into about a year when it would normally take two, perhaps three years. I thought, This is very daring and I'm going to get jumped on by all the Jungians. In actual fact, the book was very well thought of in Zurich, which gave me enormous pride. But it was not, as some critics who knew nothing about it said, a kind of potted course in Jungian analysis. Certainly not. It was a way of telling the story economically.

## INTERVIEWER

You were raised a Presbyterian, then confirmed an Anglican in your Oxford years. Now you talk about Christianity's failure to cope with either sex or evil—which I take to be two separate subjects?—and say that its insistence on striving to achieve perfection is perhaps misplaced or wrongheaded. You've often spoken most movingly about the powerful impulses of myth and legend, and the religious impulse in human life and art. Yet sometimes you seem a Gnostic. In your writing of recent years, how does all this fit in?

## DAVIES

That is something I think about a very great deal. I was certainly brought up a Presbyterian. In my childhood I acquired by heart a very valuable document which was called *The Shorter Catechism*. It was accepted by the Presbyterian Church and the Parliament of England in, I think, 1647. It contains 107 questions, the first of which is, "What is the chief end of man?" If you memorize *The Shorter Catechism* you have a kind of theological skeleton to work on. Later on this led me away from Presbyterianism, which I didn't like because of the predestination doctrine that goes with it. But that early doctrinal training still remains with me and I am grateful for it. When I became interested in Jung, I became interested in his attitude toward Christianity—which was a very honest one because he was the descendant of a long line of Lutheran pastors; so he was not an enemy of Christianity, though he recognized certain restrictions in Christianity which I think are becoming more and more apparent as the present century moves on. One is the rather meagre place it seems to have for women and all that women imply. I don't mean women as adversaries or as people different from men, but women as people who have extraordinary things to contribute to the great mass of civilized thinking, feeling, and living. Unless Christianity can reconcile itself to women as it has not done up to now, I don't see how it can continue to maintain its hold over thoughtful people. As for Gnosticism, I was once accused by the chaplain of Massey College of being a Gnostic. He was very angry with me indeed. But part of being Gnostic was using your head if you wanted to achieve salvation or even a tolerable life. That is something which the Christian church tends rather to discourage. Salvation is free for everyone. The greatest idiot and yahoo can be saved, the doctrine goes, because Christ loves him as much as he loves Albert Einstein. I don't think that is true. I think that civilization—life—has a different place for the intelligent people who try to pull us a little further out of the primal ooze than it has for the boobs who just trot along behind, dragging on the wheels. This sort of opinion has won me the reputation of being an elitist. Behold an elitist.

### INTERVIEWER

In a book of essays by Robert Louis Stevenson entitled *Men and Books* (long out of print, alas), there is an essay in which he expresses the notion that Scottish writers are more akin to North American than to English writers. Do you think that's true? As a Canadian writer, do you feel more affinity with Scottish, Celtic, or American writers than with the English?

### DAVIES

Well, no. Rather disappointingly, no. I'm very interested in the writing that goes on in Scotland and indeed in all the Celtic countries and of course in Ireland. I do not respond quite so immediately and warmly to writers in the United States, because their concerns are different from mine and their approach to them is different from mine. They seem to be infinitely concerned with very subtle details of feeling and life. I had this exemplified, for instance in many stories in *The New Yorker* where whether the family will have pumpkin pie or something else on Thanksgiving Day is a decision with infinite psychological and sexual repercussions. I take this quite seriously. I admire their subtlety but I get so sick of it. I wish they would deal with larger themes.

### INTERVIEWER

I hope you don't think *New Yorker* writers are representative of American culture across the board.

## DAVIES

Perhaps not. I just see their stories every week because I've been taking the magazine forever and I haven't the wits to stop.

## INTERVIEWER

Saul Bellow once said—and was roundly criticized for it—that American writers, presumably excepting himself, fail to grapple with what he called the central human enterprise. Grappling with the essential human enterprise may be a numbing matter, but what—in the end—*is* the aim of the novelist? You once wrote to me, "I love to make people laugh but the pull is to tears." You have also said that you write comedies, yet sometimes there is a strong tragic element in your books. Certainly they all seem to be about the central human enterprise. Then I found in one of your books the statement that novelists would be wise to explain to the readers that life is a damn rum thing.

## DAVIES

Yes. A fearful mingling of comedy, tragedy and melodrama, which is the stuff of so much of human experience.

## INTERVIEWER

Do you write comedies or do you write tragedies?

## DAVIES

I suppose I write comedies. My pull is toward comedy. And I have a very high opinion of comedy: comedy is fully as revealing in its probing of human problems as is tragedy. The thing about comedy which I greatly value is that it is infinitely harder to fake than tragedy. I have not often pulled out the *vox humana* and the *voix céleste* stops, but I know I have made quite a few people laugh, and that is not the easiest thing to do. It is extremely easy to be gloomy and to say, this is a terrible situation and everybody has got to be serious about it, and because I'm being serious about it, I am a writer of consequence.

## INTERVIEWER

Nietzsche said, "Guilt is a substitute for thought."

## DAVIES

Yes, indeed it is. But to see that life is funny and not to mock or jeer at somebody's predicament, cruelly and without understanding, simply because some aspects of it are funny—that takes a bit of doing. I saw an instance today on Fifth Avenue, a situation that was either comic or tragic depending on how you want to take it. This girl was sitting there in the rain begging, and she had a big sign which said what her trouble was. It was a quite ordinary tale of betrayal and misery and this, that and the other—if it was true, and I don't know if it was true. But the person sitting in the rain looking wretched, even if she was not an honest beggar, was tragic. That someone of her age should be sitting on the sidewalk begging may mean not that she can't do something else, but that she has chosen to do that. It's tragic. You have to balance these two things against one another. Life is, as you said, a very rum thing.

# Robertson Davies

*Timothy Findley*

The theatre has always played a central role in Robertson Davies' life as a writer. Whether as critic, playwright, or novelist, the focus of his imagination has been the stage. His earliest publication was a thesis on the subject of *Shakespeare's Boy Actors*. In his latest novel, *The Lyre of Orpheus*, one of the salient ingredients is the creation of an opera. In the interim, a dozen plays and more have seen the light of day, and some—such as *Overlaid* and *Eros at Breakfast*—are considered to be classics.

As a critic, aside from generous helpings of amusing comment on things theatrical in *The Diary* (and *The Table Talk*) *of Samuel Marchbanks*, Robertson Davies has also given us a trilogy of studies describing the creation and early years of the Stratford Festival. In 1983, he published *The Mirror of Nature*, an exploration of nineteenth century theatre and, not incidentally, a perfect example of Robertson Davies' unique approach to education as entertainment.

Still, as readers, we receive the greatest bonus from Davies' love of theatre when we come to his novels. Each and every one of them, from *Tempest-Tost* to *The Lyre of Orpheus*, is laced with a wealth of theatrical anecdote and information. Theatre and its accoutrements are also the principal source of Davies' vocabulary and imagery. In all his books, performance plays a major role. Seances, circuses, sermons and disguises abound. Some of his novels are peopled with characters whose whole lives revolve around the theatre and its various activities: singers, actors, writers, directors and magicians.

We know that Robertson Davies himself was once an actor. Once—and still is, I suspect. Recent photographs reveal not only a potential Lear and Falstaff—but an aging Petruchio and an unrepentant

Benedick. And why not? Each of these characters is possessed of a mighty gift for words.

More evident, however, than any of these, is what can be taken as the mask of Prospero.

Think of Prospero on his island—shipwrecked and in the company of the spirits he has released from the earth and the air. He creates a multitude of theatres and conjures a multitude of characters with which to people them. And this is precisely what Robertson Davies has done. His "island" is his integrity. His "shipwreck" is the necessary and emphatic seclusion of his profession. His theatres are everywhere and anywhere he bends his eye. His characters must number in the hundreds, now—just as his audience numbers in the tens of thousands.

Not his readership—but his *audience*.

The audience is always there. In his plays, of course, it is implied. But in his prose—where the audience cannot be implied—Davies creates it. He makes it a part of what he writes. Someone is always *telling*. Perhaps his characters are performing a play. Or researching a book and therefore going about *soliciting* the telling. Or one of them writes—or is about to write—his autobiography. Another is telling his story to—and having his story told by—a psychiatrist. An audience is always there as the *telling* unfolds.

*You can always read a Robertson Davies novel aloud.* Pauses, silences and all. Because he was an actor. An actor knows how important cadence is—cadence and rhythm. Timing.

But Robertson Davies' books are not just plays in disguise. What they are are *theatres*. Robertson Davies, in that respect, is not unlike an actor-manager, which means he not only gets to choose the *vehicle*, but he also gets to design the sets and costumes, audition the actors and, later on, direct them. Above and beyond all else, he always gets to play the leading role himself!

Luckily for us, one leading role is tailor-made for Robertson Davies. It is the role of *he who tells*.

# The World of Wonders of Robertson Davies

### *John Kenneth Galbraith*

**M**any years ago I learned that nothing calls forth more pleasure than the perceived failure of a presumptively educated man to know what he is supposed to know. I gave such pleasure some ten years ago when a friend of marked scholarly attainment discovered that I did not know about Robertson Davies. "And you a Canadian!"

I've since read all of Davies' non-dramatic works, and I now find occasional reward myself in encountering scholars presumably well grounded in modern language and literature who do not know Davies, or who dissemble in a highly transparent way when asked if they do. They should, indeed, be ashamed; he is one of the most learned, amusing and otherwise accomplished novelists of our time and, as I shall urge, of our century.

As to my own early ignorance, I do not admit to any special guilt because of being a Canadian. Though I am fond, in a normal way, of the land of my birth, I have never set store by that branch of literature which seeks a special Canadian identity, psyche or scene. The country is geographically too vast and ethnically too diverse to allow of anything of the sort. Robertson Davies' novels have their setting in Canada, but they are for the world.

Davies' most notable achievement is his Deptford Trilogy—*Fifth Business, The Manticore* and *World of Wonders*—all of which touch upon the life of a schoolmaster, one Dunstan Ramsay, who comes (or perhaps escapes) from a small town in southwestern Ontario. The imaginary Deptford is closely modelled on Thamesville, Ontario, a village of 500 souls some 20 or 30 miles from the slightly larger town of Dutton (population around 800 in the early part of the century) near which I was born and to which I journeyed by horse and buggy for my high school instruction.

Everything about Deptford-*cum*-Thamesville has a powerful ring of truth. The social hierarchy of Thamesville was like Dutton's; similarly, the resulting social tensions among the young. Political and other civic responsibilities were entrusted to the same solemn and extensively self-selected leaders; a rewarding sense of superiority was provided by the same jokesmiths, drunks, idlers and idiots. The Protestant denominations were the same in both towns, and the congregations were differentiated not by doctrine or faith—matters that no one discussed, much less understood—but by accident of birth. In both towns there was a deep concern for third-person misbehaviour. Sexual intercourse between consenting adults duly united in matrimony was severely suspect; any other variation was a subject for hushed but obsessive conversation: a terrible thing made worse by the frequency of occurrence. In one novel Davies tells of the prayer of the good Protestants who thus digressed: "O God, forgive me, but for God's sake keep this under Your hat."

Davies' father was the editor, publisher and owner of the weekly newspaper in Thamesville, but when his son was still young, he departed for the more considerable town of Renfrew northwest of Ottawa. It is, therefore, of a schoolboy's memories of a small town that Robertson Davies writes. He went on to Upper Canada College, the most unabashedly elitist of Canadian preparatory schools, and to Queen's University and Balliol College, Oxford. While at Oxford, he became interested in the theatre, and in the years just before the outbreak of World War II, he went to London, where he had small parts and a peripheral role in stage management at the Old Vic and in its theatre school. In later years he has written plays with, one judges, consistently disappointing results. (His productions have had limited audiences, limited runs or both.) But his knowledge of the theatre has provided him, no reader can doubt, with both material and mood for his novels. One sometimes imagines, on reading them, that he is seeing it all as on a stage.

Davies returned to Canada to become literary editor of *Saturday Night*, the Canadian journal of the arts, politics, public affairs and good thoughts, and editor and eventually publisher of the *Peterborough Examiner*, an evening newspaper in a city of some 50,000 people in the scenically attractive but agriculturally unpromising countryside 75 miles northeast of Toronto. In his 20 years at the *Examiner*, he made it into one of the best newspapers in Canada or on the continent by the simple device of insisting (as he has said) that the standards of excellence claimed by papers in New York, London or Zurich were equally applicable, if not always equally achievable, in what the untactful could call the Canadian backcountry. One reason that the paper was good was his own writing—sharp, amusing and rich in fantasy. These articles were later assembled into books purporting to be observations on the life, times, reflections and encounters of one Samuel Marchbanks.

Then, in 1962, Davies quit the routine of a newspaperman to become a professor of English at the University of Toronto and master of its Massey College, a relatively new institution devoted to graduate study. His example is one that all in the newspaper business might contemplate.

The first of the Deptford Trilogy, *Fifth Business,* came out in 1970 to a select audience; the other two came along in the five years following. The years at the university also brought a notable volume of essays, literary criticism and casual writing. Now another novel, *The Rebel Angels*, has made its appearance. It is obvious that he has carried over into his literary life the work habits of a newspaperman, and one imagines that Davies has been subject to some criticism for his offhand attitude toward the academic union rules. In the academic community anyone who writes too much or too well is in trouble.

Davies is a fine writer—deft, resourceful, diverse and, as noted, very funny. But his claim to distinction is his imagination, which he supports by a range of wholly unpredictable information. *Fifth Business* is the autobiography of Dunstan Ramsay, the longtime history master and onetime headmaster of a school for privileged boys in Toronto; it is written as a protest to the present headmaster against the account given of Ramsay's life and services on his retirement in 1969. (It could be the longest communication in the history of such discontents, and both the reader and the author forget for long chapters that it is so intended.)

The school actually figures only marginally in the story, which sketches both Ramsay's overseas service in World War I, when, slightly to his horror, he wins a Victoria Cross (and loses a leg), and his sad, affectionate association with one Mrs. Dempster (whose mental illness and confinement he traces to an accident for which he feels a continuing responsibility). There is more than a suggestion here of Davies' interest in psychology, which becomes a major theme in his later novels. But Ramsay himself has a more esoteric interest— that is, religious history and, particularly, the lives and times of the saints, a subject which seeps extensively into the novel.

In *World of Wonders,* the last volume of the trilogy, Mrs. Dempster's son (she was married to an aggressively mean local preacher) tells the story of his life as a famous magician, a profession he entered after he was abducted at an early age by a carnival coming through the town of Deptford. Here Davies reveals what seems a truly astonishing knowledge of the principles and practice of magic and assorted sleights-of-hand—and, if less surprisingly, a great knowledge of the theatre. But to mention these subjects is to do less than justice to the range of Davies' information.

Fitzgerald, Hemingway and even Faulkner dealt with a world to which the reader feels some connection. Similarly located and circum-stanced, one might see what they see. Davies deals with matters far beyond the experiences of his readers; yet, you find yourself taking his word for it, according him full faith and credit. Even if he invents the way a magician practices his art, you have to believe that the invention is at least the equal of the original.

The new novel, *The Rebel Angels*—no one should try to explain Davies' titles—yields to none of the others in either diverse and esoteric knowledge or complexity of theme. Its principal setting is the College of St. John and the Holy Ghost, one of the older church-related colleges of the University of Toronto and known to all but its rector as Spook. The action spills over into a neighbouring college called Ploughwright, which bears a certain resemblance to Massey College. (I imagine that the name, Ploughwright, owes something to the once great Massey-Harris farm equipment company that provided the Massey endowment.)

The story concerns the intricately intertwined lives of Maria Magdalena Theotoky, a supremely beautiful graduate student of Hungarian, Polish and Gypsy origin, who has a special interest in Rabelais; the Reverend Simon Darcourt, who teaches New Testament Greek; Brother John Parlabane, a brilliantly articulate and profoundly troublesome dropout from academic and religious life; and, although the list is far from complete, a highly offensive professor of Renaissance European culture and related matters named Urquhart McVarish.

The story is told in alternating chapters by Maria Theotoky and Simon Darcourt, and the device allows two different accounts and perceptions of the same flow of events. It is less confusing, once one becomes accustomed to it, than might be expected; in fact, it serves exceedingly well. The events proceed from the death of one Francis Cornish, who has made his businesslike nephew his executor and three professors (including McVarish and Darcourt) the advisers on the disposition of his estate, which includes a vast, uncatalogued collection of paintings and old and distinguished books and manuscripts. Events continue with almost everyone falling in love with Maria or having their lives hilariously disrupted by Parlabane. The book then proceeds through college dinners and Gypsy customs to an extravagant homosexual liaison and to a murder and a suicide. The lovely Maria then, in the only commonplace development of the novel, marries the most unexpected of her suitors.

I could be the only reader of the novel who will feel any twangs over the nasty McVarish's ultimate fate. He claimed to be a descendant of Sir Thomas Urquhart, the noted Scottish translator, something his colleagues much doubted, as do I. It seems more probable to me that Davies named him after my great-uncle, once-or-twice-removed, Thomas Urquhart, who was Toronto's entirely reputable mayor early in the century. If I'm right, McVarish and I would be distant cousins.

There is a convention that, in describing a novel, one should not give away the plot. But the attraction here for me is in the style of the story, the fun, and in the truly massive array of information which the book, like its predecessors, conveys: the lore of the Gypsies of eastern Europe; the scientific investigations of human feces; the work and times of Philippus Aureolus Paracelsus and of Rabelais; the theory and practice of shoplifting; the manner and morals of art collectors and their dependent scholars; and much, much more.

It is fair to say that one does not ever come into close proximity with Davies' characters. Maria Theotoky is exceedingly beautiful—so one is repeatedly told. And sexually very compelling. But the reader must take the author's word for it; her beauty and sexuality do not otherwise emerge. And with the others on the stage the reader in the audience is never deeply involved. I do not offer this as a criticism; for me at least it is pleasant to read of people who are immensely knowledgeable and interesting whom I am not impelled either to love or to hate.

Not all of the events in a Davies novel, as distinct from the information, are plausible. In *World of Wonders* the young Dempster, who eventually becomes Magnus Eisengrim, the master magician, is kidnapped from Deptford by a carnival company after a homosexual rape by one of its members. But in real life the criminals would not have escaped. They would have been pursued relentlessly anywhere in the Dominion, as it was then called, and with a certain breathless appreciation. Crime was rare and respected then.

Dunstan Ramsay's war wound and his long survival in a coma under the care of a lovely English nurse also take some believing. So, I thought, does the seduction of Maria in *The Rebel Angels,* and so does quite a bit of *The Manticore,* the second novel in the trilogy. In it, David Staunton, son of Dunstan Ramsay's friend and rival, explores through Jungian analysis his response to the death of his father, who for unknown reasons drove his Cadillac at high speed off a dock and deep into Lake Ontario. But again, if all novels excluded the unlikely, the production of them would drop rather more severely than new housing starts. That brings me back to my own field of learning, one of the few to which Robertson Davies almost never adverts.

In economic prediction there is, as all but some financial reporters and the hopelessly gullible know, a large element of wishful thought, as is now evident in the Reagan economists' account of the benign consequences of a large deficit. In literary matters things are quite different.

I have never met Robertson Davies. Making allowance for our joint provenance in the flat and generally fertile countryside of southwestern Ontario and some distant association with the same university, I can still be completely objective on the future of his novels. They will be recognized with the very best work of this century. And they will last. And those who say that they do not know about Robertson Davies will, in the years ahead, be a source of even more pleasure than was I when I so confessed.

# Rob Davies: Pioneer Playwright

*Herbert Whittaker*

I revere the international novelist that Robertson Davies' extraordinary talents have made him today, but I retain a soft spot for the pioneer Canadian dramatist I knew him as first. Our introduction was a letter dated March 17, 1946, from the editor of *The Evening Examiner*, Peterborough, to me as entertainment editor of *The Gazette*, Montreal, asking help in bringing his plays to the stage.

Identifying himself as a mutual friend of Grant Macdonald, Robertson Davies explained: "I have been writing plays for some time now and have some one-actors on Canadian themes on hand.... I would be most grateful if you would tell me where they should be sent." Macdonald was a war artist for *The Gazette* but he could be persuaded to draw for the theatre pages I edited, as his pre-war reputation had been won in London's West End.

To be a playwright in Canada was even more difficult then than it is now. Sir Barry Jackson, of England's trail-blazing Birmingham Repertory, had warned the Dominion Drama Festival (D.D.F.) that it could not develop a national theatre without its own playwrights. The D.D.F. went about compensating for this deficiency, but cautiously.

The D.D.F. by this time was no minor affair, but a national expression of Canada's need for its own theatre. It had come into being in 1933, when the Great Depression of 1929 ended our dependence on touring companies. The Earl of Bessborough, as governor-general, was easily persuaded to inaugurate a competitive festival for the many resulting non-professional community and Little Theatre groups. It had grown to involve theatrically-minded Canadians from coast to coast in local, preliminary and final competitions which reached a high level of excellence by the half-century mark, when the Canada Council came into being to support professional effort.

The outcome of that 1946 letter from Peterborough was a rare evening of one-act plays by Robertson Davies, presented at the Montreal Repertory Theatre's Guy Street Studio. Of the loftier founding members of the D.D.F., the M.R.T. was the most sophisticated, drawing on English and French Montrealers in a wide variety of presentations from Shakespeare to Obey to revue, but also heeding Sir Barry's call for indigenous playwrights. Davies' evening of plays illustrated his style and interests happily. *Hope Deferred* defends the theatre against its first enemies in New France, when Count Frontenac was blocked by the Church from staging *Tartuffe*, a notoriously anti-clerical satire by his contemporary Molière. The second, *Overlaid*, which had already won the Ottawa Little Theatre Play Contest, proclaimed the reverence for great art by the true-at-heart, represented by an old man wearing white gloves to listen to the Metropolitan Opera broadcast. The third was quite different, being a vaudeville set inside the human body. *Eros at Breakfast* had also been staged by Ottawa and was to represent Canada in the international one-act play competition in Edinburgh. So its author made a brief return to British shores as a playwright, albeit a non-professional one.

Robertson Davies enjoyed advantages few other Canadian playwrights had. His exposure to theatre in his Canadian childhood had since been sharpened by practical experience with the Oxford University Dramatic Society and then in one of the most-admired theatres, London's Old Vic, and with no less a figure than Tyrone Guthrie as mentor. His Oxford doctorate, a most perceptive work called *Shakespeare's Boy Actors*, won him the Old Vic posting: part small-part actor, part literary dog's-body. From that period survives his prologue to Oliver Goldsmith's *The Good Natur'd Man*, which began:

"Since first Man was, the Drama's task has been
Aptly to mirror Life's fantastic scene."

It then whipped on to the Restoration:

"Playwrights appear'd, a wild ungovern'd genus
Who make a molehill of thy Mount of Venus."

And wound up present-day-style with the admission:

"Applause we crave, from scorn we take defense
That have no Armour 'gainst indifference."

Young W. Robertson Davies was speaking for all fellow play-wrights there and not just for Goldsmith. He had signed on as one of the breed and was headed back to Canada, practically virgin territory for playwrights. The Old Vic not only won him the approval of the great Guthrie, but it also gave him a prize more valuable than that. He wooed and won a beautiful student actress named Brenda Mathews. Having acted in her native Australia, she was accepted into the Old Vic as actress and wound up as its first woman stage manager when the regular staff went off on a European tour. (Its youngest and prettiest too, I'll be bound).

After those Montreal one-acts at the Montreal Repertory Theatre, we climbed some tall stairs to Walter McBrome's apartment over the Guy Street studio theatre. It must have been Saturday night when we all got together, for Saturday night was a great time for late night parties. We shared our little celebration with Amelia Hall, who had first played Hepatica in *Eros at Breakfast*, and Leo Ciceri, who was Rob's Count Frontenac. Both were to remain mutual friends. That night Rob and I found we had much more in common than Grant Macdonald's friendship.

Our mutual enthusiasms might be listed, in part as The Theatre Theatrical, British Theatre Theatrical and, in particular, The Theatre Theatrical of Sir John Martin-Harvey, whose earlier tours had intro-duced us to such joys. What we also shared that moment was the Dominion Drama Festival, in which both of us competed as directors. And, oh yes, Rob Davies and I were busy newspapermen on the side. That Montreal meeting launched a correspondence which was to flower into friendship and outlast his days in theatre.

Where, he asked, for instance, could a pioneer Canadian play-wright get his work staged, beyond the annual competition of the D.D.F.? Well, summer theatres were willing to risk a new script occasionally. I introduced the Davies to the Brae Manor Playhouse, Knowlton, an off-shoot of the Montreal Repertory Theatre and a great place to spend a holiday directing eager young talent in ideal circum-stances. The Davies, director and actress, enjoyed doing *The Late Christopher Bean*, Molnar's *Olympia* and, eventually, Davies' *At My Heart's Core*.

Reading the script under high old trees, breaking for lunch in the dining-room of the Sadlers' old house, assembling in the tiny play-house the townsfolk had built for them, working with young student actors who were so eager to show off well; this was theatre at its most idyllic. The Davies made more good friends in Filmore and Marjorie Sadler, the Christian Science couple who loved everything about theatre but ran a very strict establishment. Nor were these just student actors' shows, for older actors came to share this summer season, including Amelia Hall, Leo Ciceri, Ian Fellowes, Betty Wilsen and Maud Whitmore. Cocoa and theatre-lore rounded up each evening and Rob Davies held the company spell-bound nightly. He was already teaching theatre to the young, an occupation which was to replace his original career in newspapers.

But it was Kingston's International Players who gave that former Kingston resident his full-length debut in 1948. Robertson Davies rose to the occasion brilliantly with *Fortune My Foe*. Set against the Kingston sky-line (a set designed by Grant Macdonald) it set in opposition the young professor about to succumb to the strong pull of the United States and a Czech puppeteer who expressed the country's great need for artists to remain here. It spoke directly and originally to this national dilemma.

The year 1949 was a great one for our new dramatist. It was the year of the Massey Report on the Royal Commission of the National Development of the Arts, Letters and Sciences, precursor of the Canada Council. Robertson Davies was asked to speak for the theatre. He attested wittily (in the persona of Samuel Marchbanks, his testy alter ego in *The Examiner*) and soundly to the importance of the D.D.F. and the Canadian Broadcasting Corporation dramas. As Marchbanks, he pleaded for more spacious playhouses, to replace the tiny theatres then the rule: "If you step into the wings suddenly," he said, "you will fracture your nose against the wall." Well, our playhouses have got ever larger since Marchbanks spoke up, but their wings are still clipped, which is perhaps why theatre in Canada never seems to take off as we hoped. Davies called out for the creation of a National Theatre back in 1949. Few of us recognized that in the D.D.F. we had the only kind of national theatre we were capable of then.

*Fortune My Foe* and *The Table Talk of Samuel Marchbanks* were both to be published that year; but perhaps even more satisfying for his soul was the recognition he gained as a director of Shakespeare. His staging of *The Taming of the Shrew* not only went to the D.D.F. finals at the Royal Alexandra Theatre in Toronto, but won for him the Louis Jouvet trophy for direction. There was also the satisfaction of seeing his wife, Brenda, play Katharina with such distinction, while he himself revelled in the role of the Tailor, in mauve.

I witnessed this triumph as new drama critic of *The Globe and Mail*, Toronto. One of the advantages of my move was the proximity of Peterborough, which meant a closer friendship with the Davies family. Davies as family man, in constant banter with three lively little girls, was a joy to witness, particularly when he engaged the eldest, Miranda, who was able to banter back. She would taunt him with her teacher's opinions of his fiery proclamations and he would rise to the occasion gleefully with his opinions of her teacher, to the delight of the rest of us. I shared my visits with our beloved Helena Ignatieff and, on one occasion I recall, with her bright young nephew, 11-year-old Michael. I remember that because, leaving that late fall, we ran into a blizzard which had young Michael and I manfully pushing the car out of the ditch, twice.

One summer later, at the 1950 Peterborough Summer Theatre, I reviewed *At My Heart's Core* under Michael Sadlier's direction, with a cast which included Brenda Davies, Kate Reid and Clarine Jackman, playing the territory's three literary ladies of note. In a part written for John Primm, the Devil appears to tempt them from wasting their talents on wilderness air. Further runs at Niagara Falls, Ontario, and again in Peterborough heralded the arrival of a full-fledged summer theatre in Peterborough, which gave great satisfaction to the Davies. And, as editor and critic of the local paper, Davies was able to point out the importance of theatre to the region without undue conflict of interest. Actually, that Peterborough Summer Theatre made a notable addition to the Ontario straw-hat scene. Run by Michael Sadlier and Bruce York, it attracted the best of Toronto actors, including Robert Christie, Kate Reid, Gerry Sarracini, Barbara Hamilton, Frank Perry, Anna Cameron and Charmian King, all of whom were invited to tea by Brenda Davies. Those were good, rich summers for the Davies, which I also shared as reviewer for *The Globe and Mail* and as friend of the *Peterborough Examiner*'s critic.

Davies decided to entrust his new major work *King Phoenix* to the North Toronto Theatre Guild, with myself as director. This play showed another, darker side of Davies, as he delved back to his Welsh origins to find high drama. It revealed the original King Cole as a less than jolly monarch in Druidic Britain, menaced by a particular Druid named Cadno, much given to magic. My correspondence with Davies now took on a very serious tone. On St. David's Day, 1950, he wrote:

> I am glad that Hartmann is now happy [as Cadno]; Cadno is a Fascist, just as the Pope is a Fascist for everybody's good. Yes, Cole's life is a dream; we get this worried feeling when things are going amiss with us—this feeling that we are in the grip of illusion, and the awakening will be chilly and horrible. Cole wonders if the hereafter to which he will awaken will be some ghastly cosmic icebox—he is suffering from fear and self-doubt, as even strong men do when crooks like Cadno have been badgering them.

To which he added "I hope this is clear; if not say so and I shall try again. I am anxious to give any help to the actors I can." His help and understanding paid off for one of those actors. Ron Hartmann was to dramatize and produce Davies' Deptford Trilogy for the CBC some years later, with marked success.

Davies' letters at this time also betrayed his vulnerability in the face of public adjudication by outsiders, an ordeal Canadians were exposed to in D.D.F. days. *King Phoenix* was to face one Maxwell Wray in Peterborough. "A man who confided that he expected dreadful things from 'those Canadian amateurs'," a pained Davies wrote,

> ...and proceeded to show us...with the technique of a music hall artist of the third rank, just what he had expected. It was too shaming.... He is typical of thousands of professional theatre people in that he howls piteously for new plays but does not really like anything which is not already familiar to him.... He has already faulted two of my plays for their failure to conform with some unexplained ideal of what a play should be.

After which he drew a breath and added: "Does this sound like the anguished scream of a slighted playwright? Very probably that is what it is."

Maxwell Wray fulfilled Davies' worst expectations by so pulverizing *King Phoenix*. I think the word he favoured was "artsy," one much in favour in those philistine days. The author, though declaring himself pleased with the Guild's production, staged it himself the following year at Peterborough, but won no kinder acceptance from Wray's successor. We recognized the difficulty of finding suitable experts for the long haul across the country then, but found it paining to accept the more clownish ones.

Rob Davies always had a problem accepting fools gladly, and still does, but the base performances of regional adjudicators did not sour the national importance and influence of the Dominion Drama Festival for him. He made considerable input not only as a contender but also as a Governor of the Board. On one occasion, he and I were to share one of the crises of that beloved organization. Funding a national body drove the D.D.F. to seek corporate sponsorship at the half-century mark. Seagrams, the distillers, responded handsomely, but naturally expected the Festival's top award to be named for one of its products, so "Calvert" was to replace "Bessborough" as the name of the festival's top honour. Where was the Bessborough Trophy to find a place of distinction? Davies and I, as the two newspapermen on the Board, were consulted and asked to form a committee of two to solve the Festival dilemma.

It didn't take us long. With our common respect for classic theatre, we seized the opportunity to lure Canadian groups across the country into that field. So we suggested that the Bessborough Trophy be designated the principal award of the regional festivals for the best presentation of a classic play, to be judged by the preliminary adjudicator and announced at the finals. If there had been any friendly rivalry between us, as competitors in the D.D.F., our choice inadvertently neutralized it. To match his triumph at the 1949 finals with *The Taming of the Shrew*, my *Uncle Vanya* was to win the first new Bessborough Trophy. (Later, I even won a couple of Louis Jouvet trophies to match his).

The public humiliation Davies endured over his plays, one way and another, was enough to set a man to writing novels. Not only would the less immediate demands of audience reduce the strain, but the novel also allowed the writer to relax into those perspicacious asides and observations on which the more impatient stage frowns. If Davies' first publisher, Clarke, Irwin, did not point out that the risk of acceptance for novelists was so much less than for dramatists, later publishers did. And waspish critics emphasized the point: "from scorn we take defense."

Since he was an incredibly active journalist, editor, columnist, essayist and critic, Robertson Davies did not have to confine his social commentary to plays. If he was not reaching the public he wanted, he could put aside his passion for theatre to make himself heard elsewhere. And even as a novelist he didn't need to abandon the stage entirely. His first novel, *Tempest-Tost*, with its handsome cover by Grant Macdonald, had some gentle fun at the expense of the community theatre. He picks Salterton, which sounds very much like Kingston, as his setting for the organization of an out-door production by its Little Theatre of Shakespeare's *The Tempest*, an excellent subject for ridicule to a man who understood and respected the Bard as he did.

But *Tempest-Tost* is not bitter; it is affectionate in poking fun at the Salterton thespians. But a curious transfer may be observed in this first novel. The wealth of small-town characters, the piling up of such incidents as the clergymen avid for free books and the plot's romantic entanglements, crowd the actual performance of *The Tempest* off the page. Years later, writing about a more elaborate opera in *The Lyre of Orpheus*, the same restraint is shown. There the novelist has indeed triumphed over the dramatist.

But the true lover of theatre is not easily converted. And true lovers of theatre in Canada in the early 1950s were about to see the Heavens open. Aware of the flowering of those summer theatres, and the timidity of Canada in committing itself to a full-time all-year-round, home-grown theatre, I suspected the time was ripe for a major summertime theatre festival. Because of its claims as a festival city, past and present, I thought it would locate itself at Kingston, but Peterborough had a marked advantage in the presence of Robertson Davies. I was wrong on both counts. It turned up unexpectedly in Stratford, a town with less tangible connections to drama, but one which commemorates the sacred name of Shakespeare's birthplace.

A local newsman named Tom Patterson was to make it happen by enlisting the energy and vision of none other than the Davies' old friend, Tyrone Guthrie. Guthrie burst onto the Ontario scene a true eccentric well over six feet tall and high-nosed into the bargain, eschewing conventions of attire and custom but embued with the rightness of his vision of Shakespeare, whom he regarded as something of an equal. "Guthrie showed us the big approach," his disciple Davies was to recall years later. "He showed us the rejection of provincial vulgarities when we attempted great themes, the rhythmic splendour of a finely conceived production." In short, Patterson's choice was perfect, and on July 13, 1953, the Stratford festival exploded onto the national and international scene. The Davies were uplifted, as was I writing its first review. Here was the Second Coming of our Theatre Theatrical, all the more amazing for being in a theatre-thin territory. Contact with Dr. Guthrie (as we were advised to call him) proved inspiring to all concerned, but particularly, I suspect, to the two young colonials whom he had befriended at the Old Vic over a decade before. That association was crowned by a literary collaboration with Guthrie on the first of Davies' three Stratford records, *Renown at Stratford*, made handsome by Grant Macdonald portraits.

That 1953 record was to be followed by *Twice Have the Trumpets Sounded* and *Thrice the Brindled Cat Hath Mewed* in successive years. Davies' commentary set the high-water mark for Stratford's achievement, extending on to cover the refinements made by Michael Langham, Guthrie's successor. Davies served on the Stratford Board of Governors, steering the local businessmen along the paths of high thespian art. And high it was, with the likes of Alec Guinness and Irene Worth, followed by James Mason, Paul Scofield and Siobhan McKenna from abroad, and a whole galaxy of Canada's brightest stars to match them in superb formal settings designed by Tanya Moiseiwitsch. To be part of Stratford then was to be part of great theatre.

But perhaps the greatest satisfaction for Robertson Davies was the opportunity to collaborate with Shakespeare himself. On request, he wrote a modest sequence of some sixty-four speeches for *The Merry Wives of Windsor*. The result proved seamless. Rob sent me a copy labelled the "Lost" scenes from *The Merry Wives of Windsor*, complete with his "notes" on some rich Elizabethan usages. He inscribed it with the admission: "There is nothing I like better than trying on Shakespeare's laurels."

The inspiration Stratford generated was wide-spread. It sent Douglas Campbell and the Canadian Players out across the country with an easily portable *Saint Joan*. It brought Murray and Donald Davis into Toronto from Muskoka to make over a cinema called The Crest. From the start the brothers advocated new plays as well as distinguished crowd-pleasers from abroad. The Crest's first season was graced by the North American premiere of Graham Greene's first play, *The Living Room*, but Greene's sombre work did not eclipse The Crest's opener, which was *A Jig for the Gypsy* by Robertson Davies, also under my direction. It featured the Davis brothers' sister, Barbara Chilcott, presenting a vivid celebration of the gypsy spirit in frock-coated Wales backed a strong cast which included Max Helpmann, Eric House, Norman Endicott and Neil Vipond. Davies had found his show-case, one infinitely superior to summer theatres and drama festivals, one even superior to contributing anonymous side-bars to the lofty Stratford productions.

The encouraging success of *A Jig For the Gypsy* was enough to set our playwright to fashioning another creation for The Crest, despite his heavy involvement with those Stratford Festival books and the completion of his second Salterton novel *Leaven of Malice* in 1954, which was to have such a bumpy future in dramatization. The second Crest play was called *Hunting Stuart*, which carried the high old romance of Royal Stuart succession into modern Ottawa, with a satisfying Cinderella twist. Staged by another important contributor to Davis family success, Robert Gill of Hart House Theatre, it lacked the panache of *A Jig for the Gypsy*, perhaps, but a request for a third Davies work was forthcoming as a matter of course. *Hunting Stuart and Other Plays* did not see publication until 1972 for some reason, by which time the author was already embarked on the second novel in his great Deptford Trilogy, *The Manticore*. Busy as he was, Davies was also persuaded to contribute a successor to his delightful school-boy entertainment *The Masque of Aesop* with *A Masque of Mr Punch*, making Upper Canada College unique among Canadian educational institutions in having two plays written for it by an internationally-known old boy.

But the Davies ego was to be threatened from an ungrateful source. The new play on assignment for The Crest was summarily dropped for J.B. Priestley's *The Glass Cage*. The Toronto appearance of the famous British author and playwright was highly theatrical in itself, and irresistible to the Davis family. At a reception at the University Club where the three Davis siblings made a very striking entrance, Priestley vowed then and there to write a play for them and their theatre. *The Glass Cage* was produced in the spot intended for the new Davies play *General Confession*, a work they never did stage. The Priestley premiere was given much publicity and its *success d'estime* won the financial support to take it to London after the 1955-56 season here.

The blow to Davies' pride must have been considerable, though no legal redress was sought. In the typically Canadian view, Robertson Davies "had just had it too good" for a playwright at that time. That he deserved his success fully because of his rare and special gift for theatre didn't count, but it certainly added to the pain of rejection and betrayal.

It would have been inhuman in any playwright so treated had he not taken some gleeful satisfaction from the fact that the critics were not as dazzled as the Davies family by *The Glass Cage*. Brooks Atkinson of *The New York Times* recognized that the premiere of a new Priestley play in Toronto was worth the trip, but he found *The Glass Cage* "...an interesting play about uninteresting characters." The displaced dramatist could also have enjoyed the reception of *The Glass Cage* when it reached the West End. There it was received as a minor mock-Canadian entry when compared with the gutsy vitality of another colonial import, Australia's *The Summer of the Seventeenth Doll*. Whatever his private reactions, it is significant that the next Crest Theatre season did not include a play by Robertson Davies, though it staged premieres of Jack Gray's *Bright Sun at Midnight* and *Double Image* by Roger MacDougall and Ted Allan.

But while the prodigious Deptford Trilogy progressed in all the glory of its Jungian depth psychology, Stratford still fanned that old theatrical flame. In 1960, in close collaboration with Guthrie as director, Davies dramatized *Leaven of Malice* for Broadway, under the jazzier title *Love and Libel*. But even with the great Guthrie at his side, this was to prove a sobering and aggravating experience. His moral tale of the effect of idle mischief in a small Ontario town collided head-on with a variety of tough New York conditions, among them the egotism of Dennis King, the essential Broadway star. Davies was less sympathetic to King's egotism than he was to the egoism of Sir John Martin-Harvey, whom he so sympathetically interpreted in Sir John Tresize of *World of Wonders*. In my copy of this third Deptford novel, the author has written: "Hoping you remember Sir John as affectionately as I do, Christmas 1975." He would never write that about Dennis King.

*World of Wonders* was indeed special for me, as he knew it would be. It also gave me a lesson in tolerance in its treatment of Sir John's leading lady, the old star's less-than-luminous wife, in this Jungian tale of another kind of magician, one robbed of egoism, parting sadly from the world of the Theatre Theatrical. By now I sensed, unwillingly, that a major novelist had somehow replaced the working dramatist I knew.

That Broadway had little curiosity about small-town Canadian life—or any other aspect of Canada, witness the rejection of Gratian Gelinas' *Ti-Coq*—dealt Davies a blow all the more painful because it occurred in the full glare of "The Great White Way." And the home reaction wasn't helpful. Canada has always been inclined to spitefulness when native talents impudently tackle the heights abroad.

The academic turn Robertson Davies' career took in 1963 was also bound to have a sobering influence on him. To be named first Master of Massey College was a high honour, one that implied an end to such frivolous pursuits as a country newspaperman might indulge in. More serious pursuits than theatre were called for. Curiously, even though the Master worked with Massey's architect, Ron Thom, as well as with its benefactor, the Hon. Vincent Massey himself, there was no theatre space included in the college. Yet all three men had been touched by a similar involvement with the stage.

Theatrical support-lines were not cut off, of course. For one thing the Oxonian Davies, a Balliol man, was lecturing in drama for the University. It was at a Massey College luncheon in honour of Neville Coghill, father figure of Oxford theatricals, that the question was brought forward: Was it fair that the undergraduates spending time and energy at Hart House Theatre should do so without academic credit? Naturally, Professor Coghill's opinion was sought. As I recall, it was agreed by all, save Robert Gill, father figure of University of Toronto theatre, that it was not. The establishment of the University's Centre for the Study of Drama, a graduate faculty, was the result.

There were at least two more Davies plays to come, each of which would add fuel to his publishers' argument that the rewards of the drama were meagre and depressing compared to the steadily mounting prestige and renumeration accorded an important novelist.

On the Toronto scene the building of the St. Lawrence Centre for the Arts had picked up the mission of both The Crest and Canadian Players, which had collapsed simultaneously. Its institution was a civic admission that the O'Keefe Centre, also a municipal effort, might be fine for travelling Broadway musicals and moderately fine for opera and ballet, but was not suited to legitimate drama, especially the home-product, now busily pushing up from underground. Ten years after endorsing O'Keefe, Toronto built the St. Lawrence Centre with two stages for local productions.

Leon Major, artistic director of the Centre's larger stage, was alert to the need to justify this development. How better than to enlist the talents of Robertson Davies? Davies obliged by contributing a large-scale political satire called *Question Time*. Though the play is a political satire it is also a deeper, multi-level examination of Canada's concept of government, albeit one which examines political power in a comic vein. It demands spectacle and in return offers both light and heavy symbolism. It is theatrical, incorporating displays of magic and set in a "ghastly comic icebox"; it evokes the Theatre Theatrical figure of the Double in the full *World of Wonders* mode; and also includes a giant side-swipe at Canada's national symbol, the Beaver. There is more than a touch of scornful defiance in this last major work. Not surprisingly then, it was naturally received with quite marked resistance from an unhelpful press.

But there was approval in high places, too: in the highest place of the nation, indeed. In the House, one day in 1975, Prime Minister Pierre Elliott Trudeau was spotted reading *Question Time* in a manuscript copy, gift of an alert press relations person. It is reported that its comment on the play's Leader of the Opposition brought forth the Prime Minister's glee, and a nudge to Mitchell Sharp beside him. But that was very special laughter, not widely shared.

It was not possible for the Master of Massey to put theatre out of his life, just because he was being heralded as a novelist of Nobel scale. That would have meant dismissing something that had always been part of life. But future expressions of that old passion must now be played out within the halls of academe, unless others transfer his prose to the stage. The "Masque of the Master", a farewell tribute from Massey College to Davies, with the present Master, Ann Saddlemeyer, as prime anthologist, was an example of the former. And the Stratford Festival's 1991 ambitions for *World of Wonders*, unproduced to date, suggests that the latter may well continue to be fruitful venue for Davies' work.

Davies was more directly responsible for *Pontiac and the Green Man*, an entertainment devised to mark the University's Sesquicentennial in 1977. That same graduate Centre for the study of Drama came up with the hope that a very early play called *Ponteach or The Savages of America* might be worthy of Davies' talents and interest. It was to be a collaboration with the University's Faculty of Music, using that faculty's large MacMillan Theatre. Davies agreed to work up *Ponteach* for modern-day audiences, which proved no easy task. Undaunted, he accepted the premise that it was the work of the celebrated Indian fighter, Major Robert Rogers, known for his guerilla tactics with the British troops under his command. Davies' rather elaborate conceit was that *Ponteach* be staged by a travelling troupe of players as evidence against Rogers at his court martial.

This allowed the University dramatist full rein for his fancy, producing something I characterized in a CBC review as "part pageant, part historical drama, part masque, occasionally satire and half of it theatrical revival.... *Pontiac and the Green Man* is a patchwork quilt of a play richly strung together." It was performed by such notable graduates as David Gardner, Francess Halpenny, Laurier LaPierre, Michael Tait, Rex Southgate and Ronald Bryden (who had come up with the first research), and it had Brenda Davies striking attitudes worthy of the celebrated eighteenth century actress Mrs. Yates as the leader of the troupe. It also had music by Derek Holman.

Perhaps some of the intrigues in bringing the opera *Arthur of Britain* to the stage in *The Lyre of Orpheus* (1978) were inspired by the efforts to bring *Pontiac and The Green Man* to life, for Martin Hunter, who directed it, recalls it as "one of the bloodiest shows" of his career. He does not absolve Davies, whom he greatly admires, of all blame, though he mainly took issue with the Music Faculty's contribution. Derek Holman's music was cacophonous, he holds, and the Davies script was sometimes didactic and rhetorical. As that 1978 Davies novel reminded us, "the lyre of Orpheus opens the door of the Underworld."

Martin Hunter's non-Broadway version of *Leaven of Malice* for the Centre proved more acceptable than *Love and Libel* had been, as was the Shaw Festival's subsequent staging of it by Tony van Bridge. Neither offered adequate compensation for a wounded Broadway playwright unappreciated on his home stages, especially one so gloriously established as a world-renowned novelist.

Though that playwright was in retreat at this point in Davies' career, W. Robertson Davies the actor still emerged occasionally. "I was never a very good actor," he admitted once when recalling Oxford University Old Vic days, though "I did well at the grotesques." Not a very good actor perhaps but a very good reader of his own works, like Charles Dickens, who lost his own struggle with the capricious stage. The Master's annual ghost stories for Gaudy Night at Massey College were truly masterly confections, epitomizing the special Davies blend of the topical with the mystical by a rare histrionic gift.

And like that youthful Oxonian, he could still turn his hand to an eighteenth Century prologue. He rightly refused my 1978 invitation to play the speechless Lord Burleigh in Sheridan's *The Critic* because he was too busy with major projects to fritter away evenings on a wordless theatrical joke, but he offered a generous exchange in the form of a most eloquent, and flattering, prologue to be spoken by Leah Lee Browne in the Drama Centre revival. He spoke it splendidly himself at my Big Birthday Bash in Hart House a dozen years later.

It occurred to this delighted listener then that the whole theatre span of Davies' career, so tantalizing, so frustrating, so fraught with love, might be traced back to his first public appearance in an obscure opera, *Queen Esther*, staged at the Opera House in Thamesville, where he was born.

In Peterborough days, the Davies family had taken me to Thamesville for a picnic which was part pilgrimage. We found our way into the Old Opera House with its painted drop of all Europe, a topographical marvel. Here he had only been part of the Chorus of Israelite Children, but he was not lost in the crowd. The Israelite child with Mohammed's crescent in his Jewish turban was the Boy Davies.

That sunny day in Thamesville we were exploring the origins of the theatrical Davies. From here could be traced Upper Canada College triumphs on stage, others from the Oxford University Dramatic Society, the Old Vic, the plays—long and short—which so enriched a fledgling theatre, the contributions to The Crest and Stratford and that crashing Broadway flight, persisting down through the years towards another Biblical work about Nabob, Ahab and the notorious Queen Jezebel. This latter work is his libretto for an oratorio composed by the same Derek Holman, reportedly forthcoming.

Another trip I consider illuminating was one Rob and I once took to visit his father, the formidable Senator Rupert Davies, sometime Lord Lieutenant of Cardiff, but then confined to a Canadian hospital bed. Standing with his already distinguished son at the foot of the bed,

I was treated as a boy also. In my amateur Freudian way, I wondered if this parental attitude hadn't driven Rob to create for himself the image of the imposing patriarch of today, beautifully bearded and benign. But when we were *en famille*, Rob could be as jolly, as mischievous, as peevish and gossipy as any friend of one's own age should be. And in correspondence, he could sign a note to me "Barney O'Lunacy" without my wondering who it was from. All the same, it was years before I discovered that I was three years older than he was.

The great trilogies, the collections of essays, the learned studies are all now accepted as the contribution of a distinguished international author. But the early plays are the abstract and brief chronicles of our own time when our own drama shook itself and took its place in the spotlight. It is as such that this ill-considered part of the Davies legacy survives, as does my affection for him as a pioneer Canadian dramatist.

# Magister Ludi:
# The Mask of Robertson Davies

*Martin Hunter*

My first encounter with Robertson Davies took place on a windy spring day some forty years ago when he called at the house of the Cunningham family who were later to become my in-laws. He stepped from his Jaguar with a gleeful grin, the cape sleeves of his exquisitely cut Ulster fluttering in the breeze. He raised his broad-brimmed hat in greeting so that his magnificent head of already silvery hair blew wildly about, totally obscuring his vision. He tried in vain to get his unruly mane under control and eventually had to get back into the Jaguar to recompose his coiffure before coming into the house. It was a brilliantly eccentric comic entrance and he made the most of it, playing his chosen role of the unrepentant dandy hoist by his own petard with the utmost relish.

Over the next forty years I came to know Davies in many roles: first as drama adjudicator, then as university teacher, later as colleague at the Graduate Centre for the Study of Drama, where I directed two of his plays, and, finally as the subject of a radio biography which I prepared. I have had the opportunity to watch him play out many variations of his public persona and have never ceased to marvel at his ability to bring unflagging energy and *brio* to his portrayal of that most engaging of all his created characters—himself.

On the dust-jacket blurbs of his books, Robertson Davies is generally credited with having had three careers, the first being that of actor. Stage-struck from boyhood, he appeared as a schoolboy in several operettas at Upper Canada College under the direction of Richard Tattersall singing the comic patter songs of Sir Joseph Porter and Major-General Stanley. He was evidently adept at spitting out Gilbert's witty lyrics and opted for a thespian career.

In his early twenties he was a minor actor in Tyrone Guthrie's productions at the Old Vic's 1939-40 season, playing comic roles such as Snout in *A Midsummer Night's Dream*. He abandoned acting because, by his own admission, he found it difficult to inhabit the skin of another being and to construct a dramatic character distinct from his own; he preferred instead to elaborate and project his own colourful personality. He gave up on being an actor but became a consummate performer.

As a performer he is highly accomplished. He can hold the stage for an hour, amuse and stimulate a classroom throughout a morning-long seminar, dominate a dinner party for an entire evening. Even in informal situations, the persona seems always to be in place. My brother-in-law, James Cunningham, who used to stay at the Davies house in Peterborough in the 40s, tells me Davies never failed to give a performance at his own dinner table. Cunningham was led to wonder how this busy man could be bothered to expend so much enthusiasm just to garner a few laughs from his wife and daughters and one fourteen-year-old visitor.

Davies' performance has developed in both subtlety and depth during the four decades I have observed him. In the late 40s he was already a skilled clown, adept at milking chuckle after chuckle from his audience. (Only two performers in my experience have matched his ability to tickle the funnybone of the average Ontario farmer— Donald Harron and William Hutt—though I suspect Stephen Leacock was equally skilful at connecting with this type of audience.) Davies the performer is in the tradition of Stephen Leacock, Mark Twain and Charles Dickens; all of them loved to get up on a stage, engage an audience face to face and win them over by a mixture of pithy audacity and curmudgeonly charm.

In addition to literary figures, Davies has undoubtedly based his public personality on some living models. When I was preparing a profile of Davies for the CBC programme *Ideas*, I asked him who had been his principal mentors or role-models and, perhaps not surprisingly for a trilogist, he named three, the first of whom was his natural father Rupert Davies. A Welshman of considerable resource and vivacity, Rupert Davies was an almost archetypal, self-made man. He came to Canada as a boy and apprenticed as a printer's devil, eventually becoming owner and publisher of a string of newspapers and a Canadian senator before he retired to Wales to live in a castle in the town where he had been born.

As a rich man's son, Robertson Davies could not shape his life to quite the same pattern, but he too set out to become a sort of self-made personality. His fascination with the process of self-creation is evident in his work as a novelist. He first explored this theme in depth in *A Mixture of Frailties* by tracing the development of the singer Monica Gall, giving careful delineation not only of her technical musical training, but also of the relationship of her emotional development to her success as a performer.

The process is more exhaustively explored in the Deptford Trilogy where all three of Davies major characters consciously construct their own personalities, overcoming physical and/or emotional handicaps (Ramsay's Calvinist upbringing and wooden leg; Liesl's unusual height and physical ugliness; Eisengrim's abused and deprived childhood). In spite of these impediments, they realize their potential as performers, each in his special sphere. All three are unlikely heroes who, by exploring their own inner resources and adopting new names, eventually manage to express their true natures. Each becomes in some sense his own creation. Underneath the social and psychological complexities of these books there is the upbeat energy of a G.A. Henty romance. It is partly this optimistic underpinning that makes the books so satisfying to their readers.

Robertson Davies is at heart a crowd-pleaser, and this is never more evident than when he makes a public appearance. He radiates a sort of crusty geniality. He takes his audience into his confidence, employing the raised eyebrow, the sly wink, the mock suspension of judgment that will later be paid off by the knowing look of the inveterate sceptic. Davies lets us see he isn't easily fooled and his manner assures us he knows we aren't either.

Davies' early public appearances were to some degree an extension of the character he developed under the pseudonym of Samuel Marchbanks, a figure whose real identity was once a mystery to the readers of the *Peterborough Examiner*, but who is now so closely identified with his creator that recent editions print mirror images of Davies and Marchbanks on the front cover. Davies in the 40s was like Marchbanks come to life. (His daughter Miranda once told me that she watched him dressing for the part of Marchbanks, consciously preening in front of a mirror before he set out to address an audience of Rotarians or IODE matrons.)

Marchbanks/Davies, the entertainer of the 50s, presented a somewhat different aspect than the public Davies currently on display. He was an eccentric in the days when wearing a beard was in itself a badge of eccentricity. (There had been earlier experiments with affectation: one of his schoolmasters, Freddy Mallett, told me Davies sported a monocle in class at Upper Canada College, though he may have merely been rehearsing the effect for a Gilbert and Sullivan role.) The beard is supposed to have been grown during an illness, but may also have been inspired by a reading of *Antic Hay*, the Aldous Huxley novel which Davies admits had a profound influence on his early development. (Its bland hero dons a false beard, a disguise which permits him to participate in various outrageous adventures.)

Marchbanks/Davies was not merely eccentric; he was also a satirist. He attacked institutions and individuals and was actively hostile to elements in society he didn't like: the complacent, the mean-minded, the Philistine. He could be vindictive, especially when he appeared as a drama adjudicator. He would unmercifully flay the weakness of one production in order to set up the virtues of another. As someone who benefited from his use of this ploy, I was aware of its effectiveness and also intrigued to find him using it in the 60s in his new role of university teacher. In his classes he had favourites whose causes he advanced, while there were others he vilified. I was lucky enough to be one of the former, and I would be ungrateful if I did not record that Davies provided me with more positive reinforcement as a writer than anyone else in the literary establishment. Nevertheless, I have sometimes winced for his victims.

Like many of the finest critics, Davies was unashamedly partisan. He saw himself as the scourge of confining convention. He extolled the power of mind and heart over the virtues of consistency and unfailing common sense. He celebrated the creative spirit, which he saw as irrepressible and anarchic. He amplified the persona of Marchbanks, the social critic, when he created the characters of Pops in *Overlaid* and Mr. Punch in *The Masque of Mr. Punch*. Either role might have been written for himself, though perhaps they are a bit too extreme for Davies ever to abandon his waistcoat and cravat to actually play them on the stage.

Another figure from Davies' early writing who partakes of an unruly satirical spirit is Humphrey Cobbler, the drunken organist who weaves his way in and out of the Salterton novels. Cobbler is perhaps the most attractive figure in Davies' stage adaptation of *Leaven of Malice* which Tyrone Guthrie directed under the title of *Love and Libel*. This play failed in New York, but I was permitted to revive it in a somewhat rewritten version at Hart House Theatre in 1973 where it was well received by a university audience who easily recognized the petty but deadly academic intrigue that provides the mainspring of the plot. Davies once confessed to me that the joyous if messy domesticity of Humphrey Cobbler and his wife Molly was to some extent modelled on the home life of Judy and Tony Guthrie. It is interesting to note that the central scene of the play takes place in a bed where Molly and Humphrey entertain the young Canadian academic and would-be writer Solly Bridgetower. The scene is not erotic; instead, it is pervaded by a harmony that combines alcohol-fortified frankness with intellectual passion, an image of fulfilment that would be echoed in the Deptford Trilogy where the consummation of the relationship between Dunstan Ramsay, Liselotte Vitzlipützli and Magnus Eisengrim also involves three in a bed, sharing brandy, free confession and what are described as "high old times."

Whether or not the young Davies was ever invited to enter the Guthrie bed, there is no doubt Guthrie had a strong influence on the writer's early creative life. Davies named him as the second of his mentors, and Guthrie was apparently fond of claiming to be the young author's "Father in Art." When Davies was part of Guthrie's Old Vic company, he had a sort of special status as "resident pedant." However, Guthrie was not above intervening in the personal lives of his protégés and he tried to persuade Brenda Mathews, then his stage manager, that she should not marry young Robertson.

Brenda and Davies ignored Guthrie's advice; they wed and returned to Canada, where Brenda assumed the role of consort, as well as a sort of permanent stage manager for the continuing Davies show. Davies did not hold a grudge against Guthrie, but used his influence to help bring the eminent director to Canada to head the Stratford Festival. He was rewarded by being given the chance to function as of dramaturge during Guthrie's years there. He adapted Ben Jonson's *Bartholomew Fair* to a rural Ontario setting, but Guthrie didn't get around to producing it.

Guthrie did agree to direct *Love and Libel*, for which Davies not only wrote the script but also helped arrange financing. When the New York critics pilloried the production, Guthrie abandoned the project. There was disappointment on both sides and Davies believes that in the final years of their relationship, Guthrie, who had begun to fancy himself as a writer, came to resent Davies' rising success as a novelist.

In spite of the fact that he wrote a string of plays which were professionally produced and achieved public success unequalled at the time in English Canada, Davies more or less abandoned the theatre after the failure of *Love and Libel* and decided to concentrate on writing novels. It is generally thought today his plays are not stageworthy. In time some of them will get productions that may revise this verdict. However, it seems to me that some of the plays are coloured by a didacticism that makes them difficult to accept. It is as if Davies wants to tell us what to think of his characters instead of leaving it to the actors to do what only they can do: make the characters come to life by inhabiting them and allowing them free emotional range. The limitations of Davies, the would-be actor, may somehow have carried over to inhibit the full expression of his talents as a dramatist.

Davies underwent a psychological change during the early 60s when he faced and coped with a medical diagnosis of cancer. He began work on *Fifth Business*, a novel that signalled this change in outlook. Like his hero, Dunstan Ramsay, he came to terms with a personal reality which could not be dealt with merely by standing back and making wisecracks. In Ramsay he found a voice with deeper reverberations. Ramsay is a teacher and as such he too performs. He can "get off a good one," but he also seeks a plain style that allows for the expression of ethical truths. Ramsay is cantankerous but compassionate, unconventional but responsible. Just as the young Davies had taken on the character of his creation Marchbanks, now, in middle age, Davies the academic began to evince the qualities of his more mature creation, Dunstan Ramsay.

At the same time Davies retained something of the Guthrie style: a manipulative subtlety in addition to a certain grandeur and generosity. Guthrie came across as a big man, not merely physically, but in outlook. He arrived in the artistically colonial Canada like a big white hunter, stalking rare aesthetic game. He gave lavish dinner parties for his actors, provoked them with unexpected intellectual queries, and opened up places for them on the stage alongside international stars like Alec Guinness and James Mason.

It was this same spirit that found expression when Davies, assisted by Brenda, always his sartorial and conversational match, set the social and intellectual tone for Massey College, a tone that was warmly welcoming, if at the same time somewhat self-consciously aristocratic. Guthrie's longtime collaborator, designer Tanya Moiseiwitsch, once told me that the great director turned every rehearsal into a sort of Victorian picnic. I remembered this image years later at a rehearsal for Davies' play *Question Time* at the St. Lawrence Centre when Robertson and Brenda sat in the back of the theatre watching the actors. Between them was a large wicker basket from which they fortified themselves with lobster sandwiches and cold hock, which they magnanimously offered to anyone who came within their range.

By this time Robertson Davies was firmly established as the Master of Massey College, and his public persona was beginning to evolve beyond the limitations of the stern schoolmaster Dunstan Ramsay. In the free-wheeling late 60s he had become less the attacker of hidebound conformity than the defender and, indeed, establisher of tradition. Marchbanks was replaced by a presence who was less a satirist than a stylist, less a quirky young pedant than a passionate magus. Wit was still in evidence and so was a sense of enjoyment, but there was a new emphasis on ceremony. If Marchbanks had been half Touchstone, half Jacques, the Master of Massey was half Falstaff, half Prospero—with perhaps just a dash of the Wizard of Oz.

It is possible to discern in this new figure the influence of the third of Davies' acknowledged mentors: Vincent Massey, the man who chose him to breathe life into his newly founded graduate college. Massey had worshipped at the altar of upper-class British taste before he returned home to make himself the High Priest of Canadian Culture. He was formal and rather frozen-faced in public, but privately something of a cynic and a consummate manipulator. Davies has admitted he learned much from Massey in both areas. As Davies worked to build up an endowment for his new college by cultivating Torontonians with financial and intellectual clout, he and Brenda organized a variety of glittering social occasions: high-table dinners with eminent scholars from around the globe, elegant receptions with musical accompaniment or dramatic entertainment and, above all, the annual Christmas Gaudy Night, which was one of the highlights of the Toronto season.

"Gaudy" is a term borrowed from Oxford and signifies a celebration; under Davies' shaping aegis it became an event both gaudy and rich—in more than one sense of the word. Financiers and grand dames rubbed shoulders with academic celebrities such as Marshall McLuhan and Tuzo Wilson. Original music commissioned from Harry Somers or John Beckwith was sung by the Massey choir and poets like Robert Finch and Earle Birney recited original verse. But the star turn of the evening was Davies himself reading the original Ghost Story he wrote each year for the occasion. Here Davies was in his element, affable and self-mocking, elegant and hilarious. He was no longer the outsider but "The Master" at the centre of a world he had himself created, a world of intelligence and decorum spiked by a spirit that could be sly or sardonic but was no longer sour. He had come into his own and he was enjoying it hugely.

During this period, Davies the Writer achieved literary recognition with his Deptford novels. Davies the Master provided a complement to this literary work at the same time as he promoted it. The success stories of Ramsay and Eisengrim were parallelled and given credibility by the real-life success of Robertson Davies. Like most effective salesmen, Davies knew better than to do anything as vulgar as tout his wares; he established a presence and connected with his audience.

Gradually the cantankerousness of the Presbyterian Ramsay gave way to the more mellow, more vulnerable personality of the priest Father Simon Darcourt, a central figure in the Cornish Trilogy. Darcourt has a certain authority, though he is also disarmingly aware of his own failings. And with the loving delineation of the fictional character of Darcourt, Davies has continued to modify his own persona, shaping it more expertly than ever, so that it becomes wholly consistent with his literary eminence. He has deepened and ripened as the years have advanced, until now, as he nears eighty, he seems altogether wise and guileless. He commands respect and admiration on a scale that any statesman or philosopher might envy. Robertson Davies the Sage is one of his most endearing characters.

The persona serves him well as he travels the globe, entertaining his readers and propounding his ideas. He may have been a failed actor, but now all the world is indeed his stage. Wherever he appears

Davies is a Master of Revels which are no mere kicking up of the heels, but a celebration of the complication and unpredictability of life itself. His dance of life—a unique blend of Highland reel, minuet and fandango—is still spirited and sprightly, though it must one day inevitably come to an end. One can imagine the obsequies will be splendid. Already the urns that will hold his and Brenda's ashes wait on the mantelpiece of their house in Caledon. Meanwhile the mask is held high. Now smiling benignly, now frowning reprovingly, the contours of the mask shift subtly, like the lineaments of a living picture of Dorian Gray. An intricate creation with a life of its own, the mask of Robertson Davies must be acknowledged one of his most compelling works of art.

# The Mask of Satire: Character and Symbolic Pattern in Robertson Davies' Fiction

*Hugo McPherson*

V ery well, if you wish it, I shall talk to someone else," says Samuel Marchbanks to one of his many vacuous dinner partners. "I do not believe in wasting good talk on people who are plainly unable to appreciate it."[1] This testy, Johnsonian pronouncement might stand as the key signature of Robertson Davies' writing. In the past dozen years he has produced fifteen volumes of drama, fiction and discussion of the theatre. Many of them are very good talk indeed, yet Davies' reviewers—like Marchbanks' dinner partners—have generally failed to grasp the full import of his astringent and irreverent statement. They praise his wit, ribaldry and invective, and even join in his laughter at Canadian conformity and stodginess; but in the end they label him a clown—ubiquitous and erudite to be sure, but scarcely a serious thinker.

Unquestionably Davies *is* the *enfant terrible* of Canadian letters, but behind the puckered mask of the satirist lives a serious writer of romance. His novels study in symbolic fashion a problem that has concerned Canadian writers since Susanna Moodie; the plight of the imagination in this chilly cultural climate. This central theme in his work has generally gone unrecognized because the genre of satirical romance is unfamiliar to Canadians (Davies is its only native practitioner), and because, having come to the novel from drama and the essay, he has had difficulty creating characters who live *on the page*. As a result he has been judged upon the most prominent features of his work—his explicit ideas and his burlesques of Canadian manners.

AN APPRECIATION                                                67

In this essay, therefore, I propose to redress the balance by going back to the beginning of his fiction—to the irascible Samuel Marchbanks—and examining the symbolic structure and statement of his novels, and the problems of characterization which, until *A Mixture of Frailties,* have plagued him.

Robertson Davies had been writing plays, studying the theatre and writing for newspapers since Neville Chamberlain's great umbrella-waving year, 1939, but he did not publish a volume of fiction until 1947; and even then his approach was oblique. A few years earlier he had created in the columns of the *Peterborough Examiner* a dyspeptic gentleman called Samuel Marchbanks—a disaffected Canadian whose attacks on contemporary manners borrowed heavily on the capital of Pepys, Addison, Swift, Samuel Butler, Shaw and, in desperate moments, H.L. Mencken and Sinclair Lewis. Marchbanks was at once the apostle of intelligence, the champion of live-and-let-live-eccentricity and the defender of the principle that ideas, like mothers-in-law, are to be entertained rather than maintained. So voluble was his talk that it finally overflowed the *Examiner* and filled two book-length volumes—*The Diary of Samuel Marchbanks* (1947)[2] and *The Table Talk of Samuel Marchbanks* (1949).

These informal essays or "confessions" gave Davies most of the advantages of the novelist with almost none of the responsibilities. He could disregard plot; a simple day-to-day chronology sufficed. He had no need of consistently-developed characters; the persons of the diary are clever caricatures who perform their antics on the stage of Samuel Marchbanks' observation. As in Davies' models, the ruling principle is the play of idea and opinion; nothing is sacred, and Marchbanks wastes no opportunity, trivial or profound, of whacking the provincial backsides of his Canadian and American compatriots. By turn self-pitying, ironic, antic, savage or sweetly reasonable, he applies his lash impartially to Hollywood films—"the apotheosis of the Yahoo" (*Diary*, p. 38)—to pious politicians and salesladies, to medical fads, and to chocolate-stuffed children who allow balloons to "disembarrass themselves of their wind" (*Table Talk*, p. 17) in adults' faces. But above all, Marchbanks fights the glum sobriety of Calvinism, the morality which calls any bovine female a Lady so long as she is "Good," and the mentality of "young fogies...fellows who, at thirty, are well content with beaten paths and reach-me-down opinions;

[whose] very conservatism is second-hand, [because] they don't know what they are conserving" (*Table Talk*, p. 118).

Mixed in with all this is a dash of ribaldry. In parodying the synopsis of a French play, for example, Marchbanks gives the characters such names as Alphamet, Feenaminte, Flanalette, Clitore, Merde and Vespasienne (*Table Talk*, p. 55). This particular example is unfortunately juvenile; nevertheless, Davies uses crude humour deliberately, for he will not indulge readers who would like to think Marchbanks "proper." To *l'homme moyen sensuel*, everything is proper—in its place, Marchbanks' all-encompassing complaint, then, is the narrowness of Canadian thinking and the reflection of this narrowness in Canadian manners.

Marchbanks' talk is very good medicine. Canadians, who "don't like to be kidded or mimicked, though they are extremely fond of kidding or mimicking others" (*Diary*, p. 82), might take a course of the tonic every spring and fall. And yet the impact of the Marchbanks chronicles is not nearly as great as it might be. It is tempting to argue that their weakness is a malady to which even the best journalism is prone. The newspaper columnist, constantly under pressure to say something bright or challenging, almost inevitably descends to well-worn formulas or wit or impudence, to the superficial glance at people, or to controversy for its own sake. However, Robertson Davies seldom falls into these traps. His problem is that Samuel Marchbanks, for all his energy, never really comes alive as a character. Davies knows that:

> Every man and woman is a mystery, built like those Chinese puzzles which consist of one box inside another, so that ten or twelve boxes have to be opened before the final solution is found (*Diary*, pp. 26-27).

Yet he shows us little more than the bows, the gaudy seals and the tissue of ideas that conceal the deepest reaches of Marchbanks' character. Hence, far from emerging as a mordant critic in the vein of Swift, Johnson or Shaw, Marchbanks appears as an essentially theatrical creation who strikes attitudes instead of expressing convictions; who screens identity instead of revealing it. And the reader, lacking some glimpse of the "final solution" to his character, sees him as a pastiche of earlier and more assured diarists. Thus, even before

Robertson Davies began writing novels, characterization became the *bête noire* of his art.

In turning to this problem of character creation I am not abandoning my original intention of examining the statement and structure of Davies' novels, for both their content and form are contingent upon his conception of character. From what we have seen of Samuel Marchbanks it is clear that his temper is neo-classical rather than romantic; he is confident that he can take care of his own soul, and his prime demand is the freedom to enjoy his own private labyrinth without the pious intrusions of do-gooders and well-meaning acquaintances. But he will not attain this freedom and privacy until his community has achieved a measure of urbanity and sophistication. The aim of Marchbanks' talk, then, is to reveal the deformity or atrophy, the folly or self-deception of individuals as they present themselves in society.

Unquestionably Robertson Davies shares this general view of character. Unlike Hugh MacLennan, who has sought to discover *what* our national character is, and *why* it is, Davies rejects altogether the introspective search for identity. The last thing he wants is to delve into the recesses of Calvinist or Catholic hearts; in their Canadian habiliments they are too pinched and regimented to warrant close attention. On the assumption, then, that everybody *has* an identity, however mean, he focuses his attention on the conflict of ideas and on the spectacle of manners in the community. Character, in short, is a private affair (its privacy guaranteed—or violated—by the manners of others); and it is properly studied through its public manifestations.

Now this conception of character works very well in the theatre, where we watch an action from the outside, or in the essay, where we are concerned with ideas and opinions, but it raises serious problems in the novel. If the characters are to be observed from the outside, then we must have a narrator like the author-impresario in *Tom Jones* whose judgment we know and trust; or alternatively, as in Hemingway, we must be left entirely free to judge the facts on their own merits. In his first novel, *Tempest-Tost* (1951),[3] Davies, still very much the playwright and essayist, was unable to adopt either of these narrative methods. Precisely because of his unwillingness to create anything but "public" characters, he gives us no counterpart of Fielding's intimate narrator to direct our responses, yet he will not, like Hemingway, withdraw entirely from the scene. Instead he gives us a group of externally observed characters and a narrator who, like Alice's Cheshire cat, has disappeared, leaving only a savage Marchbanksian grin and a disembodied voice that makes acidulous, intrusive comments on the action.

In consequence *Tempest-Tost* is rather like an elaborate puppet show with interminable stage directions describing the setting and the appearance, background and motives of the characters; at the same time, an offstage M.C. urges us to see the stupidity of the performance. The story presents for our inspection the kind of people who organize Shakespearean productions in the Little Theatres of provincial Canadian cities—in this case Salterton (or Kingston) Ontario. Almost everybody concerned is so hopelessly second-rate that we are not sorry to see their pretensions exposed. But because the characters are never more than caricatures we are not inclined to look for any meaning beyond their surface absurdities. *Tempest-Tost*, we decide, is a frequently trivial and generally heavy-handed jibe at the provincialism of Canadian Little Theatre.

Having reached such a comforting conclusion we might, like Marchbanks' dinner partner, turn indifferently away from Mr. Davies' talk. But one nagging thought deters us: surely it is inconceivable that a man of Davies' talent and experience in the theatre could produce such a banal account of a Shakespearean production. The play itself, moreover, is not discussed at all. Why not? Surely Davies regards it as a great work of literature? It is when we ask this question about *The Tempest* and its meaning that the whole strategy of Davies' novel suddenly flashes upon us. Its action—so slight when viewed as a topical satire— is really an ironic off-stage re-enactment of Shakespeare's allegory, with a cast of Canadian characters. Robertson Davies not only understands the full import of Shakespeare's play, but he has looked about in a long-established Canadian community for the nearest equivalents he can find to the characters of the ageless romance. The result is a series of chilling ironies.

*The Tempest*, we recall, dramatizes the conflict between the humane powers of Duke Prospero and the grasping materialism of the King of Naples. Prospero lost his power because he neglected the practical needs of his state for the delights of his library. On the desert island to which he was banished, however, he learned to control the forces of imagination and intellect (Ariel) and the physical forces of the body and of nature (Caliban). And because Prospero mastered the "magic" of these forces, the play ends in a happy marriage between Ferdinand and Miranda—a creative union of the imaginative and materialistic forces or "families" which had so long been in opposition. In sum, *The Tempest* is Shakespeare's sweetest affirmation of faith in the imagination and its power to make man a genuinely humane and enlightened creature.

In the jejune and complacent community of Salterton, however, it is almost impossible to find people who might be appropriately cast in the various roles of *The Tempest*. Everybody agrees that the production is a daring enterprise; it could not be undertaken at all without the aid of an American-trained director, Valentine Rich (Davies' names are often symbolic), and a despised composer and organist of the Church of England, Humphrey Cobbler. Nevertheless the casting does take place, with piercingly ironic results. The person who is determined to play Prospero, the learned nobleman and loving father, is Professor Vambrace, an egotistical and cloistered pedant from the classics department of Waverley University. Naturally the Salterton Miranda is Vambrace's daughter Pearl, who, unlike Shakespeare's heroine, has had a narrow and ignoble upbringing and who—though potentially beautiful—can only be described as glum and repressed. Ferdinand, the gentle prince who loves Miranda at sight, is an egocentric young officer from Salterton's military college who prides himself on a long list of seductions.

But if the leading characters of the Salterton "Tempest" suffer a sea-change into something gauche and strange, the transformation of the secondary characters is even more ludicrous. The wise old councillor Gonzalo becomes Hector Mackilwraith, a Salterton mathematics teacher and son of an ineffectual Presbyterian minister; Hector's greatest wisdom is thrift, orderliness and a slavish reliance on the Puritan logic of *Pro* and *Contra*. Salterton's Caliban, not unexpectedly, is a crude practical joker who works in the local store of the Liquor Control Board of Ontario.

The greatest casting problem, of course, is Ariel, the ubiquitous spirit of intellect, imagination and beauty. (For Davies, as for Shakespeare, music is the symbol of these qualities.) After great deliberation, the Salterton thespians award this role to Griselda Webster, a pretty girl whose singing voice and I.Q. are acceptable though not exceptional. The *real* reason for their decision is that Ariel's father is the richest man in town; moreover, he will lend his garden to the Little Theatre for its *Tempest*. Thus the community's unacknowledged but slavish worship of wealth as the "highest good" is revealed in the casting of Ariel.

From this point on, the ironies of *Tempest-Tost* multiply and proliferate. In Salterton nobody but Valentine Rich (the Canadian artist who must make her living abroad) recognizes the potential of Pearl Vambrace, the Canadian Miranda. Instead, the three bachelors of the story yearn foolishly after Ariel, the affluent "impatient Griselda": Lieutenant Tasset (Prince Ferdinand) covets the physical pleasures which she promises; Hector Mackilwraith (Gonzalo) worships her as a pure and chaste ideal; and Solly Bridgetower, an indecisive young English professor at Waverley (who is the best assistant-director that Valentine Rich can find in Salterton) moons after her weakly. None succeeds in his suit, however, for this shrewd Canadian Ariel is aloof to them all.

In Salterton's eyes, of course, the whole production of *The Tempest* is a frivolous affair. Mrs. Caesar Augustus Conquerwood, the leading patron, departs in the middle of the first performance. What Salterton society really values is revealed in two long episodes which at first appear extraneous to the theme of the novel: the great ball at the military college, and the distribution of the library collected by Valentine Rich's father. The military ball is an overpoweringly stuffy affair, replete with major-generals, MPP's, civic officials, ageing representatives of Loyalist families, Waverley dignitaries and whoever else can procure tickets (from whatever source). In Salterton people must be cajoled into seeing a play, but everybody wants to be seen at the ball and to have his status confirmed in the social columns of the *Evening Bellman*. The ball, with all its gold braid and medals, is an anti-masque within the Salterton "tempest."

The episode of Valentine Rich's inherited library is more complex. The will of the late Adam Savage, Valentine's father, bequeaths his library to the clergy of Salterton; they may choose from it what will be useful to them. On the morning when the books are made available there is a near riot at the Savage home; more than two hundred black-clad gentlemen invade the library and strip it like a horde of army ants. In the confusion, rabbis find themselves with commentaries on the New Testament, and a shovel-hatted priest ends up with ten volumes of a Scottish metaphysician. Even for Canada's second estate, books are impressive *per se*, whatever their contents.

But there is a final irony: Professor Savage willed to Valentine a wrapped bundle of books which inadvertently fall into the auctioneer's hands and are sold to a New York dealer for the astounding sum (in Salterton commerce) of fifty dollars. As collectors' items the books are worth several thousands; they are the main asset of the Professor's estate. But Valentine—intent on the riches of art rather than the market—has failed to discover their dollar value. The Canadian heritage, it would appear, is chiefly valuable as a collection of marketable antiques; Professor Savage's legacy of *ideas* is exactly nil. Salterton's best hope is that people like Valentine may kindle the cold Canadian imagination.

Robertson Davies is clearly not optimistic about Salterton's cultural future. As the novel ends, Canada's Puritan Gonzalo, Hector Mackilwraith, attempts suicide, believing that he has lost his gilt-edged Ariel to the lustful Ferdinand. Ariel's younger sister (Shakespeare's messenger Iris) attributes Hector's despair to the oppressive influence of "oppressive religion," and proceeds with her youthful project of brewing champagne in Canada. Cobbler, the musical director, warns her that it cannot be champagne—"Just good cider with ideas above its station." And the badly-shaken Hector-Gonzalo decides (God help us!) to accept a job in the Ontario Department of Education, a decision which Ariel rewards with a formal kiss.

The foregoing, I believe, is the essential statement of *Tempest-Tost*. Beneath the surface satire, Robertson Davies has developed a major theme; but his external handling of character and his failure to get beyond the dramatist's impersonal method has so muffled his statement that the book must be accounted a failure. In the Preface to his drama *At My Heart's Core* (1950), Davies recognized that a play loses a great deal on the printed page. "The playwright's work," he says,

> is completed by the actor; the reader is not often so imaginative as to be able to discover in the text of the play...the qualities which would be revealed in it by a group of capable actors and an able director who had worked on it for a month.[4]

In *Tempest-Tost* he lacked the aid of a "group of capable actors" but had not yet reconciled himself to the novelist's need for some means of revealing more than the outer layer of the Chinese puzzle of character.

*Leaven of Malice* (1954),[5] a tightly plotted satirical romance, is a much better work. It is not surprising to learn that Davies has already adapted it as a play which Tyrone Guthrie will produce in New York, for the hand of the dramatist, carefully building up scenes and climaxes, still dominates. There is as yet no genuinely living character, but the citizens of Salterton are more sharply observed, and the satire has the therapeutic bite of a mustard plaster. (An academic party, replete with games, vile punch and an overweening sociology instructor as host, is one of the most uproarious chapters in Canadian fiction.) The author-playwright has now withdrawn almost entirely into the wings and distributed his ideas among Humphrey Cobbler, Gloster Ridley, editor of the *Evening Bellman*, and Dean Jevon Knapp of St. Nicholas' Cathedral. And finally, the action reveals more clearly than in *Tempest-Tost* the complementary elements of surface satire and symbolic implication.

Regarded as a waspish satire with a healing moral, *Leaven of Malice* tells of a crude practical joke. A false announcement that Pearl Vambrace is engaged to Solly Bridgetower sets aflame a ready-laid fire of animosities in Salterton. Ultimately the culprit is unmasked, but not until his false charge has led Pearl and Solly into each others' arms, and allowed Dean Knapp to point a moral. Malice, he says,

> works like a leaven; it stirs, and swells, and changes all that surrounds it.... It may cause the greatest misery and distress in many unexpected quarters. I have even known it to have quite unforeseen good results. But those things which it invades will never be quite the same again (*Leaven*, pp. 266-67).

But exactly what *are* the things that malice has invaded, and how has it changed them? If we look again at the persons of Robertson Davies' story and consider them as representative of various "forces" at work in Salterton society rather than mere satirical butts, we see that the author is once more talking about the failure of Canada's imagination; in contrast to *Tempest-Tost*, however, this action ends in a "marriage" which may portend a new era.

Gloster Ridley, though not the hero of the romance, is its main character. A self-educated intellectual who takes himself a few degrees too seriously, he has nevertheless transformed the *Evening Bellman* from an unprofitable and provincial curiosity to an alert and thriving newspaper which serves all segments of the community intelligently. But in achieving this revolution he has antagonized Salterton's "old guard"—the smug, sentimentally Anglophile, tradition-bound antiques who regard themselves as the community's social and intellectual arbiters. This group, which includes granddaughters of Brigadiers, widows of Waverley Deans, and persons claiming distant kinship with British nobility, would not demean themselves to fight Ridley openly, but all are privately delighted when the spurious announcement exposes Ridley, Pearl and Solly to ridicule. Nor is it surprising that the person who secretly performed this malicious act is a toady to the "old guard." He is Bevill Higgin, a maddeningly genteel old country "artist" whose writing, acting, singing and piano-playing epitomize the "old Guard's" worst failings in taste and education.

But Higgin's essential shoddiness does not pass undetected everywhere: a girl whom he imagines to be Pearl Vambrace refuses him university library privileges; Solly Bridgetower rejects his impudent offer to recite Shakespeare to students; and Ridley refuses to print his precious essays in the *Bellman*. Higgin's spiteful hoax wounds the three victims, but it also drives them to self-assessment and positive action. For example, Pearl's father (the egotistical Prospero of *Tempest-Tost*) regards the hoax as an attack on his personal honour, and in the family rows that ensue Pearl is freed from the tyranny and coldness of her home. She even adopts a new name—Veronica. Solly, whose department head has advised him to "jump right into Amcan" and publish a work on the great Canadian dramatist Charles Heavysege, recognizes that he wants to *create* some Canadian literature rather than study its relics. And Ridley, who had hoped for an honourary degree from Waverley as visible proof of his achievement, realizes that he needs no such external reassurances.

As is usual in romance, the maligned parties are aided by benign and intelligent friends—particularly Dean Knapp and Humphrey Cobbler, who represent the genuine humanity and taste of the British tradition as opposed to Higgin's pseudo-culture. Since music is equated with imagination in Davies, it is the happy Cobbler who counsels Solly to defy his "old guard" mother, marry his Pearl-Veronica, and begin to create. Finally, then, through the working of malice, the creative intelligence of Salterton finds its independence, or at least seems about to find it.

The statement of *Leaven of Malice* is hopeful, but despite the great ingenuity of its action and the sharpness of its observation it is not a warm book. In Gloster Ridley we meet a character who is highly lifelike, yet not entirely alive. Robertson Davies has not yet penetrated beyond the second or third box of the Chinese puzzle. His point of view is still the "public," wide-angled perspective of the dramatist, and though we watch *Leaven of Malice* with pleasure, we do not live *in* it.

In *A Mixture of Frailties*, however, Davies finally takes the step—so alien to the Marchbanksian side of his sensibility—which makes him a novelist, as distinct from a playwright. Here for the first time in his fiction he creates a protagonist whom we know fully and through whose eyes we see the action unfold. Now, instead of looking across the footlights, we are on stage and at the center of the action. The career of Monica Gall—a Canadian Cinderella who becomes a great singer—is *our* career; we suffer and learn with her. Because Davies is not entirely at home with this technique of characterization, there are many awkwardly-handled moments in Monica's story, but the access of warmth and intimacy which the method makes possible far outweighs these defects. There is no doubt now that the author intends much more than a topical satire of Canadian provinciality.

Davies' symbolic theme is still the struggle of the Canadian imagination to free itself from second-rateness, parochialism and dullness, but it moves beyond the situation of *Leaven of Malice*. He has explored the prospects of the educated Canadian intellectual, Solly Bridgetower, as far as he is able. Solly will "produce" it if he can. The question now is: What happens when a gifted but completely untutored Canadian is exposed to the best that Europe can offer? The story of Monica Gall is Davies' answer.

The machinery which sets Monica's story in motion is farcical though not, as a sequel to *Leaven of Malice*, improbable. The first year of Solly Bridgetower's marriage is blighted by the shadow of his "old guard" mother. The newlyweds live in her forbidding Victorian house, and even her death does not release them from the "Dead Hand" of her tradition. They will inherit her fortune only when they produce a male heir—a new Solomon. Until then a board of trustees is to spend the income from the estate on the artistic education of some talented young woman from Salterton. Monica Gall, Humphrey Cobbler's candidate, becomes the beneficiary.

As Monica's experience unfolds, we become aware that Davies' characters, while still as much the targets of satire as the caricatures of the earlier novels, now have a new relevance. Such persons as Monica's colleagues in the Heart and Hope Gospel Quartet, her callow, materialistic lover at the Glue Works, her wistful confidante Aunt Ellen, lost in a never-never world of music—these people reveal to us dramatically, existentially, what Monica *is*. Chief among them is Ma Gall, an image of the repressed Canadian imagination—of what Monica might have been:

> Ma, when she told tall stories, when she rasped her family with rough, sardonic jokes, when she rebelled against the circumstances of her life in coarse abuse, and when she cut through a fog of nonsense with the beam of her insight, was an artist—a spoiled artist, one who had never made anything, who was unaware of the nature or genesis of her own discontent, but who nevertheless possessed the artist's temperament; in her that temperament, misunderstood, denied and gone sour, had become a poison which had turned against the very sources of life itself. Nevertheless [Monica] was like Ma, and she must not go astray as Ma—not wholly through her own fault—had gone.[6]

In the same way, Monica's training in England is at once a highly absorbing narrative, full of humour, action and brilliant talk, and a symbolic study of the forces which the artist must recognize and learn to control if he is to become a genuine creator. Monica's director is Sir Benedict Domdaniel, a great British conductor. He sends her first to Murtagh Molloy, a voice coach who teaches her technique—the control of her physical resources—and then to Giles Revelstoke, a composer who initiates her into the mysteries of passion and joy which are the sources of art. The tension between these two aspects of her art, between technique and content, are worked out dramatically—even melodramatically. Monica soon falls slavishly in love with Revelstoke who, as befits the representative of the bardic spirit, comes from a primitive part of Wales, wears a signet ring bearing the image of Orpheus, and publishes a little magazine called *Lantern*. But as we might expect, though Revelstoke takes Monica as his mistress, he cannot be harnessed in marriage, nor can he be mothered; true to his nature, he is an isolated, brilliant, absolutely candid and easily exacerbated force. But if Monica cannot *possess* the creative spirit whom she loves, she will not become the mistress of technique. At a costume ball her voice coach, Molloy, attempts to seduce her and is rebuffed. "He can't resist a good pupil," says Mrs. Molloy, "he wants to run away with 'em all" (*Mixture*, p. 260).

Finally, after a violent quarrel, Revelstoke and Monica separate, and when she returns to him in the belief that she must accept his weaknesses along with his strengths, she finds him dead. On the surface level of the narrative this chapter is complex and awkwardly-contrived melodrama; but Revelstoke's death, seen as a final step in Monica's artistic development, is inevitable. The artist cannot remain indefinitely in servitude to an undisciplined creative spirit. Yet Monica's love for Revelstoke does not die; though she is freed from his domination, she inherits the files of his *Lantern*, and his talismanic Orpheus ring. Now her education is complete: she can return to Canada a free, self-determining individual. But the voices of Revelstoke and Ma Gall, though no longer dominating, will always counsel her; she will be "as one that hath a familiar spirit" (*Mixture*, p. 372).

This account of the structure of *A Mixture of Frailties* does no justice to the subtlety and richness of its execution, but that is the subject of another essay. In typical fashion, the romance closes with a rite. Davies gives us a daringly executed final chapter in which fragments of a sermon on the Magi are interwoven with Monica's thoughts and with passages of a letter in which Sir Benedict Domdaniel asks Monica to marry him. It is St. Nicholas' Day, the second anniversary of the Bridgetower Trust, and just before the memorial service begins we learn that Solly's wife has given birth to a healthy male heir. At last the "Dead Hand" of the Victorian past has relaxed its grip. The promise extended at the conclusion of *Leaven of Malice* has been fulfilled. As the congregation leaves the church, the irrepressible Cobbler plays "For unto us a child is born." Monica, we suspect, will accept Sir Benedict's proposal, but this is a matter of small concern, for Monica—a symbol of the Canadian imagination reaching its maturity—is now a citizen of the world.

Robertson Davies, I think, will yet write even better novels than *A Mixture of Frailties*, for he has learned that though the novelist may not lay bare the contents of the Chinese box, he must at least find a means of suggesting its contents. He may never abandon his role as Peterborough's Bad Boy (indeed I hope that he does not) but his most important achievement is his imaginative insight into the problems and the prospects of his culture. That insight, combined with his unfailing wit, bespeaks a gift that is all too rare in Canadian letters.

# Notes

1  Robertson Davies, *The Table Talk of Samuel Marchbanks* (Toronto: Clarke, Irwin & Co., 1949), p. 17.

2  Robertson Davies, *The Diary of Samuel Marchbanks* (Toronto: Clarke, Irwin & Co., 1947).

3  Robertson Davies, *Tempest-Tost* (Toronto: Clarke, Irwin & Co., 1958).

4  Robertson Davies, "Preface," in *At My Heart's Core* (Toronto: Clarke, Irwin & Co., 1950), p. *vii*.

5  Robertson Davies, *Leaven of Malice* (Toronto: Clarke, Irwin & Co., 1954).

6  Robertson Davies, *A Mixture of Frailties* (Toronto: Macmillan, 1958), p. 303.

# Robertson Davies' *Fifth Business* and "That Old Fantastical Duke Of Dark Corners, C.G. Jung"

*Gordon Roper*

D unstan Ramsay, the narrator of Robertson Davies' novel *Fifth Business*, in mid-life says of his closest friend and enemy, Boy Staunton:

> If his social life interested me, his private life fascinated me. I have never known anyone in whose life sex played such a dominant part. He didn't think so. He once told me that he thought this fellow Freud must be a madman, bringing everything down to sex in the way he did. I attempted no defence of Freud; by this time I was myself much concerned with that old fantastical duke of dark corners, C.G. Jung, but I had read a great deal of Freud and remembered his injunction against arguing in favour of psycho-analysis with those who clearly hated it.[1]

As the narrator of his own spiritual history in *Fifth Business*, Dunstan is a master of indirection and of understatement; this is his single allusion by name to Jung, in a book whose form and substance is overwhelmingly Jungian.

But Jungian in what sense? Jung explored so many dark corners in his long and far-reaching career. In his pursuit of knowledge and understanding of the soul of man he ranged through mythology and fairy tale, alchemy, anthropology, clinical cases of neuroses, art and literature, politics, the present and future and religions east and west. His collected work alone forms eighteen volumes in the Bollingen Series XX, and he published many other papers, essays, lectures and studies, notably in *Modern Man in Search of His Soul* (1933), *Man and his Symbols* (1964) and his remarkable spiritual autobiography, *Memories, Dreams, Reflections* (1961).

Robertson Davies, like his character Dunstan Ramsay, read widely in Freud's writings and then even more widely in Jung's. In the decade before he wrote *Fifth Business*, Jung had become his "Wise Old Man." His deepening commitment to a Jungian angle of vision rarely emerged in his writing in the 1960s, since most of that writing was scholarly or occasional. But how the spiritual wind was blowing as he started to write *Fifth Business* was evident in a talk he gave to students in February, 1968:

> Great as Freud was, and unassailable as his position is among the great liberators of the human mind, his actual technique seems more suited to the consulting-room than to the university lecture room; his mind dealt more strikingly with problems of neuroses than with matters of aesthetics, and his cast of mind was powerfully reductive. After the Freudian treatment, most things look a little shabby—needlessly so. Jung's depth psychology on the other hand, is much more aesthetic and humanistic in its effects on artistic experience. The light it throws on matters of literature and on the temperament of the writer is extremely useful and revealing.[2]

Today most lay readers know something of Jung and his depth psychology, but that knowledge is not apt to be extensive or precise. So before looking at what light depth psychology can throw on *Fifth Business* let me—as a lay reader—attempt to provide a working sketch of what was in Jung's temperament and thought that may have provided a matrix for Robertson Davies' book. For the sake of clarity, this sketch is overly diagrammatic.

Although his training was medical and scientific, Jung by temperament was unusually open to the power of the unknown. He felt strongly that the greatest force that shapes the lives of men—call it God, Fate, Destiny, Nature or the Unconscious—was infinite and ungraspable. Yet something drives men to know and to understand. As a way of looking into the darkness, Jung placed his faith in the tireless observation of and speculation about the individual. In his *Memories, Dreams, Reflections*, he wrote:

> My life has been permeated and held together by one idea and one goal: namely, to penetrate into the secret of the personality. Everything can be explained from this central point, and all my works relate to this one theme.[3]

Jung assumed that the individual was made up of an interacting body and psyche (or soul or spirit). The psyche, like the body, has had centuries of development, a development which each individual inherits from the collective past and individuates within his own capacity. Jung's most revolutionary concept was that the psyche in each individual—the total personality—is made up of three components. The only component we know directly is our ego, that small spark of consciousness or awareness of the self and what is perceptible to us through our senses. This spark floats in a sea of unconsciousness of two distinguishable kinds. The sea closest to our consciousness Jung termed the "personal unconscious," and assumed that it was made up of memories, feelings or states of mind which once were within the consciousness but now have slipped or were pushed outside. Beneath the personal unconscious lies the greater, unknown force of the "collective unconscious," common to all men in the primitive past and working still in each individual in forms Jung called "archetypes" which sometimes erupt in consciousness as "archetypal images" or "archetypal ideas or felt situations." Archetypal images manifest themselves to us in dreams, myths and legends and fairy tales, works of art or religious symbols.[4]

Jung also assumed that as biological life is a form of energy, so too is psychic life. Psychic energy he called the "libido," and the law of its dynamics, he believed, was a constant flow between opposing poles, or "opposites."

> Old Heraclitus, who was indeed a very great sage, discovered the most marvellous of all psychological laws; the regulative function of opposites. He called it *enantiodromia*, a running contrariwise, by which he meant that sooner or later everything runs into its opposite.[5]

Thus if the consciousness represses strongly the unconscious forces within the personality, the unconscious will surge back into the consciousness in the form of oppressive dreams, violent sudden emotion, bodily pain or illness. The invasion will continue until the conscious part of the personality somehow recognizes the opposing force and comes to some accommodation with it, a balancing which often requires outside help to achieve.

Jung's hypothesis of the polarity of psychic forces led him to posit tensions between parts of the personality—the conscious, and the personal and collective unconscious. He observed that as the individual grows, the conscious part, or ego, tends to develop those functions (or roles, or qualities) which come easiest to it, and which are encouraged by the physical and social world outside of it. Indeed, it develops a special side of itself, the persona (or mask) which it interposes between itself and the world, and which the world mistakes as the whole personality of that ego. Meanwhile as consciousness grows in the individual's earliest years, the ego tends to suppress or to drive into the personal unconscious those functions which oppose its development. This suppressed part of the personality, gathering force in the personal unconscious, Jung called "the shadow." By "shadow" he meant that it was the dark or more primitive side of consciousness, not that it was immoral or evil.

As our ego grows, our shadow grows. And under certain conditions the shadow will erupt into our consciousness. Then we find ourselves feeling or doing something which startles us because it seems out of character. After, we may say "I was not myself," or "I was beside myself." Or the shadow may manifest itself when we meet someone of the same sex and feel a sudden, intense enmity, envy or contempt for him. Since Jung assumed that our perception of all outside of us is highly (if not fully) subjective, he believed that when we responded to others in this unreasonable way what really happened was that the shadow part of our personality was projecting an image of itself onto that other person, to which our repressing ego reacted. An ego which refuses for long to recognize the existence and force of its shadow is inviting disruption. A healthy ego expands its consciousness by recognizing its shadow and by accepting its reality. This is one way of coming to know one's Self.

Jung also identified another pair of opposites—the ego and the anima (or animus). From his observation of thousands of clinical cases and of individuals outside clinics, he concluded that in each male personality is hidden a female force and in each woman a male force. He believed that these pairs of opposing forces were laid down deep in the collective unconscious. In men, this compelling attraction to the opposite sex—a yearning for completion, or for wholeness—projected itself as an "anima" image; in women, as an "animus" image. In men the force of the anima makes itself first felt to the individual in his image of his mother, the female image which he projects from within his collective unconscious to satisfy his deepest needs—and probably an image that bears little resemblance to his mother's actual personality.

When the bearer of this image fails him, as fail she must, he is driven in search of his anima to other women, finding one aspect in one particular woman and other aspects in other women, for at different times in his life his anima will express itself in different figures, some appearing to him as beneficent, some as malign, some as enigmatic. Some will be highly attractive, some highly repulsive, some a mingling of the highly attractive and repulsive. The man who approaches psychic wholeness is he who, along with other things, has found a satisfying anima in one individual woman—the Great Mother archetypal image, who is mother of himself and of his children, mistress, companion, spiritual guide and burier of the dead.[6]

These concepts of the shadow and of the anima helped Robertson Davies to shape his characters and their interactions in *Fifth Business*. The structure of the novel as a whole was shaped, I believe, by his interpretation of the concept at the heart of Jung's view of man—the concept of the growth of the individual personality towards wholeness, a process Jung called "individuation." In his spiritual autobiography, *Memories, Dreams, Reflections*, Jung wrote: "The central concept of my psychology [is] the process of individuation." In the same book he wrote:

> Individuation means becoming a single, homogeneous being, and, in so far as "individuality" embraces an innermost, last, and incomparable uniqueness, it also implies becoming one's own self.[7]

"Self" here appears to mean what it usually does in Jung's writing, the whole personality, made up of consciousness (with the persona or mask turned towards the public), the private unconsciousness and the collective unconsciousness.

> Conscious and unconscious do not make a whole when one of them is suppressed and injured by the other. If they must contend, let it

be at least a fair fight with equal rights on both sides. Both are aspects of life. Consciousness should defend its reason and protect itself, and the chaotic life of the unconscious should be given the chance of having its way too—as much as we can stand. This means open conflict and open collaboration at once. That, evidently, is the way human life should be. It is the old game of hammer and anvil: between them the patient iron is forged into an indestructible whole, an "individual." This, roughly, is what I mean by the individuation process.[8]

Coming to know the self, or getting to one's inner centre and making contact with the living mystery of the unconscious, alone and unaided, is difficult and dangerous; indeed, it is impossible for some.

Jung believed that the individual life unfolded itself in stages—early years and maturity. Each stage had its own nature and appropriate functions. Youth extends from puberty to middle age, which begins between thirty-five and forty. He described the stages:

Take for comparison the daily course of the sun—but a sun that is endowed with human feeling and man's limited consciousness: In the morning it rises from the nocturnal sea of unconsciousness and looks upon the wide, bright world which lies before it in an expanse that steadily widens the higher it climbs in the firmament. In this extension of its field of action caused by its own rising, the sun will discover its significance; it will see the attainment of the greatest possible height and the widest possible dissemination of its blessing, as its goal. In this conviction the sun pursues its course to the unforeseen zenith—unforeseen because its career is unique and individual. At the stroke of noon the descent begins. And the descent means the reversal of all the ideals and values that were cherished in the morning.[9]

After he had started to write *Fifth Business*, Robertson Davies commented on this change in the middle years of life:

What is the nature of this change? It is part of intellectual and spiritual growth. As Jung explains it, in the early part of life—roughly the first half of it—man's chief aims are personal and social. He must grow up, he must find his work, he must find out what kind of sex life he is going to lead, he must achieve some place in the world and attempt to get security within it, or else decide that security is not important to him. But when he has achieved these ends, or come to some sort of *understanding* with this part of existence, his attention is turned to matters that are broader in scope, and sometimes disturbing to contemplate. His physical strength is waning rather than growing; he has found out what sex is, and though it may be very important to him it can do little to surprise him; he realizes that some day he is really going to die and that the way he approaches death is of importance to him; he finds that without God (using that name to comprehend all the great and inexplicable things and the redemptive or destructive powers that lie outside human command and understanding), his life lacks a factor that it greatly needs; he finds that, in Jung's phrase, he is not the master of his fate except in a very modest degree and that he is in fact the object of a supraordinate subject. And he seeks wisdom rather than power—though the circumstances of his early life may continue to thrust power into his hands. [10]

Later in his talk, Davies continued:

The values that are proper and all-absorbing during the first half of life will not sustain a man during the second half. If he has the courage and wisdom to advance courageously into the new realm of values and emotions he will age physically of course, but his intellect and spiritual growth will continue, and will give satisfaction to himself and to all those associated with him. And such courage and wisdom are by no means rare; they may show themselves among many people who never have thought along these lines at all but who have a knack of living life wisely; and they also are to be found among those who regard self-awareness as one of the primary duties of a good life. [11]

As *Fifth Business* bodies forth so powerfully, the afternoon and evening of life can bring disaster to the individual who cannot adapt. As Jung warned, adaptation does not come easily; it comes only after the severest shocks. To adapt, the individual must turn inward; he must expand his conscious grasp of the unconscious that is master of his Fate. His consciousness grows by coming to recognize his shadow in his own personal unconsciousness. It grows by coming to cope with the more powerful and less graspable anima in the collective unconscious. And the anima is only one of the "archetypes" with which he must somehow integrate.

Jung thought of archetypes in various contexts as "the original components of the psyche" or "the great decisive forces" that bring about all events in individual and collective life. He likened them to biological instincts and to primordial patterns of psychic energy flow.

The language of the archetypes is symbolic. They speak to our consciousness from nature and from our cultural past, through certain shapes—mandalas, circles or crosses. They speak through certain actions, such as journeys, ascents or descents, or metamorphoses and rebirths, or they speak through certain natural places or scenes, or our fantasies of Gardens, Paradises or Hells. They make their presence felt in our dreams; through our senses; in rituals and celebrations; in myths, legends, fairy stories, folk lore; in religions; in music, dance, sculpture, painting, story or poem. Archetypal images are multitudinous; the symbolic forms in which they present themselves are unendingly various and shifting. But some basic symbols seem to occur most frequently. Besides the shadow and the anima, Jung identified as basic the Great Mother; the Father in his many forms, the Hero in all his guises as God-man, vanquisher of monsters, saviour of all people; the Wise Old Man who counsels and directs us in crises. Jung also identified other figures, such as the Rich Young Prince, the Sleeping Princess, the Devil in his many roles (often variants of the Father, Hero, or Wise Old Man), the Magus, or Magician and the Witch or She-Devil.

Whatever their symbolic form, archetypes are always felt by the effects of their unmistakable force—what Jung called their "luminosity"—in our consciousness. Our ego must recognize them as the symbolic language of our Fate speaking to us, and must somehow align itself with their force if it is to grow towards wholeness of Self.

> You can know all about the saints, sages, prophets, and other godly men, and all the great mothers of the world. But if they are mere images whose numinosity you have never experienced, it will be as if you were talking in a dream, for you will not know what you are talking about. The mere words you use will be empty and valueless. They gain life and meaning only when you try to take into account their numinosity—i.e., their relationship to the living individual. Only then do you begin to understand that their names mean very little, whereas the way they are *related* to you is all-important.[12]

Jung made a vital distinction between his use of "symbol" and "sign." For him a symbol must have numinosity. It expresses itself in an unpredictable variety of forms and its "meaning" is in the way it affects the individual consciousness. Conversely, consciousness cannot assign fixed meanings to symbols without reducing and distorting their force and so misapprehending them. It cannot decode them for it cannot grasp a key to the code. It can establish a code of signs, a short-hand system of referents to what it knows. The cross is a sign to many Christians, but it is not a symbol in the Jungian sense unless it has a numinosity to the individual—be he Christian or non Christian. Robertson Davies is fully aware of Jung's distinction between the nature of symbol and sign, and the reader who decodes *Fifth Business* according to a system of fixed signs will be working against its grain.

The grain of *Fifth Business* is, I suggest, that of modern myth. Jung believed that myth was a symbolic dramatization in story form which the forces of the collective unconscious bring into being in the imaginations of men, and perpetuate so long as the psychic energy expressed through it moves its auditors. He assumed that serious writers could create from the unconscious new myths or variants of the old which would speak eloquently to contemporary readers. In matter and manner, *Fifth Business* is a modern myth, and has been responded to as such by many readers.

At the most immediate level, *Fifth Business* is a memoir written by Dunstan Ramsay to the Headmaster of Colborne College, the prep school from which Ramsay has retired after years of teaching history. His writing is triggered by a farewell article in the college paper which stereotypes him flippantly as a Mr. Chips. This cheapening of his public image as a history master also violates his inner sense of himself: his commitment to life, his training as a scholar and his years of passionate questing into mythology and the mysteries of sainthood. As a man (and as a teacher) he must tell the truth about his whole life, especially about that hidden life which has been so much more adventurous and strange than his public life.

What he writes here at seventy-two, from high in the Swiss mountains, reveals that by temperament he is introverted, an individual of intense, complex feeling, driven by something within to break through the shell imposed upon him by his Scots Presbyterian upbringing. To protect himself, he has learned long ago to walk alone, to deal out personal revelations cautiously, hedging them with indirection and understatement. From mid-life his view of himself and the world around him has been ordered by his reading of Jung, although characteristically he only mentions this reading once, almost casually. Now at seventy-two, from near St. Gall, with his companions Liesl and the artist-magician Paul, he has achieved some sense of wholeness; from here he tells his story.

Dunstan orders his story, it seems, to dramatize how two interlocking constellations of characters play their parts in his unfolding physical and spiritual life. One constellation asserts forces primarily on his outer, public life and at the end of the story enables him to recognize himself as "Fifth Business," his shadow side. This constellation includes Boyd (Boy) Staunton, Boy's first and second wives, Leola and Denyse and Paul Dempster, son of Mrs. Mary Dempster. The other constellation dramatizes his inner search for his anima: his mother, Mrs. Mary Dempster, Leola, Diana Marfleet and, finally, Liesl. Two priests, one in his village and one in his private life, add their direction: Father Regan dogmatically warns him against pursuing a "fool saint"; Father Blazon acts as his Wise Old Man, and directs the pursuit of the spirit inward. Mary Dempster, in her changing aspects, is the major interlocking force between the two constellations.

Dunstan's journey is at once an inner and outer one. Let me, at the risk of distortion, suggest the central thrust of his inner journey: his search for his anima. After his secret involvement with Mrs. Dempster, his mother attaches him to Mrs. Dempster as helper and watchdog. When he is fourteen he undergoes a traumatic experience with his mother. And bereft of a mother he seeks that image in Mrs. Dempster. Mrs. Dempster becomes more deranged, and outrages the villagers by her charity to a tramp in the gravel pit. She is tied up within her home, but Dunny (Dunstan) seeks her aid when he believes his brother has died, and she performs her second miracle. Mrs. Ramsay tries to retain possession of "her wee laddie," but Dunny evades her force by slipping away from home to join the army.

In the second chapter, Dunny encounters two more anima figures. He is violently wounded at Passchendaele in November, 1917. Before he loses consciousness, he sees a vision of a Madonna with the face of Mrs. Dempster. He regains consciousness in an English hospital in May, 1918, terribly scarred and without a left leg. After this season in the dark he is "reborn," and initiated into manhood by his nurse, Diana Marfleet. When he realizes his attraction to her may lead to a possession by another mother, a wife-mother, he extricates himself, and she rechristens him Dunstan (after St. Dunstan) on Christmas

Day. When he returns to his village with a Victoria Cross awarded by his King, he is given a village hero's welcome. He also finds that his friend and rival, Percy Boyd Staunton, has claimed the village princess, Leola, to whom Dunny was attracted in a teen-age way. His mother and father have died in the influenza epidemic in 1918, and he feels freed. He also learns that Paul had run away with a circus when he was ten and Mrs. Dempster has been taken to live with an aunt near Toronto.

After his University years he becomes a history master at Colborne College in Toronto, and his search for his anima takes two paths. He visits Mrs. Dempster, and finally has her placed in an asylum, as the sad, best thing he can do to help her. Meanwhile, his association with her, and what to him were her three miracles, has led him to devote all of his private time to research into the lives of the saints. This leads him to a village in the Tyrol in search of knowledge about St. Uncumber, and there he meets Paul, now a magician in a small travelling show. When Dunstan is in Toronto, he keeps in touch with Boy Staunton and his wife Leola, for whom Dunstan has little feeling other than pity now. On another European research trip to the Bollandists he meets the Jesuit, Father Blazon, who turns out to be his Wise Old Man. Father Blazon counsels him in Jungian language not to seek the meaning of sainthood in Mrs. Dempster or in the Lives of the Saints, but within himself:

> I do not suggest that you should fail in your duty toward her; if she has no friends but you, care for her by all means. But stop trying to be God, making it up to her that you are sane and she is mad. Turn your mind to the real problem: who is she? Oh, I don't mean her police identification or what her name was before she was married. I mean, who is she in your personal world? What figure is she in your personal mythology? If she appeared to save you on the battlefield, as you say, it has just as much to do with you as it had with her—much more probably. Lots of men have visions of their mother in time of danger. Why not you? Why was it this woman? Who is she? That is what you must discover, Ramezay, and you must find your answer in psychological truth, not in objective truth.[13]

In Chapter Five, "Liesl," Dunstan again meets with Paul while on a research trip in Mexico. Paul is now Magnus Eisengrim, masterly artist at his craft, and is managed by a strangely repulsive-attractive woman, Liesl. After an infatuation with Faustina, the young trouper, he comes to know Liesl in a rousing bedroom scene. She convinces him that he has "a whole great piece of life that is unlived, denied, set aside" and urges him to live his unlived life, to shake hands with his own devil. He does more than just shake hands. Finally she hurls at him:

> Here you are, twice-born, and nearer your death than your birth, and you have still to make a real life.
> Who are you? Where do you fit into poetry and myth? Do you know who I think you are, Ramsay? I think you are Fifth Business.

And she proceeds to tell him in detail what "Fifth Business" means.[14] He discovers that he is indeed Fifth Business in his room with Paul and Boy on the night of Boy's death. At Eisengrim's performance at the Royal Alexandra the next night, it is Liesl, speaking through the Brazen Head, who answers cryptically the question "Who killed Boy Staunton?" and it is Liesl who writes to Dunstan, after his heart attack, to invite him to join her and Paul in the mountains of Switzerland, and so in the end it seems Dunstan finds his anima.

Dunstan's outer journey is made largely through the effect on him of his relation to Percy Boyd Staunton and Paul Dempster. Staunton (who later rechristens himself "Boy") from village days has been to Dunstan his opposite. Boy is an extrovert, with a single-minded genius for acquiring money and power. His father has become rich by village standards: Boy becomes much richer. To Dunstan he seems an envied Rich Young Prince; he marries Leola, the village Princess. He models himself on that Ideal Prince of the 1920s, the Prince of Wales. Dunstan admires the young Prince's father, the King. Boy gives his sexual drive free rein, while Dunstan, scarred by his physical and psychic wounds, subdues his in pursuit of the spirit. Boy treats women as objects; Dunstan sees them as individuals.

Apparently Boy has suppressed completely any awareness of his relation to Mrs. Dempster. But Dunstan and he feel a bond, a responsibility for each other. Boy helps Dunstan with financial advice and guides him to a modest financial security. Dunstan is disturbed by Boy's enigmatic behaviour in the "Gyges and King Candaules" episode. He worries about Boy's spiritual unawareness and urges him to come to know himself, although, at the same time, Dunstan himself is unaware of how his own shadow projects its images onto Boy. It is Father Blazon who begins Dunstan's enlightenment about his relation with Boy, and later it is Liesl who advances that enlightenment.

Boy continues to believe in his image of himself as the Rich Young Prince well into his middle years. But when his ideal collapses in the Abdication of 1936, Boy falls into a private hell. His family disintegrates (in a way told by his son David in *The Manticore*). Leola attempts desperately to save herself by turning to Dunstan; he runs away (as he later says), although after her attempt at suicide he does return to try to help clean up the emotional mess. Leola dies, and Boy apparently feels little loss; when Mrs. Dempster dies later, Dunstan loses one of "the fixed stars in my life." Boy marries (or is married by) Denyse, a woman "of masculine mind" without recognizing that she will devour him. He thinks of death; it comes through Paul, now the great magician, whom he meets in Dunstan's college rooms after a performance.

Dunstan's shadow—his Fifth Business side—breaks through his conscious image of himself to tell Paul how Boy became related to both their lives in village days. Boy is found dead in his submerged car in Toronto Harbour, with a stone in his mouth, the stone that Dunstan has treasured since Boy threw it in a snowball years before. So Boy is killed, by the four principals and Fifth Business. Dunstan collapses, but his acceptance later of Liesl's invitation to join her and Paul in Switzerland suggests that he has come to know his shadow side and to live with it, as in his inner journey he has arrived at a harmony of forces. So he attains some fused inner and outer state of wholeness in the mountains at St. Gall.

This is one reading of the myth of individuation which seems to structure *Fifth Business*—a structure enriched by many archetypal images, ideas and situations, and enhanced by interwoven signs. Presented in this reductive way, it may suggest that Robertson Davies has worked consciously from a scheme of fixed Jungian concepts. But such a conclusion would go contrary to his mode of working and to Jung's mode of thought. As Jung wrote in Part II of his "Aion":

> Therefore, in describing the living process of the psyche, I deliberately and consciously give preference to a dramatic, myth-ological way of thinking and speaking, because this is not only the

more expressive, but also more exact than an abstract scientific terminology, which is wont to flirt with the notion that its theoretical formulations may one fine day be resolved into algebraic equations. [15]

Davies' way of thinking and speaking is also intuitive, dramatic and mythological. For some years Jung's angle of vision has coincided with his own, and Jung has become for him a spring of wisdom. From that spring the archetypal forms flow, and the writer's task is to body them forth in words so their effect will be felt by the reader. The process of bodying forth is that of the unconscious and the conscious working together, often in a way that the consciousness cannot control or recognize. When he is expressing myths the writer does not know what he is doing; when he is inventing signs, he does know. *Fifth Business* is made up of both myth and sign. These working together give it a strange power. And this was Davies' aim, for, like his magician Paul, he desires to move his audience to wonder. When Dunstan and Paul talk in Mexico City after Paul's performance, Paul says:

> You see what we are doing.... We are building up a magic show of unique quality.... You know that nowadays the theatre has almost abandoned charm; actors want to be sweaty and real; playwrights want to scratch their scabs in public. Very well; it is the mood of the times. But there is always another mood, one precisely contrary to what seems to be the fashion. Nowadays this concealed longing is for romance and marvels. Well, that is what we can offer, but it is not done with the back bent and a cringing smile; it must be offered with authority...

Dunstan asks him: "What do you want? To be feared?" and Paul replies:

> To be wondered at. This is not egotism. People want to marvel at something, and the whole spirit of our time is not to let them do it... [16]

Like Paul, Robertson Davies offers his *Fifth Business* with authority arising from a brilliant performance and from a wisdom that is old and forever new. Perhaps Davies also has done in words some thing similar, and for similar reasons, to what Jung did when he built his house on the lake shore near Zurich when he was nearing fifty:

> I had to achieve a kind of representation in stone of my innermost thoughts and the knowledge I had acquired. Or to put it another way, I had to make a confession of faith in stone. That was the beginning of the 'Tower,' the house which I built for myself at Bollingen...so in 1922 I bought some land.... It was situated in the area of St. Meinrad, and is old church land, having formerly belonged to the monastery of St. Gall.[17]

# Notes

1 Robertson Davies, *Fifth Business* (Toronto: Macmillan, 1970), p. 213.

2 Robertson Davies, "The Conscience of the Writer," a talk given to students at Glendon College, York University, on February 15,1968, and printed in *One Half of Robertson Davies* (Toronto: Macmillan, 1977), p. 126.

3 C.G. Jung. *Memories, Reflections, Dreams*, recorded and edited by Aniela Jaffé (New York: Alfred Knopf, 1961), p. 206.

4 See Jung's discussion of the nature of the psyche in *Collected Works* (hereafter referred to as CW) 9, parts I and II (Princeton: Bollingen Series XX, Princeton University Press).

5 C.G. Jung, "Two Essays on Analytical Psychology," CW 7, paragraph 111.

6 For Jung on the shadow and anima, see particularly CW 4, 11.

7 C.G. Jung, *Memories, Dreams, Reflections*, p. 209.

8 C.G. Jung, CW 9, 1, paragraphs 522-523.

9 C.G. Jung, "The Stages of Life," CW 8, paragraph 778.

10 Robertson Davies, "The Conscience of the Writer," pp. 127-128.

11 *Ibid.*, p. 128.

12 C.G. Jung, *Man and his Symbols* (Garden City, N.Y.: Doubleday, 1954). Rpt. (New York: Dell, 1968), p. 88.

13 Robertson Davies, *Fifth Business*, pp. 198-208.

14 *Ibid.*, pp. 259-267.

15 C.G. Jung, CW 9, part II.

16 Robertson Davies, *Fifth Business*, p. 244.

17 C.G. Jung, *Memories, Dreams, Reflections.* p. 223. The following paragraphs are also of interest.

# Miracle and Art in *Fifth Business* or Who the Devil is Liselotte Vitzlipützli?

*Wilfred Cude*

P erhaps scholars fall a little too easily into the habit of adopting long-established categories with a minimum of scrutiny. To many an academic mind, the categories of "fiction" and "nonfiction" are of a mutually exclusive nature, and works listed under the one are to be carefully disassociated from those listed under the other. It is almost as if fiction were deemed more enjoyable, but somehow less respectable, than nonfiction: as if it were deemed imaginative and recreational, but simply not real. This sort of categorization, however admissible to scholars still deferring to Plato's censure of the fanciful follies of poets, has been flatly rejected by many serious writers of fiction. Henry Fielding wrote of his novels as histories. Henry James insisted that fiction emanate the odour of reality. Ernest Hemingway demanded that the author of fiction confine himself rigorously to the realm of personal knowledge. For such writers, art was not to be divorced from reality: rather, it evolved out of reality, and it existed to provide another means of approaching reality. As Joseph Conrad put the matter, the task of the writer is to make you see. Fiction is not literary sleight of hand, fun tainted with tricksterism: fiction is an artistic miracle whereby those afflicted in their imaginations can be made to experience again the remarkable world about them. Within the long tradition of works that challenge us to appreciate this truth, *Fifth Business* by Robertson Davies is a vital newcomer.

In Dunstan Ramsay, the narrator of the novel, Davies has created a character who seems to have a comprehensive grasp of reality. Despite his worldly demeanour, Dunny lives by an academic philosophy that is austere to the point of asceticism. He is quite prepared to come to grips with any mode of thought that passes his way.

> I clung to my notion, ill defined though it was, that a serious study of any important body of human knowledge, or theory, or belief, if undertaken with a critical but not a cruel mind, would in the end yield some secret, some valuable permanent insight, into the nature of life and the true end of man.[1]

Suiting his practice to what he preaches, Dunny grapples heroically with a curriculum that would daunt anyone but the most dedicated of polymaths. One subject after another, he wrestles into submission entire kingdoms of learning: magic, history, zoology, religious studies, French, German, Latin, Italian, Greek, and medieval and renaissance art and architecture. Nor is he content only with a mastery of the mechanics of several disciplines: nothing less than a confrontation with "the reality of the spirit" (p. 102) will satisfy him, and so he sets himself to an engagement with the entire phenomenon of faith.

> I was trying to get at the subject without wearing either the pink spectacles of faith or the green spectacles of science. All I had managed by the time I found myself sitting in the basilica of Guadalupe was a certainty that faith was a psychological reality, and that where it was not invited to fasten itself on things unseen, it invaded and raised bloody hell with things seen (p. 179).

As Dunny's personality emerges from his narrative, he stands out as one who has the courage to attempt much and the vision to perceive wonders; he stands out, in effect, as a formidable and devoted scholar. "Illiteracy was my abhorrence" (p. 111), he laconically observes: and, from the evidence he supplies, we may well believe him.

And yet, even while he delineates his own scholarship and insight, Dunny does not appear affected or smug. He is alert to the pathetic delusions fostered by self-deception. "This is one of the cruelties of the theatre of life; we all think of ourselves as stars and rarely recognize it when we are indeed mere supporting characters or even supernumeraries" (p. 20). He is alert to the multiplicity of masks that every human being might wear in life. "I cannot remember a time when I did not take it as understood that everybody has at least two, if not twenty-two, sides to him" (pp. 65-66). And because he is a hard-headed Scot, he is far too practical to assume that his behaviour is any exception to the norm. He knows that he is a man: that is to say, he knows that he has a flair for duplicity, an egalitarian talent that impartially misleads him as well as others.

> She wanted to know all about me, and I told her as honestly as I could; but as I was barely twenty, and a romantic myself, I know now that I lied in every word I uttered—lied not in fact but in emphasis, in colour, and in intention (p. 74).

This is a genuine humility. Its essence is not a sanctimonious self-abasement, but a wary consciousness of the elusive qualities of the human soul. And by rendering his central character so intensely aware of the intricacies of things spiritual, Davies is intimating to us that much in the novel could be other than it seems.

## II

The complexities of the interplay between fiction and fact should initially strike us when we deduce that the down-to-earth Dunny is very wrong about being Fifth Business. At the opening of the novel, he writes with assurance: "I have been cast by Fate and my own character for the vital though never glorious role of Fifth Business" (p. 14). This is a self-imposed fiction, for the facts of the novel are altogether otherwise. Once we examine the definition of Fifth Business that Davies provides on the flyleaf, we must conclude that Dunny just cannot be cast for the role.

> Those roles which, being neither those of Hero nor Heroine, Confidante nor Villain, but which were nonetheless essential to bring about the Recognition or the dénouement, were called the Fifth Business in drama and opera companies organized according to the old style; the player who acted these parts was often referred to as Fifth Business (p. 5).

If Dunny were Fifth Business, he would of necessity be a subordinate in the work. He would perform somewhat as, for example, Nelly Dean in *Wuthering Heights*, presenting the story, making observations, even contributing to some of the minor crises, but, always focusing the attention of the reader on the other characters. And Dunny Ramsay has no such role. Surely he is closer to Hero, Confidant, even Villain, than Fifth Business. We follow him, not the others. They exist to shed light on him, on his activities—not the other way around. When Dunny begins his narrative, the first paragraph is most informative.

> My lifelong involvement with Mrs. Dempster began at 5:58 o'clock p.m. on the 27th of December, 1908, at which time I was ten years and seven months old (p. 9).

Clearly, we have learned a good deal more about Dunny than Mrs. Dempster. She is named only as a person with whom he had "a lifelong involvement." But he is introduced as narrator, in a spate of personal details that suggest he will be the major figure in the work. We are introduced to a boy who will grow up to be a scholar, a strange adventurer embarking upon a lifelong quest for sainthood: and the story we are reading is most definitely the story of his life.

After all, what reason does Dunny advance for setting down his story in the first place? He is not interested in writing about Mary Dempster or Boy Staunton: he is interested in writing strictly about himself. He is determined to correct an article published in the Colborne College paper, an article purporting to give a summary of his career.

> But why, you will ask, am I writing to you at all? Why, after a professional association of so many years, during which I have been reticent about my personal affairs, am I impelled now to offer you such a statement as this?
>
> It is because I was deeply offended by the idiotic piece that appeared in the *College Chronicle* in the issue of mid-summer 1969. It is not merely its illiteracy of tone that disgusts me (though I think the quarterly publication of a famous Canadian school ought to do better), but its presentation to the public of a portrait of myself as a typical old schoolmaster doddering into retirement with tears in his eyes and a drop hanging from his nose (pp. 12-13).

"The Cork" is a caricature, a beaver-clad Mr. Chips, a travesty spawned from the stereotypes that clutter the brain of Lorne Packer, MA and aspirant to a PhD, and Dunny will have none of it. In rebuttal to Packer's fiction, he produces his own statement of fact. He is, to use the politician's phrase, setting the record straight.

Although Dunny's anger goads him into writing a lengthy account of his life, it is typical of him that his indignation stems in equal measure from personal and professional considerations. An author and scholar himself, he has infinite contempt for Packer and Packer's work. "Packer and his scientific view of history! Oh God!" (p. 14) The offending article is representative of a regrettable sub-genre of academic composition: it is spun so completely out of preconceptions that its fabric rarely displays the slightest wisp of reality. Packer thinks of Lorne Packer as a product of a fine private school, and so he enumerates with an almost Homeric zest the splendours of those associated with Colborne College. The College Old Boys could muster up "several MPs and two cabinet ministers" and "four heads of history departments," to say nothing of the virtually vice-regal shade of "late Boy Staunton, D.S.O., C.B.E." Packer wishes to hint coyly at the brilliance of those who (like Lorne Packer) have moved beyond the simplicities of school-level history, and so he modestly works in a reference to those worthies. They are to be found among "countless boys," Dunny's victims, and they are the elect who "have gone on to a more scientific study of the subject in the universities." Packer chooses to laud Lorne Packer's concept of history, and so he sweeps Dunny's research aside as the foibles of an old dingbat. Dunny has "taught history, as he sees it." Dunny's studies are best touched upon "humorously" in "a generous, non-critical tribute" by a "scientific" historian (p. 13). The offending article fails to mention that Dunny had won the Victoria Cross, had written ten substantial books and had lived a life of travel, gallantry and romance. Dunny is understandably irked.

> But what most galls me is the patronizing, dismissive tone of the piece—as if I had never had a life outside the classroom, had never risen to the full stature of a man, had never rejoiced or sorrowed or known love or hate, and never, in short, been anything except what lies within the comprehension of the donkey Packer.... (p. 14)

To be precise, Dunny is accusing Packer of gross distortion—of omitting relevant material, of being oblivious to the spiritual timbre of human events, of manipulating attitudes, of twisting the marvels of actuality almost beyond recognition.[2] This is an egregious imbecility on the part of an old pupil, and Dunny has no intention of sparing the corrective rod.

Solely as an alternative to Packer's piece, then, we are invited to accept the full text of the novel. We are whimsically cast by Davies in the role of Headmaster, and we should not lose sight of the implications of this. We are invited to judge between Packer's writing and Dunny's writing, between Packer's way and Dunny's way, and—ultimately—between Packer and Dunny. Should we decide to accept Dunny's narrative, Dunny's analysis of the course of his life, we are warned by his frankness that his work must be flawed by human fallibility. Obviously enough, he cannot see that it is flawed: but we are the Headmaster, we are possessed of the facts from other vantage-points, and we are able to sort out the misconstructions. As we have already discovered, Dunny cannot be Fifth Business. His humility, which armours him against the sin of pride, also encumbers him when he attempts to assess the part he played in his own story. Even as he occupies the centre of the stage, he is encouraged by the bizarre but enchanting Liselotte Vitzlipützli to regard himself as an auxiliary player. It should be noted that she tempts him by suggesting the possibility and leaving the conclusion to him. "Are you Fifth Business? You had better find out" (p. 203). Handicapped for once by his consistent refusal to set himself apart from the generality of mankind, he unhesitatingly answers in the affirmative, overlooking that he knows Liesl to be the very devil of a woman. As the agent of a magician seeking an accomplished ghost writer, as an insatiable seductress seeking a victim of integrity, she has her reasons for seeing Dunny as Fifth Business. However, we do not share her reasons: Fifth Business he may be to others, but categorically not to us.

## III

Given that Dunny can be mistaken about his own role, we should feel obliged to review at length the recurrent question of the novel: is Mary Dempster actually a saint? Certainly Dunny never wavers in his conviction of her sanctity. In book six, entitled "The Soirée of Illusions," he protests:

> I had once been fully persuaded that Mary Dempster was a saint and even of late years I had not really changed my mind. There were the three miracles, after all; miracles to me, if to no one else (pp. 218-19).

The phrase "if to no one else" is a necessary qualification, for Dunny has retained his conviction in the face of extensive scepticism. Mary's prayerful intercession or not, Dr. McCausland is hardly about to countenance any intimations of Willie's miraculous return from immortality. "I think you may safely leave it to me to say when people are dead, Dunny" (p. 56). The doctor's scientific pronouncement receives religious confirmation from Father Regan. "A few minutes with no signs of life. Well, that's hardly Lazarus, now, is it?" Nor is the good Father inclined in the least to embrace either of the other miracles. He mocks the conversion of a nameless and hungry would-be-rapist into the zealous Mr. Joel Surgeoner. "A tramp reformed. I've reformed a tramp or two myself; they get spells of repentance, like most people." He scoffs at the vision of the little Madonna at Passchendaele. "And your own experience when you were wounded—man, you were out of your head" (p. 124). In the estimation of Father Regan, Mary is nothing more than a fool-saint.

> A fool-saint is somebody who seems to be full of holiness and loves everybody and does every good act he can, but because he's a fool it all comes to nothing—to worse than nothing, because it is virtue tainted with madness, and you can't tell where it'll end up (p. 125).

Resent these opinions though he may, Dunny's scrupulous sense of scholarship compels him to record them, and thereby to offer them to the Headmaster for consideration. And what are we to make of them?

When we attempt to thread our way through the maze of these contrary views, we could do much worse than follow the thought of Father Blazon, the Jesuit and Bollandist, who guides Dunny around some of the convolutions of sainthood. Father Blazon does not overly concern himself with miracles as such, for he tends to regard all existence as miraculous. "Life itself is too great a miracle for us to make so much fuss about potty little reversals of what we pompously assume to be the natural order" (p. 157). Because he thus sees the universe, he tries to avoid the issue of Mary's miracles, advising Dunny not to worry unduly about technicalities. "As for the miracles, you and I have looked too deeply into miracles to dogmatize; you believe in them, and your belief has coloured your life with beauty and goodness; too much scientizing will not help you" (pp. 221-22). Of far greater relevance to Father Blazon's deliberations is the matter of Dunny's relationship with his fool-saint. Much to Dunny's consternation, he postulates that Mary could be part of God's plan for an unheralded Canadian schoolmaster.

> And while you are searching, get on with your own life and accept the possibility that it may be purchased at the price of hers and that this may be God's plan for you and her.
>
> You think that dreadful? For her, poor sacrifice, and for you who must accept the sacrifice? Listen, Ramezay, have you heard what Einstein says—Einstein, the great scientist, not some Jesuit like old Blazon. He says, 'God is subtle, but He is not cruel.' There is some sound Jewish wisdom for your muddled Protestant mind. Try to understand the subtlety, and stop whimpering about the cruelty. Maybe God wants you for something special. Maybe so much that you are worth a woman's sanity (p. 160).

After a contemplation of the strange story his younger colleague brought him, a contemplation sustained over a period of years, the old Jesuit concludes that Mary "would never have got past the Bollandists" (p. 221); but he nonetheless urges Dunny to accept her as one who brought some measure of illumination into his life.

Like all of Father Blazon's counsel, this is solid good sense. Stress how he will Mary's good nature, Dunny cannot turn his fool-saint into a true saint, since her path to virtue is undermined by her lack of awareness, her simplicity, her folly. Her reaction to Dunny's worried hovering over her and the infant Paul is to laugh at the boy's concern. Her idea of charity is to traipse round the community presenting wilted rhubarb or rank lettuce to bewildered recipients who had no use for these unsolicited gifts. And her contribution to each of the three miracles is marred by touches of innocent mindlessness. Caught in the depths of the gravel pit Gehenna, wrenched from the copulation that proves instrumental in the redemption of the fanatical Joel

Surgeoner, she explains her motives to her husband with the fabulous response: "He was very civil, 'Masa. And he wanted it so badly" (p. 44). Shepherded from the bedside of the revived Willie, she pauses an instant to blow him a kiss (p. 55). Just before the manifestation of the little Madonna at Passchendaele, Dunny recalls the practical commonplace Mary left him with, and he thrusts her thought away as an absurdity disclosed by the flames of war. "Mrs. Dempster, I said aloud, was a fool" (p. 70). Though he will not suppress these hard facts, he also will not investigate them critically; and his reticence conceals from himself and others the possibility that the miracles inspiring his reverence could with greater justice be attributed to him.

We should scrutinize this possibility with care, because Dunny's scholarly sharpness is least incisive when the subject for examination is Mrs. Dempster. His dissection of the three miracles is hopelessly botched, a classic demonstration of the *post hoc ergo propter hoc* procedure. Mary was a part of the miracles: very well then, Mary was the cause of the miracles. But in each instance, Mary was the passive agent—and Dunny was the active agent. Were it not for Dunny, the traumatic interruption of the copulation that made the new Joel Surgeoner could never have occurred, for Dunny was the one who discovered the couple. Were it not for Dunny, Mary could never have prayed over the stricken Willie: for Dunny ran to get her, Dunny released her, and Dunny conducted her to the invalid's bed. Were it not for Dunny, the appearance of the little Madonna at Passchendaele would have been meaningless. As Father Blazon so accurately sums it up to his friend: "If she appeared to save you on the battlefield, as you say, it has just as much to do with you as it has with her—much more probably" (p. 159). Moreover, unlike Mary's simple antics, Dunny's participation in each event sprang from a conscious moral impulse. He went to the gravel pit in search of the lost Mary; he ran from Willie's side to get help for his stricken brother; he gazed up from the mud into the fiery heavens of Passchendaele while serving above and beyond the call of military duty. All these facts cry out for recognition, and indicate a hypothesis vastly different from the one Dunny has brought himself to accept.

Mary's odour of sanctity is Chanel Number Five. Very much like the perfume sprinkled over her corpse by the decent undertaker, Mary's saintly exploits are well-intentioned moral cosmetics fabricated by Dunny to disguise a sad reality. Father Blazon is completely right: Mary, whose ashes appropriately carry the epitaph "Here is the patience and faith of the saints" (p. 234), existed to become part of Dunny's mission in life. Time and again, the novel restates this basic truth. The devilish Liesl says it with a sting.

> You make yourself responsible for other people's troubles. It is your hobby. You take on the care of a poor madwoman you knew as a boy. You put up with subtle insult and being taken for granted by a boyhood friend—this big sugar-man who is such a power in your part of the world. You are a friend to this woman—Leola, what a name!—who gave you your *congé* when she wanted to marry Mr. Sugar. And you are secret and stiff-rumped about it all, and never admit it is damned good of you (p. 201).

Liesl's flamboyant minion Eisengrim says it almost with regret.

> Many people feel these irrational responsibilities and cannot crush them. Like Ramsay's loyalty to my mother, for instance, I am sure it was an impediment to him, and certainly it must have been a heavy expense, but he did not fail her. I suppose he loved her. I might have done so if I had ever known her (p. 232).

How does it happen that Mary's ashes are "the patience and faith of the saints?" They are all that is left of some of the holy work of Dunstan Ramsay, the one true saint that the novel is depicting.

## IV

To fully comprehend this, the central Recognition of the novel, we must search for the character who makes the plot work. We must find for ourselves "the odd man out, the person who has no opposite of the other sex" (p. 203). We can readily fix upon him in Padre Blazon, the real Fifth Business of this dramatic company organized according to the old style. Translate the title, and Davies has playfully assigned Father Blazon the same initials as Fifth Business: but he has also provided grounds of greater substance to convey to us the part played by the old Jesuit. Father Blazon is the one person who satisfies all the requirements of the title role. Not only does Dunny not suit the definition on the flyleaf, he scarcely matches the description advanced by the temptress Liesl. How could he be considered as having "no opposite of the other sex" when he is sitting at his ease in bed with a semi-nude woman passionately intent upon seducing him? No such objection could be raised with respect to Father Blazon, Dunny's spiritual mentor; notwithstanding the regular matinal guarantee that he could have been a great lover, he is still able to trumpet forth his pride in his unassailable chastity. "Behold me, Ramezay, a virgin at the age of seventy-six" (p. 157)! Yes, in this novel, Father Blazon must be "the odd man out." There never was, and never could be, an "opposite of the other sex" for him. Nor can he be regarded as anything remotely resembling a Hero, a Confidant, or a Villain. His part is never glorious, but vital: he furnishes the details we need to see what is really before us. It "is not spectacular, but a good line of work;" and most conclusively we can agree that Father Blazon "outlasts the golden voices" (p. 203). And who does our Fifth Business reveal Dunny to be? Why, of course, a Canadian St. Dunstan—born again "a thousand years after his time" (p. 223).

It is axiomatic that the revelations of Fifth Business will be consistent with the total structure of the work, and so we find it to be in this case. In the second book, entitled "I Am Born Again," Davies makes us witness to the induction of a modern saint. When Dunny is wounded after his capture of a machine-gun nest at Passchendaele, he crawls into the ruins of a church to collapse in agony: and while he is thus reduced to the shreds of his elemental being, he partakes of an event he will later account a miracle.

> It was then that one of the things happened that make my life strange—one of the experiences that other people have not had or do not admit to—one of the things that makes me so resentful of Packer's estimate of me as a dim man to whom nothing important has ever happened (p. 70).

In the garish light of a descending flare, he sees a statue of a little Madonna, and recognizes her as "the Crowned Woman in *Revelation*—she who had the moon beneath her feet and was menaced by the Red Dragon" (p. 70). He falls unconscious and remains so for six months, lapsing into a state of existence that medical science decides to label as shell-shock coma, but that he prefers to consider as something marvellously akin to paradise.

> Years later, when for the first time I read Coleridge's *Kubla Khan* and came on—

> Weave a circle round him thrice,
> And close your eyes with holy dread,
> For he on honey-dew hath fed,
> And drunk the milk of Paradise.

—I almost jumped out of my skin, for the words so perfectly described my state before I woke up in hospital. I had been wonderfully at ease and healingly at peace; though from time to time voices spoke to me I was under no obligation to hear what they said or to make a reply; I felt that everything was good, that my spirit was wholly my own, and that though all was strange nothing was evil (p. 71).

He revives in an English hospital, to learn that most of his clothes and all of his identification had been consumed by the flare and the Flanders mud. He has left the old Dunstable Ramsay behind, and is—physically, mentally, spiritually—every bit a new man.

Physically, he is rather the worse for wear. The harrowing experience of executing his secular duty has cost him a leg and severe burns across his chest and left side. Mentally, he is awakened to what he has become. At the ceremony at Buckingham Palace, as the King is awarding him the Victoria Cross, Dunny has a revelation concerning the nature he has assumed.

> We are public icons, we two; he an icon of kingship, and I an icon of heroism, unreal yet very necessary; we have obligations above what is merely personal, and to let personal feelings obscure the obligations would be failing in one's duty (p. 79).

Spiritually, he is vaguely aware that he has a destiny to explore all on his own.

> I agree that I was sure there was more to me than that, but I didn't know what it was and I needed time to find out. Furthermore, I knew that the finding out must be done alone (p. 83).

The new Dunny is arisen, literally from the flames, and he requires only a second name to enter the company of the twice-born.

The delectable Diana Marfleet, the angel of mercy who ministers to Dunny while he is in his state of transition, is the one chosen to consecrate him in his new identity. She commences by explaining why he should take the name Dunstan.

> You'll never get anywhere in the world named Dumbledum
> Ramsay. Why don't you change it to Dunstan? St. Dunstan was a
> marvellous person and very much like you—mad about learning,
> terribly stiff and stern and scowly, and an absolute wizard at
> withstanding temptation. Do you know that the Devil once came
> to tempt him in the form of a fascinating woman, and he caught
> her nose in his goldsmith's tongs and gave it a terrible twist (p.
> 84)?

Following a brief tussle, in which he gives her nose a twist, he allows
her to pour port over his head and rename him. By undergoing a
baptism of fiery spirits at the hands of a good and beautiful woman,
Dunstan Ramsay is prepared to take up his life's work afresh.

Diana's brief romance of St. Dunstan corresponds nicely with
Father Blazon's crowning assessment of Dunny. If Dunny had no
goldsmith's tongs, he at least had very strong fingers that were
accustomed (thanks to his own shrewdness and his faith in Boy's
skilled tuition) to handling not inconsiderable amounts of today's gold
in currency. And with these fingers, this man of learning, "terribly
stiff and stern and scowly, and an absolute wizard at withstanding
temptation," catches the nose of the Satanic temptress and gives it a
cracking good twist. Not once, but twice. The first occasion is when
he contends with the alluring Diana who intends to reduce him to a
creation of hers, something she fashioned from a broken wreck in a
hospital bed. The second occasion is when he contends with the
beguiling Liesl, who intends to reduce him to a creature of hers, a
thing she ripped loose from a soul of unyielding integrity. Under the
circumstances of these assaults, his recourse to the tweaking of his
adversary's nose is beyond the shadow of a doubt exactly what Father
Blazon calls it: "St. Dunstan seizing the Devil's snout in his tongs"
(p. 223).

## V

With all of this to work from, a Headmaster moved by a normal
instinct for pedantry could scarcely resist the impulse to inspect the
Dunstan legend more closely. And should we find ourselves impelled
to do so, we cannot help but revel in the ingenious good fun of the
parallel Davies has drawn with the old story of the Celtic saint. Born
a native of Wessex, the Celtic West of England, Dunstan grew to

maturity in an era scarred by wars between the English and the Teutonic hordes of the Continent. As a young man, he became a member of the court of King Athelstan, and the ladies of the court befriended him and instructed him in the social graces. He proved adept at more than polite intercourse: a painstaking scholar, he pursued not only the study of letters in several languages, but also the study of various arts and crafts—tapestries and paintings, architecture and metalwork. And always he took the greatest delight in tales of spiritual adventure, a delight that led him to collect and comment upon the lives of the saints. Yet this exemplary youth was not without enemies. In the words of one biographer:

> Dunstan's desire, and it was eager, to fulfil his duty to his neighbour was fenced around by a reserve, by a craving for that solitude in which alone he could find what his soul, his mind, his hands, offered him. It was hard for him to suffer fools gladly....[3]

Falsely accused of studying magic, of exposing his soul to heathen spells and sinister legends, he was exiled from the court a number of times—once even as far afield as Flanders. There, in that region torn by conflict between the Germans and the French, he was vouchsafed a vision confirming his destiny as a scholar and reformer. Soon thereafter, he was recalled from Flanders to become the advisor to King Edgar. The experience of his earlier rule as Abbot of Glastonbury, a monastic community of men and boys, stood him in good stead when his regal friend elevated him to the See of Canterbury. But Edgar was a gay blade with the ladies, and his amours tended to complicate the career of his scholarly confessor. Shortly after the death of his first wife, Edgar married again, taking an ambitious widow for his second bride. The new queen conceived an aversion to Dunstan, and deftly excluded him from the royal circle. This discourtesy was underscored by the act of a more formidable foe. While Dunstan was involved with the dedication of a new church, a stone hurtled from nowhere, narrowly missing his head: and tradition has it that the missile came from the hand of the Devil himself. Be that as it may, the Archbishop turned with relief from the turmoil of the court, and devoted himself to the monastic and scholastic reforms for which he is celebrated. According to another biographer, he died with the verse of the Psalmist on his lips: "The merciful and gracious Lord hath made a remembrance of His marvellous works; He hath given food to them that fear Him."[4] St. Dunstan's Day is the nineteenth of May, a date generally accepted as being in the vicinity of his birthday.

Well now, if that doesn't just sound like somebody we know. Dunny's exact birthdate is never given, but a rough computation backwards from the data in the opening paragraph would place it somewhere in the last half of May. And Dunny is a native of Southern Ontario, a region of the British empire settled by Scots and Irish in the last century, a region that could qualify admirably as the Celtic West of England. During his boyhood years, Dunny's home village of Deptford is dominated by a family named Athelstan. Over the passage of time, the rule of the Athelstans is usurped by Doc Staunton, whom Dunny describes as "not yet a Sugar-Beet King, but...well on his way to it—a sort of Sticky Duke" (p. 101). Dunny is educated in the train of these luminaries, acquiring many of his accomplishments courtesy of the first ladies of this odd little realm. His mother and Mary Dempster have one characteristic in common, a characteristic that Diana and Liesl will also come to share: each of them contributes to Dunny's initiation into the mysteries of life. Coping with the smothering possessiveness of his mother, he develops a firm self-discipline and an obsessive determination to make his own way. "If I could manage it, I had no intention of being anybody's own dear laddie, ever again" (p. 80). Discharging what he has taken to be his obligation to Mary, he commits himself to the supervision of her son Paul; and he entertains himself and his first pupil with his studies of magic and the saints. "I needed an audience, to judge how well I was doing, and I found one readily in Paul Dempster" (p. 34). Innocent as his activities are, they constantly get Dunny into trouble. The Reverend Amasa Dempster denounces him for exposing his son to vile gambling practices and evil Papist superstitions.

> I did not feel I had done wrong, though I had been a fool to forget how dead set Baptists were against cards. As for the stories about saints, they were tales of wonders....(p. 39)

His subsequent banishment from the Dempster household cannot alter Dunny's stubborn adherence to his singular pursuits. Indeed, he intensifies his eccentricities, and his refusal to modify them brings him into a confrontation with the village elite: Dr. McCausland, the Reverend Phelps and his own mother. "Deep inside myself I knew that to yield, and promise what she wanted, would be the end of anything that was any good in me" (p. 58). Rather than submit, he enlists in the Canadian Army. And in this militant manner, he accepts his exile to Flanders: exile to the mud and flames, to the vision that will enrol him in the ranks of the saints.

One consequence of the miracle of the vision is to bring Dunny into contact with Diana, the daughter of English nobility who smoothes over his gruff rusticity with the polish of the social graces. With the reassurance of Diana by his side, he can stand in the presence of his Sovereign: and with the confidence imparted by his memories of Diana, he can return to Canada and resume his association with the courtly Boy on something approaching equal terms. For the son of the Sticky Duke, secure in the state of his father's riches and intent upon wielding the sceptre of political authority, "knew that he too had a crown awaiting him" (p. 101). Selecting as his model Edward Albert Christian George Andrew Patrick David, the Prince of Wales, Boy works hard at cultivating the demeanour of "one of the lords of creation" (p. 103). He assembles about himself all of the trappings of university aristocracy: a fast car, a number of fast girls, a pretty fiancée, and a companion of a contemplative cast of mind. And who better to fill the office of philosophic confidant than his old friend Dunny? Never one to curb his tongue, Dunny describes his new alliance with Boy in a style suitably dour: "brilliant young men seem to need a dull listener, just as pretty girls need a plain friend, to set them off" (p. 99).

Apart from his penchant for grumping about like Diogenes, Dunny does not minimize the benefits he derives from his place in Boy's entourage. As Boy gathers to himself the regalia of power, he sees that Dunny receives a share, and Dunny dutifully records all the circumstances. From the beginning to the end of the Depression, in a stock market that only a financial king can master, Boy makes his hundreds of thousands and ensures that Dunny makes his hundreds. Across the span of World War II, in an era disrupted by the chaos of Europe and Asia, Boy rises to cabinet minister and ensures that Dunny rises to headmaster. However, Dunny is a saint, not a courtier: he takes what comes to him as the wages due a good and faithful servant, knowing full well that the hand dispensing largesse might also brush him aside. And so it comes to pass. To appease the murmurs of a handful of unimaginative parents, Boy removes Dunny from the headship of the college. To appease the atheist whim of his second wife, Boy gradually eases Dunny out of the family circle. None of this, not one of the gifts or one of the slights, can astonish or disconcert Dunstan Ramsay. Since their childhood days together, he has been Boy's scholarly confessor, the "keeper of his conscience and keeper of the stone" (p. 237).

As in the original legend, the stone comes to loom large in the story of our Dunstan. Of itself, the stone was nothing: "an ordinary piece of pinkish granite about the size of a small egg" (p. 224). Yet it was the core of the snowball that Boy hurled at Dunny, a nasty bit of rock flung out of the encroaching darkness of a late December evening. To Dunny's mother, who must struggle to keep life in an infant pushed prematurely into the world, the one throwing the missile was directed by the Father of Lies. "Whoever it was, the Devil guided his hand" (p. 23). To Boy Staunton, who will never confess the brutality of what he has done, the missile was a fact to be repressed forever. "An ordinary bit of stone.... It doesn't remind me of anything" (p. 235). To Dunny, who can do nothing with Boy's guilt save make it his own burden, the missile must rest beside the ashes of Mary Dempster, two curious relics symbolizing "a form of piety" and "a sense of guilt unexpiated" (p. 235). And whatever else it might have been, it is undeniably the Devil's own work. In a fatal circuit of sixty years that takes it from Boy's hand to Boy's mouth, it never really touches Dunstan, but it leaves a shadow between king and confessor, always a reminder of the dark powers that menace even the saints.

Once Denyse and the stone have released him from the pressures of Boy's life, Dunny is free to outline for the Headmaster the scholarly reform that had been his destiny. Here and there in the novel, others offer hints of what Dunny has done for scholarship. Into the dry expanse of academic research, an arid desolation of what Joel Surgeoner calls "police-court facts" (p. 119), Dunny has brought a stimulating draught of the marvellous. Liesl states his accomplishment in suitably flattering terms.

> But you, who have written so persuasively about the saints—slipping under the guard of the skeptic with a candour that is brilliantly

disingenuous, treating marvels with the seriousness of fact—you
are just the man for us (p. 188).

How fittingly we might apply this statement to the full text of Dunny's
story. And this would be quite as it should, since the full text of his
story is the exemplum of the system that Dunny has espoused. In
writing of the possibility of a Canadian miracle, Dunny admits: "I
was far too much a Canadian, deeply if unconsciously convinced of
the inferiority of my own country and its people, to think it could
happen in Toronto, to a man I could see" (p. 117). So it is with this
narrative. Composed by a veteran, it is indeed compounded out of
stodgy Canadian fact: Southern Ontario, no less, complete with a
village with outhouses, a lieutenant-governor designate, and a Toronto that seems to conform to every vitriolic line scribbled about
Toronto. Yet the writer perceives fact with eyes that have witnessed
marvels, and he writes to establish that the essence of miracle is
inseparable from the stuff of reality. The narrative is a miracle of
art, transmuting the dullness of Canadian academic life into the
wonders of sainthood. Written to bring reformation to the Packers,
the scientific huns of an academic dark age, it is a miracle that might
bring a measure of enlightenment to us as well.

## VI

If a proper scientific historian such as Packer were asked to endorse
a frank designation for the saints, he would undoubtedly applaud Boy
Staunton's dismissal of them: "wonder-workers and holy wizards
and juiceless women" (p. 176). And if a proper scientific historian
such as Packer were told that Dunstan Ramsay was a saint, he would
undoubtedly object that Dunny couldn't possibly be one, since many
facts absolutely preclude this sort of contingency. What about the
men he killed, the three Germans he shot at point-blank range in the
machine-gun nest? What about the women he loved, Diana and Liesl
and the implausibly-named triad of Agnes Day, Gloria Mundy and
Libby Doe?[5] What about the boys he thrashed, the slashing verbal
cruelties he indulged in, the scepticism he never could totally
renounce? As we ponder these facts, believable human traits that
science would insist upon and that religion could not deny, we should
begin to understand the serious aspect of this parallel with St.

Dunstan. In Dunstan Ramsay, Robertson Davies has created for us a figure that retains his humanity while he struggles towards sainthood.

During an interview for *Maclean's* magazine, Davies explains why he is intrigued by "the condition of Sainthood."

> It is just as interesting as evil. What makes a saint? You look at the lives of some of the very great saints and you find that they were fascinating people. Just as fascinating as great criminals or great conquerors. Most saints have been almost unbearable nuisances in life. Some were reformers, some were sages, some were visionaries, but all were intensely alive, and thus a living rebuke to people who were not.[6]

By giving us *Fifth Business*, Davies renders this perception more tangible, scrubbing off the pious patina embossing "the condition of sainthood" to show the human reality that necessarily embodies the legends. The novel centres upon a man living a life of wonderment. The emphasis throughout is on his humanity; it rests with us to see his sanctity. And thus it has always been, because saints are notoriously incapable of surmising that they are saints: this annoying peculiarity is derived, not from holy humbug, but from a level-headed evaluation of their own humanity. We don't see this because, across a lapse of time, without the irritating human fact that we have often ourselves obliterated in some rash pique, the saint's humanity becomes enshrouded as the saint becomes inhumanly good. Dunstan Ramsay was created to demonstrate that the saint becomes humanly good. "A selfish, envious, cankered wretch, wasn't I?" (p. 105) he asks, leaving the answer to the Headmaster. This is no mean artistic feat.

Naturally, it would remain with Father Blazon to tell us something of what the Creator intended for the saint. The old incorrigible gleefully expounds upon a counter-tradition of shabby stories in hagiology, a seamy underside to the splendid fables of the saints.

> St. Joseph hears more prayers about cuckoldry than he does about house-hunting or confectionery, I can assure you. Indeed, in the underworld hagiology of which I promised to tell you, it is whispered that the Virgin herself, who was born to Joachim and Anna through God's personal intervention, was a divine daughter

as well as a divine mate; the Greeks could hardly improve on that, could they (pp. 154-55)?

His purpose in repeating this naughtiness is not to erode faith, but to shore it up on a more secure foundation. He realistically argues that the saint is significant, not for being free of sin, but for doing battle with sin.

> But all this terrible talk about the saints is not disrespect, Ramezay. Far from it! It is faith! It is love! It takes the saint to the heart by supplying the other side of his character that history or legend has suppressed—that he may very well have suppressed himself in his struggle toward sainthood. The saint triumphs over sin (p. 155).

Father Blazon takes the stand that, by dwelling upon the flaws of the saint, we acknowledge our kinship with the saint: and, somewhat paradoxically, we therefore acknowledge that we also share his potential for the good.

> If they, these holy ones who have lived so greatly but who still carry their shadows with them, can approach God, well then, there is hope for the worst of us (p. 155).

Now, since even the beatified have their human blemishes, how do we go about the recognition of the true saint? This is the mystery that confounds the experts, priests and popes and inquisitors, let alone scientific historians. Yet to Father Blazon, the fundamental reality is sufficiently straightforward. "Heroism in God's cause is the mark of the saint, Ramezay, not conjuring tricks" (p. 222).

With the direction of Fifth Business, one need not be a hagiographer to discern Dunny's authentic sanctity. Should we turn again to the Dunstan legend, we will have little difficulty disinterring analogues for Dunny's tumbles from grace. The education of the original Dunstan was shaped by a number of women, whose charms he cherished and whose wiles he eluded. The career of the original Dunstan was dedicated to the instruction of others, many of whom felt the flat of his hand or the edge of his tongue. And the course of the original Dunstan was stained by blood that he was forced to shed. When sitting in judgment in a court of law, he found three coiners guilty and condemned them to the mandatory penalty: at his orders, they were taken to a place of execution, and their right hands were struck off. As a man of God, he found the action repugnant; but as a provost of the King, he found the action to be his secular duty, and he saw no alternative to the imposition of what was tantamount to a sentence of death. Dunny's behaviour, seen in this light, is consistent with that of his saintly predecessor.

Of even greater import, however, is Dunny's undisputed possession of the one attribute Father Blazon selects as the mark of the saint: "heroism in God's cause." This is not the same heroism that so distinguished him in the service of his King, though it is a kindred quality. Instead, it is the heroism that led him to shield Mary Dempster, in her sickness and her sorrow, from a world in which she could never survive. It is the heroism that led him to champion Leola and David and Caroline, in defiance of Boy's intemperate abuse of his autocratic power. "Boy told me that if I had to behave like one of the bloody saints I was always yapping about, he wished I would do it somewhere else" (p. 167). It is the heroism that led him to accept guidance from Destiny, to bend his will before the Will of the universe.

> For I was, as you have already guessed, a collaborator with Destiny, not one who put a pistol to its head and demanded particular treasures. The only thing for me to do was to keep on keeping on, to have faith in my whim, and remember that for me, as for the saints, illumination when it came would probably come from some unexpected source (p. 152).

This is courage of an unconventional form, the courage of the true individual who can dare the currently unfashionable, the courage that can bow the intellectual in prayer. Alone with the body of Mary, he faces himself and his efforts, and he strikes down his pride in an act of contrition.

> I prayed for the repose of the soul of Mary Dempster, somewhere and somehow unspecified, under the benevolence of some power unidentified but deeply felt. It was the sort of prayer that supported all the arguments of Denyse Staunton against religion, but I was in the grip of an impulsion that it would have been spiritual suicide to deny. And then I begged forgiveness for myself because, though I had done what I imagined was my best, I had not been loving enough, or wise enough, or generous enough in my dealings with her (p. 218).

Ours is a worldly time, obsessed with the machinery of the physical, not given to any deference to the spiritual. In the context of such a time, Dunny's quiet acceptance of God elevates his work from philanthropy to religion: it places him under the banner of belief, marshalling him with the saints.

## VII

To realize how fully this fiction brings us home to fact, we must go back to where we started, to Packer's fatuous article. Counterparts of equal fatuity might in truth be found in numerous publications, for authors of every school woodenly contort things Canadian in conformity with preconceptions from abroad. What you see is what you get, *bien sur,* in Canadian letters. Packer is in good company. Voltaire saw *"quelques arpents de neige."* Francis Parkman saw seigneurs and peasants and savages. Rupert Brooke saw great empty plains with a lamentable paucity of ghosts. Ernest Hemingway and Wyndham Lewis saw dingy and tasteless metropolises, hopelessly tedious cultural wastelands. And our own Margaret Atwood industriously pounded the first fruits of these perceptions into a pemmican of victims, a mass of inarticulate exiles lumped together in snow-blasted spaces or culturally-bankrupt hamlets, stuck with each other in the mythless heritage of Canada. The good Canadian Packer, with the hand-me-down imagination of all the good Canada Packers, just dishes up a native product with the methodology of another culture. No wonder that what he serves is unpalatable and second-rate.

The alternative for all of us, scholars and scientists, saints and sinners, is to emulate the approach of Dunstan Ramsay. The ore of his manufacture is mined from the rocky ground of his homeland; he merely works it his own way. He is pedestrian, meticulous, balanced—very much the Canadian, very much the teacher. He takes the raw materials of his existence, the quaint elements of Southern Ontario, and welds them into a mosaic that glows alive with digression, qualification and illumination. In this regard, the fictional Dunstan Ramsay and the factual Robertson Davies are one. It goes beyond coincidence that they share the same initials, howbeit in reversed order; for reversed order is what *Fifth Business* is about. According to Davies, Canadians get themselves backwards because they cannot reconcile their reality with their image.

A lot of people complain that my novels aren't about Canada. I think they are, because I see Canada as a country torn between a very northern, rather extraordinary, mystical spirit which it fears and its desire to present itself to the world as a Scotch banker. This makes for tension. Tension is the very stuff of art.[7]

The art of Davies mirrors for us a different reflection of ourselves. Look again, says *Fifth Business*, with eyes open to the miraculous—and see what marvels there are.

We Canadians should relish the irony that our national compulsion to view ourselves as provincial and uninteresting is itself derivative. A similar compulsion moved the scholars of Oxford to study the dramas of Classic antiquity when they might have watched Shakespeare acting one of his plays. A similar compulsion moved the brahmins of Boston to send to England for Dickens when they might have visited Hawthorne or Thoreau or Melville. But Canada today is no less a source of art than the Ireland of Joyce or the Norway of Ibsen. To see this, we only have to look again. Davies reminds us that what is needful is the miracle of the artistic eye.

# Note

1   Robertson Davies, *Fifth Business* (New York: Viking Press, 1970), p. 152. All subsequent page references to the novel will be given in parentheses in the text of the essay.

2   It is interesting that Davies' fiction has a counterpart in the supposedly separate category of contemporary non-fiction. Like *Fifth Business*, Norman Mailer's *The Armies of the Night* attempts to utilize the techniques of the novel to reveal the subtleties of reality. Much in the style of Dunny's attack on Packer's article, Mailer commences with a devastating attack on a *Time* article that he prints in full in his opening chapter. Mailer's point is Dunny's: the article postures in an ostensibly objective manner while it distorts by omitting details, evading spiritual considerations, and offering judgments in a patronizing tone. Both *Fifth Business* and *The Armies of the Night* remind the reader to look again at the world we all take for granted.

3   Eleanor Shipley Duckett, *Saint Dunstan of Canterbury* (New York: Norton Press, 1955), p. 207.

4   David Knowles, *Saints and Scholars* (Cambridge: Cambridge University Press, 1962), p. 20.

5  *Agnus Dei, Gloria Mundi,* and Libido. Should we be tempted to censure Davies for his little games with words, we should also bear in mind that worse can be found in the plays of Shakespeare and the epics of Milton.

6  Peter C. Newman, "The Master's Voice," *Maclean's* (August, 1972), p. 43.

7  *Ibid.*

# Confessions of a Sorcerer's Apprentice: *World of Wonders* and the Deptford Trilogy of Robertson Davies

*Patricia Monk*

With the publication of *World of Wonders* Robertson Davies has completed the trilogy begun by *Fifth Business* and continued by *The Manticore*.[1] Characteristically, the completion it provides manages to be both unlikely and inevitable. It is unlikely for two reasons: because of its apparently tangential relationship to *The Manticore*, and because of its apparent change of subject for the last section of three (a mere twenty-three pages). So tangential does the relationship to *The Manticore* appear that I began by wondering if this trilogy was going to have four parts, since any reader wanting to know the fate of David Staunton after the end of *The Manticore* is left in suspense after reading *World of Wonders*, which leaps back in space and time to pick up from *Fifth Business* the life of Paul Dempster at the moment when he disappeared from Deptford.

At the opening of *World of Wonders*, Paul, now Magnus Eisengrim and a world-renowned illusionist, is completing the filming of a BBC feature film about the nineteenth-century French illusionist Robert-Houdin, at Sorgenfrei, Liesl's "Gothic gingerbread" home in Switzerland, where he and Dunstan Ramsay are Liesl's permanent house-guests and her occasional lovers. Ramsay takes over the narration of this frame story and introduces the other main characters: Lind, the Swedish director; his Danish cameraman, Kinghovn; and

Ronald Ingestree, the BBC producer in charge of the film. As the result of a slightly less than amicable wrangle with the rest of the group, Eisengrim offers them a "sub-text" for the film in the form of the story of his life, from the day when, as he says of himself, "I descended into hell."

"Hell" is his life in a carnival freak show, as pathic to Willard the Wizard, who rapes him, steals him, teaches him the art of the illusionist and obsesses him throughout a long and painful servitude. He begins by spending his time in the bowels of a card-playing automaton, but later becomes Willard's understudy, as they move through the Canadian and American mid-West carnival and vaudeville circuits at the lowest possible level, observing distantly, but never making contact with, the world outside the show. From this, after Willard's death, Eisengrim moves on to a life as the leading actor's double in Sir John Tresize's old-fashioned theatre company in London (and later on tour in Canada), where his life is more comfortable, but equally anonymous. The carnival (Wanless' World of Wonders, from which the book not insignificantly takes its name) demands to be described as bizarre, grotesque, nightmarish—but still impresses itself as being uncomfortably real, solid and credible. Eisengrim's life with the theatre company has a similar effect, though rather less nightmarish and rather less easy to describe; "stagey" is perhaps too glib; "romantic" ignores Davies' obviously firsthand experience of the less romantic aspects of theatre life. From this theatre company Eisengrim moves on again, pursuing his earlier hobby of clockwork in order to earn his living, to his encounter with Liesl, and to the point of his re-emergence into the life of Dunstan Ramsay.

Set into this narrative, somewhat in the manner of choric episodes, are the conversations in which his listeners (whether before his face or behind his back) discuss the events and implications of his story. These discussions centre on the nature of good and evil, of God and the Devil, and of truth and illusion, although Davies, in the person of his narrator Ramsay, is wise enough to point out that, "I'm not expecting to untangle anything. But I'm making a record—a document" (*World*, p. 358).

The apparent change of subject for the last section ("Le Lit de Justice"), which is the second reason for the apparent unlikeliness of *World of Wonders* as the completion of the trilogy, develops from Ramsay's insistence as a historian and as Eisengrim's biographer, on getting a true record. He believes that Eisengrim knows more about the death of Boy Staunton than he has been willing to say. Here we are given Eisengrim's previously withheld account of his encounter with Boy Staunton on the night of the latter's death-plunge into the muddy waters of Toronto harbour, holding firmly in his mouth the stone long-hoarded by Ramsay from the snowball thrown at him by Boy, which felled Mrs. Dempster. In this section, the emphasis suddenly shifts from Eisengrim; he, the egoist who has made quite sure the emphasis rested in the right place (him) up to this point, now himself shifts it to Boy Staunton—whom we have previously seen only as second lead in *Fifth Business* as Ramsay's "lifelong friend and enemy," and as villain in *The Manticore* haunting and almost destroying his son David. Paradoxically (I was tempted to write perversely), Davies turns this seeming irrelevance into the key to the trilogy, and it is to this last section, which slots into place the last few pieces of the jigsaw puzzle of Boy's death, that *World of Wonders* owes its inevitability as the completion of the trilogy.

It is, in fact, the iceberg tip of the fourth part of the trilogy. This is not, however, the fourth book which the tangential relationship between *The Manticore* and *World of Wonders* seemed to require: it is the narrative continually implied in the narratives of Dunstan Ramsay, David Staunton, and Magnus Eisengrim: the story of Boy Staunton. Eisengrim provides the key to it when he says that in becoming Sir John Tresize's double he "entered upon a long apprenticeship to an egoism," and describes Ramsay as "a ferocious egoist" (*World*, pp. 191-92). On this level the trilogy is about four egoisms: Eisengrim, Ramsay, David Staunton and Boy. But of the four, it is Boy Staunton's which is the lever and motive force of the trilogy as a whole. Just as on the story level the events of the trilogy follow his outward action (a product of his egoism), the thematic development follows the distorting effect which his egoism has upon the inner lives of those whose outer lives are most deeply affected by the snowball's action (including Mrs. Dempster whose life is so closely bound up with Ramsay's). Boy's own egoism is so profound that he can distort an egoism as profound and independent of his own as Ramsay's; he can divert a new mind into egoism, as he does Paul Dempster's; and he can create it as a consequence of sheer opposition to himself, as he does with his son David. His influence is consistently disruptive;

his force moves the other characters centrifugally from the central point of his own ego at this particular point in time.

It is for this reason that the shape of the trilogy appears to be so unorthodox; the three novels radiate from a common source in different directions. But they are bound together again finally, in spite of their divergence, by the presence of Liesl. For where Boy is the centre all three heroes flee, Liesl is the centre they all (though David to a lesser extent than Ramsay and Eisengrim) seek.

This is not, however, the only factor involved in the distance between *The Manticore* and *World of Wonders*. Another is that Davies, while apparently abandoning the Jungian machinery, nevertheless creates a polarity of character between David Staunton and Magnus Eisengrim which is explicable in Jungian terms. David's problem, as Frau Doktor von Haller makes clear to him, is that he is too much of a thinker—he depends too much on intellect and analysis. Magnus, on the other hand, has "no brain" (according to Liesl), but depends entirely on feeling to understand and control the world around him. The relationship between the two men is one of affinity; David, during his stay at Sorgenfrei, finds himself liking and wanting to know more about Eisengrim, thus reflecting in a curious way what Jung said about modern man—that he "wants...to know how he is to reconcile himself with his own nature—how he is to love the enemy in his own heart and call the wolf his brother."[2] For Eisengrim is the wolf, as his name (chosen for him by Liesl out of the medieval Beast *Epic*) indicates, and the wolf brother, the enemy within, is the archetypal Shadow which every individual carries within his or her psyche.

A further ironic contrast (and therefore distancing) between David and Eisengrim is produced by the trajectory of the journey which each takes in search of himself. David's is begun at least under the hygienic auspices of psychotherapy—a process which is designed in modern man to replace the lost mythic pattern of initiation. But Eisengrim's is a true initiation, carried out fully in the primitive terms of myth, and is explicitly identified as such. In the argument which follows Eisengrim's narration of Willard's death, Ramsay draws attention to the mythic quality of Eisengrim's life:

> What I want is to defend Eisengrim against the charge of being a villain.... You must look at his history in the light of myth.... What is the mythical element in his story? Simply the very old tale of

the man who is in search of his soul, and who must struggle with a monster to secure it (*World*, pp. 153-55).

The same mythical element has been visible in *The Manticore* in the life of David Staunton as an implied counterpoint to the trajectory of his *anamnesis*, and more overtly in the story of his expedition to the prehistoric bear-cult cave with Liesl, which plunges him back into the deepest levels of the past and of his own soul. It was implied, too, in the story of Dunstan Ramsay, by his "death" on a battlefield of World War I and his later rebirth. In the lives of all three men, the pattern of the hero is unmistakable—the symbolic events and objects and figures of the quest myth reappear, all variously disguised, yet always retaining beneath the disguises their own unalterable identity. However, the story of Magnus Eisengrim demonstrates the mythic quality of feeling involved, partly because of the author's treatment of evil, and partly because of his control of his material.

In the narrative of Magnus Eisengrim we experience the events of his life from the viewpoint of a man who relates to the world through his feelings, rather than through his intellect (as do Ramsay and David Staunton). Eisengrim is acutely sensitive to every element of his environment. As we are locked firmly into his viewpoint by the first-person narration, and are only released temporarily for the conversation and comments which follow each episode of his story, so we are consequently locked into Eisengrim's feelings about what has happened to him. His judgements on this may for various reasons be unreliable, as Ramsay points out; his feelings are not. They exist unchanged by time or later experience, and they are conveyed to us in all their raw pungency by a technique of understatement which Davies has finely honed for the purpose. Eisengrim's narration makes his audience within the story, and consequently the reader, suffer vicariously all the isolation, terror and mystery of each stage of his mythic journey in unwitting search of his soul. Thus they experience not only the particularities of Eisengrim's quest, but also the very pattern of the quest itself.

This level of feeling involved in Eisengrim's experience helps to produce the second contribution to the clarity with which the mythic pattern of his experience is exposed. For Eisengrim does not analyze and discuss the nature of evil (as both Ramsay and David Staunton do); he encounters it at full strength through his hypersensitive feelings and in very concrete terms. The rape of children has not yet become acceptable as material for popular literature (at least, not in the part of it which is distributed through the usual commercial publishing outlets). For although it is human evil in one of its extremest manifestations, it remains *undisguisably* evil, recognizable as such by everyone, and it cannot be prettied up for general consumption and titillation. Davies presents it as the evil it is, without sentimentality or decoration, but with overwhelming vividness, through the wide-open sensitivities *and* the wide-open senses of its victim. His technique in this presentation, in contrast to that of understatement in the presentation of feeling, is the use of sensuous detail in his descriptions. The accuracy of his observation of detail and his skilful manipulation of it play no small part in convincing the reader that (to use one key scene as an example) evil is truly present in the darkened stinking latrine of an Ontario fairground, truly manifest in the person of Willard, and truly acted out in his rape of ten-year-old Paul Dempster.

The fact that the boy is ten years old is not mentioned casually, for Paul's age is important thematically, and Davies' fine control of his material is demonstrated in this placing of the experience of evil in Paul's life-span. Paul is a rather young ten-year-old in some ways, it is true, since he is a minister's son, although he is old in some others because of his mother's condition. But developmentally speaking he is just the right age for the meaning of what has happened to him—"blasphemy" (*World*, p. 45) he calls it, and he is right—to be clear to him. His descent into darkness in quest of his soul begins with this dawning of awareness and self-awareness. It is not merely that the psychology of it is right. It is right within the pattern of myth that the development of the hero should be precocious. So that even in this, Davies' manipulation of his material serves to present the strength of the mythic element in Paul Dempster's metamorphosis into Magnus Eisengrim.

This mythic element remains implicitly, rather than explicitly, presented, except for Ramsay's remarks. But clearly it is here that the centre of gravity of the Deptford trilogy lies. As I have pointed out, however, this trilogy has four parts. In what mythic pattern can the story of Boy Staunton be placed?

The question is asked not of Boy's role in relationship to each of the three main characters of the trilogy, but of his role in his own life (so to speak). There are a few suggestive details in the trilogy, of which I can only sketch in the two most promising here: the first is that Boy's life may be interpreted in terms of the Faust myth. This myth has been implicitly present in the trilogy from the first brief mention when Paul Dempster appears as Faustus Legrand in *Fifth Business*. It is reiterated later in the book with the appearance of the girl, Faustina, and by the theme of the illusion in which she has a part ("The Vision of Dr. Faustus"). In many ways, not only here, but later in *The Manticore*, the myth is again suggested by the relationship between Eisengrim and Liesl, which curiously hints at that between Faust and his demonic servant, Mephistopheles. But *World of Wonders*, which brings the Faust theme to full articulation in Liesl's explication of her stage surname of Vitzlipützli, also disposes of Eisengrim as a candidate for the Faust role. For at the same time Liesl also draws the portrait of Eisengrim as a Magian soul in terms of Spengler's theory set out in *Der Untergang des Abendlandes*. This, so easy to dismiss as "gadgetry" or a "red herring," is neither. It is a clear and definite pointer to the nature of Boy Staunton's life-role.

The Magian World View or "Weltanschauung" is described in relation to Eisengrim:

> It was a sense of the unfathomable wonder of the invisible world that existed side by side with a hard recognition of the cruelty and day-to-day demands of the tangible world. It was a readiness to see demons where nowadays we see neuroses, and to see the hand of a guardian angel in what we are apt to shrug off ungratefully as a stroke of luck. It was a religion, but a religion with a thousand gods, none of them all-powerful and most of them ambiguous in their attitude toward man. It was poetry and wonder which might reveal themselves in the dunghill, and it was an understanding of the dunghill that lurks in poetry and wonder. It was a sense of living in what Spengler called a quivering cavern-light always in danger of being swallowed up in the surrounding impenetrable darkness (*World*, pp. 323-24).

It is clear that this Magian world view is not only that of Eisengrim, but also of Ramsay (in his exploration of the borderland between history and myth) and of David Staunton (in his progress towards what he speculates might be called *esse in anima*). Each of these men who goes in search of his soul returns victoriously with a new self, but also with this sense of "poetry and wonder" of Spengler's formulation.

But the fourth story in the trilogy, that of Boy Staunton, is that of a man who rejects any search for his soul. In its symbolic form as the egg-shaped piece of granite, he throws it away as an act of childish egoism and reclaims it only at the point of his death, to take it down to death with him in the dirty waters of Toronto harbour.[3] If the Spenglerian formulation, as I believe, can be interpreted so that the Magian soul is the successful quest hero, then the hero who rejects or refuses the quest for his soul may be described by Spengler's term for the opposite type to the Magian, which is the Faustian—named after the legendary Dr. Faustus of German tradition, in whom Spengler appears to have seen the crystallization of the lesser, later age which followed the Magian (in historical terms the Magian being Medieval and the Faustian Renaissance). Through this interpretation, the story of Boy Staunton becomes much clearer in its trajectory, its meaning, and its relation to the other three major characters.

This interpretation of Boy also brings into focus the second thematic role which he plays in the trilogy—that of some sort of polar opposite to Liesl. I have pointed out above that structurally Boy is the centre which the other heroes (Ramsay, Eisengrim, and David Staunton) flee, and that Liesl is the other centre which they all seek, since structurally the novels diverge from Boy's egoist action with the stone in the snowball, just as structurally they all converge on Liesl (specifically on Liesl's bed, although admittedly in David's case this is only by implication).

The polarization of Boy as some sort of "evil" force (disruptive, or destructive) and of Liesl as some sort of "good" force (healing, or synthesizing) begins to take on a rather heavy weight of significance in view of the discussions which take place in *World of Wonders* about good or evil, and especially about God and the Devil (especially when we remember the earlier identification of Liesl with the Devil in *Fifth Business*). Therefore there is more than a simple irony involved in Ramsay's final remark on the nature of God and the Devil: "It's the moment of decision—of will—when those Two nab us, and as they both speak so compellingly it's tricky work to know who's talking" (*World*, p. 358). The revision of our notions of good and evil is never very far from Davies' line of attack, either here or in *Fifth Business*.

Although the Spenglerian distinction, by pointing out this polar-ization of good and evil forces within the novel, throws an important light on a large area of the thematic organization of the book, it is not to be taken as an invitation to interpret the novel in Spenglerian terms. Without the trappings of hagiography or Jungian psychology, *World of Wonders* is a plain tale, and clearly announced as such. According to Eisengrim himself, a great magician is "a man who can stand stark naked in the midst of a crowd and keep it gaping for an hour while he manipulates a few coins, or cards, or billiard balls" (*World*, p. 4). Eisengrim's remark about the naked magician clearly points to the writer himself—the great writer is one who can, as Davies does in this novel, dispense with the trappings of his craft, the trappings of wonder, and still create a sense of wonder in the reader.

*World of Wonders* is a fitting conclusion to the Deptford trilogy. We must all hope that Davies has other "coins, or cards" with which to fascinate us in the future.

# Notes

1   Robertson Davies, *World of Wonders* (Toronto: Macmillan, 1975), *Fifth Business* (Toronto: Macmillan, 1970) and *The Manticore* (New York: Viking Press, 1972).

2   C.G. Jung, "Psychotherapist or the Clergy," *Collected Works*, 2, *Psychology and Religion: West and East* (Princeton: Princeton University Press, 1958), p. 341.

3   I am grateful to Jerome Morgan of the Dalhousie English Department for pointing out an interesting parallel between this and the Indian rite described in Howard O'Hagan's *Tay John*.

# Structural Unity in the Deptford Trilogy: Robertson Davies as Egoist

*James Neufeld*

W hether or not Robertson Davies intended from the outset to write a trilogy based on Deptford story material, the fact remains that he has now presented his readers with three books—*Fifth Business, The Manticore* and *World of Wonders*—that are closely related in story and theme. The word "trilogy," however, sets up certain expectations of continuity and symmetry which this trio of books does not always fulfil. They do not, for example, tell a continuing story in orderly, chronological sequence. Instead, they indulge in a considerable amount of doubling back, commenting on a single event, like Boy Staunton's death, from various points of view. Furthermore, the emphasis on David Staunton and his story in *The Manticore* throws the entire trilogy slightly out of focus. It does not present the same story (the one beginning with the snowball incident of the 27th of December, 1908) told from the points of view of the three characters (Dunstan Ramsay, Boy Staunton and Magnus Eisengrim) most directly concerned with it. David Staunton represents the wrong generation for that kind of symmetrical organization and his story is not as centrally connected with the Deptford event as one might expect. The connections between these three books are real, but they are not obvious. In this they resemble the famous pronouncement by the Brazen Head regarding Boy Staunton's death. Its five categories suggest a neat division of characters and responsibilities connected with the death. But no two people, either inside or outside the books, can agree *which* five characters ought to fit into the categories. In similar fashion, Davies has suggested a neat symmetry to the organization of his material by using the trilogy structure, but has perversely refused to develop that material with the obvious neatness the structure implies. This paper will attempt to explore some of the links between these three books as Davies develops them.

These links serve to unify the trilogy because they emphasize a common theme that binds the three books together and that receives significant development from one book to the next. Quite simply put, the characters in *World of Wonders* know more about themselves than they do in *Fifth Business* and the basis for that increased self-knowledge is most explicitly presented in *The Manticore*. David Staunton, in some ways odd man out, provides the key to the trilogy's thematic unity.

> Thinking of Netty puts me in mind of Pargetter's warning about the witnesses, or clients, whose creed is *esse in re*; to such people the world is absolutely clear because they cannot understand that our personal point of view colours what we perceive; they think everything seems exactly the same to everyone as it does to themselves. After all, they say, the world is utterly objective; it is plain before our eyes; therefore what the ordinary intelligent man (this is always themselves) sees is all there is to be seen, and anyone who sees differently is mad, or malign, or just plain stupid. An astonishing number of judges seem to belong in this category....
>
> Netty was certainly one of those, and I never really knew why I was always at odds with her (while really loving the old girl, I must confess) till Pargetter rebuked me for being an equally wrong-headed, though more complex and amusing creature, whose creed is *esse in intellectu solo*. "You think the world is your idea," he said one November day at a tutorial when I had been offering him some fancy theorizing, "and if you don't understand that and check it now it will make your whole life a gigantic hallucination." Which, in spite of my success, is pretty much what happened, and my extended experiments as a booze artist were chiefly directed to checking any incursions of unwelcome truth into my illusion.
>
> But what am I headed for? Where has Dr. Johanna been taking me? I suspect toward a new ground of belief that wouldn't have occurred to Pargetter, which might be called *esse in anima*: I am beginning to recognize the objectivity of the world, while knowing also that because I am who and what I am, I both perceive the

world in terms of who and what I am and project onto the world a great deal of who and what I am. If I know this, I ought to be able to escape the stupider kinds of illusion. The absolute nature of things is independent of my senses (which are all I have to perceive with), and what I perceive is an image in my own psyche.

All very fine. Not too hard to formulate and accept intellectually. But to *know* it; to bring it into daily life—that's the problem. And it would be real humility, not just the mock-modesty that generally passes for humility.[1]

The lengthy quotation is necessary because of its centrality to Davies' theme. The opposition and eventual compromise between the objective and subjective views of the world occupy Davies and his characters throughout the trilogy. These ideas even influence the narrative devices through which he presents his story. And their eventual resolution in *World of Wonders* reveals Davies' characters as egoists who may be genuinely humble without a trace of modesty. But in order to see the relevance of this passage to the trilogy as a whole, it will be best to examine in detail some of its connecting links, features common to all three books that serve to bind them together with some kind of unity.

The first of these connecting links is geography. Although the three books range over a considerable terrain, all three share a common set of geographical limits. Each story begins in Deptford and ends, metaphorically at least, in Sorgenfrei. Deptford and Sorgenfrei thus act as important poles, or points of reference, for each book in the trilogy and for each of its central characters. And the constancy of these two points of reference helps to provide a consistent sense of stability for the reader working his way through the confusing variety of events and locales Davies presents. Wherever Davies may lead his characters in search of adventure, the reader can rest assured that Deptford and Sorgenfrei are never really very far away. Dunstan Ramsay establishes the pattern in *Fifth Business*. Born and raised in one, he chooses to end his days in the other. And although Sorgenfrei itself is mentioned in *Fifth Business* only in passing, as "this house among the mountains—a house that itself holds the truths behind many illusions,"[2] it exerts a powerful influence on the shaping of Dunstan Ramsay's tale. Only after one has completed the entire trilogy can one appreciate fully the fact that it is Sorgenfrei that provides Ramsay with the peace and security to prepare his story for the headmaster of

Colborne College. David Staunton upholds this pattern in *The Manticore*. Although born in Toronto, he must begin the search for his personal past in Deptford, where he spent his childhood summers (and to which he refers as "my Arcadia"[3]); he ends his story in Sorgenfrei, facing a decision which must take him beyond it. And in *World of Wonders*, Magnus Eisengrim acknowledges the importance of Deptford by the action of spitting on it. "I had not settled any scores, or altered my feelings, but I had done something of importance. Nobody knew it, but Paul Dempster had visited his childhood home."[4] By the time he tells his story, Sorgenfrei has become his permanent, and most appropriate, home. Thus, for each of the three narrators, Deptford in some sense begins the story he has to tell and Sorgenfrei ends it. Why?

In part, because Davies is making a point about the importance of the past, and Deptford represents the past for Ramsay, David Staunton and Eisengrim. Ramsay's acknowledgment of the continuing significance of Deptford in his life applies, with varying degrees of force, to David Staunton and Eisengrim as well.

> I had tried to get Deptford out of my head, just as Boy had done, and for the same reason; I wanted a new life. What Surgeoner told me made it clear that any new life must include Deptford. There was to be no release by muffling up the past.[5]

The trilogy continually emphasizes the importance of the past in the shaping of the present and the future; the repeated references to Deptford illustrate this point in the personal lives of the three central characters.

Davies' use of Deptford as the small Ontario town which none of its natives can ever quite escape resembles Stephen Leacock's evocation of Mariposa, in the last chapter of *Sunshine Sketches of a Little Town*, as the small Ontario town to which none of its natives can ever return. Both authors, through the use of the small town, express their interest in a common past. But one sees the past as something that cannot be evaded while the other views it nostalgically as something that cannot be recaptured.

But as well as emphasizing the importance of the past, Davies wants to introduce an air of romance and mystery into his story. Sorgenfrei stands opposite prosy Deptford as one of the principal sources of romance and mystery in all three novels. Like Liesl, its owner, Sorgenfrei is "monstrous but fascinating,"[6] the appropriate place for intimate revelations and spiritual adventures. But for Ramsay, David Staunton and Eisengrim, the mystery that culminates in Sorgenfrei has its roots in Deptford. Davies has related the two locales to each other in such a way that the mysteries implicit in ordinary Deptford are made explicit in exotic Sorgenfrei. Those mysteries are concerned with the development and full realization of the human spirit, as David Staunton comes to know. Unlike Liesl, Davies, through the connection of Deptford and Sorgenfrei, seems to suggest that Canada *is* "a country where big spiritual adventures are possible."[7]

Another important way in which Davies unifies the trilogy, and stresses once again the importance of Deptford as the source of the adventure, is his recurring use of Deptford characters, both major and minor, in different contexts throughout the novels. These characters rarely look exactly the same from one appearance to the next. In the cases of major figures like Ramsay, Boy Staunton or Eisengrim, the changing perspectives on character that are thus created provide one of the major sources of interest in following the trilogy through to its conclusion. But a less central example of the technique will illustrate the shocking force with which it can work. David Staunton describes a Deptford character in *The Manticore* whose identity and significance are not specified:

> It seems there had been some woman there when she [Netty] was a little girl who had always been "at it" and had eventually been discovered in a gravel pit, "at it" with a tramp; of course this woman had gone stark, staring mad and had had to be kept in her house, tied up.[8]

The reader of *Fifth Business*, however, recognizes immediately the saintly Mary Dempster and may experience real indignation at the injustice of Netty's description of her.

But is her description unjust? Or is it simply a description from a different point of view? Before becoming too irate, the reader does well to remember that Dunstan's portrait of Mary Dempster as a saint is not necessarily any more objective than Netty's picture of her as a whore. This dramatic shift in the significance of a character, depending on the context in which she appears, illustrates forcefully David Staunton's discovery that "the absolute nature of things is independent of my senses (which are all I have to perceive with), and what I perceive is an image in my own psyche." By showing us Mary Dempster as she appears to two different characters, Davies illuminates his central theme of the relativity of the objective world. Thus the device that binds the three books together superficially, by reintroducing characters from one book in the next, also reflects the common theme that connects the novels at a more basic level.

But perhaps the most significant of the unifying links in the trilogy is Davies' use of framing devices for the presentation and qualification of the various narratives. Each novel has one of these framing devices and they become progressively more complicated during the course of the trilogy. Their purpose is not merely to provide an occasion for the telling of each story, although they do perform that function. Rather, they are designed to make the reader question the interpretation which each narrator places on events. By calling into question the trustworthiness of each narrator, these framing devices lead the reader to a more complex apprehension of the "truth" than the one any single narrator presents. This awareness builds cumulatively over the course of the three novels and contributes substantially to the effective presentation of Davies' central theme.

*Fifth Business* employs the simplest and least obtrusive of these framing devices. Davies casts the entire novel as a letter addressed by Dunstan Ramsay to the headmaster of Colborne College and occasioned by Lorne Packer's condescending account of Ramsay's retirement in the *College Chronicle*. Consequently, Ramsay's tone throughout is one of outraged self-defence. The headmaster makes an ideal hypothetical audience because of his absence. He cannot talk back or question Ramsay and so Ramsay has complete freedom to put "the emphasis where I think it belongs."[9] But the very passion of his self-defence belies his objectivity and leads the reader to be a little sceptical. Ramsay does not always present a complete picture, particularly of himself. A tantalizing indication of a side that has remained undescribed occurs when Boy Staunton accuses Ramsay of being an eccentric.

> 'Eccentric? Me!'
> 'Yes, you. Good God, don't you think the way you rootle in

> your ear with your little finger delights the boys? And the way you waggle your eyebrows—great wild things like moustaches, I don't know why you don't trim them—and those terrible Harris tweed suits you wear and never have pressed. And that disgusting trick of blowing your nose and looking into your handkerchief as if you expected to prophesy something from the mess.'[10]

The details in themselves are trivial but they are enough to startle Ramsay and so lead the reader to question him as a narrator. Consequently, a picture of Ramsay greater than the one he presents of himself is implied by Davies. Although Ramsay as narrator works by direct and emphatic statement, Davies as novelist works by implication to present a fully-rounded picture of his narrator and central character.

He uses a more complex and sophisticated framing device in *The Manticore*. The story of David Staunton's life comes to the reader filtered through a hypothetical legal defence (prepared by David himself as part of his treatment), a dialogue between doctor and patient in the course of Jungian analysis, and some entries from David's private journal. In all cases, David himself is the narrator, but his narrative is constantly qualified by his own legal training and by Dr. von Haller's questions. And although David initially declares his scepticism about the value of analysis, Dr. von Haller in the role of analyst proves to be a formidable and troublesome commentator. She asks the kind of questions one would like to ask of Ramsay in *Fifth Business* and David Staunton, as a consequence, has a good deal more difficulty than does Ramsay in placing the emphasis where he thinks it belongs. Indeed, the reader's conclusions, particularly about the nature of the relationship between David and his father, come as much from Dr. von Haller's unanswered questions as they do from David's account of himself. The point cannot be illustrated by a single quotation. The repeated insertion of question and commentary after David's prolonged passages of narration builds up, during the course of the novel, an impression of Dr. von Haller's opinions as very different from those of David. Once again, Davies uses a narrative device to present the contrast between the objective and the subjective perceptions of a single phenomenon. The reader must be careful not to choose between the two accounts, accepting one and rejecting the other, but to blend them in a fashion compatible with David's realization of *esse in anima*. If one is following only the story, the framing device of *The Manticore* may seem intrusive and artificial. But as it contributes to the vivid realization of Davies' theme, it is an essential development beyond the apparent simplicity of *Fifth Business*. The way in which Davies tells his story has become as important as the story itself.

*World of Wonders* alters this balance. The framing device used here is even more complex than that of *The Manticore* and the manner of telling the story becomes *more* important than the story itself. The narrator proper is Magnus Eisengrim, but his words are reported by Dunstan Ramsay. Eisengrim tells his story, ostensibly because he believes in the specious theory that it has validity as a "sub-text" to the film biography of Robert-Houdin, but actually because, as Liesl puts it, he "has come to the confessional moment in his life."[11] What may be Eisengrim's principal motive—the desire to unmask Ingestree—remains unstated at the outset of the novel, and the story, whether sub-text or confession, begins. But the interruptions come even more frequently and disturbingly than Dr. von Haller's in *The Manticore*. *World of Wonders* has two sets of commentators—Lind, Kinghovn and Ingestree as commentators on the sub-text and Ramsay and Liesl as commentators on the confession. The number of narrative filters and qualifiers threatens to obscure the story completely as each one presents a rival interpretation of the significance of Eisengrim's tale.

Of all these commentators, Roland Ingestree is perhaps the most important. He is certainly the most fatuous, as his condescending attitude towards God and the Bible, important presences in all three novels in the trilogy, would indicate:

> "Eisengrim talks a lot about God," said Ingestree, "and God seems still to be a tremendous reality to him.... I really must read the Bible some time; there are such marvellous goodies in it, just waiting to be picked up. But even these Bibles Designed to be Read as Literature are so bloody thick! I suppose one could browse, but when I browse I never seem to find anything except tiresome stud-book stuff about Aminadab begetting Jonadab and that kind of thing."[12]

But even the fool can be important, as Ingestree proves in two ways. First, he becomes drawn into Eisengrim's story itself in a way that reveals much about Eisengrim's character and the malice underlying his decision to tell. But more important, despite his fatuousness, he tells Eisengrim an important and uncomfortable truth about himself. The most foolish commentator is, on one important point, also the most profound, as Eisengrim himself acknowledges:

> I loved him [Sir John Tresize] and served him faithfully right up to the end, but in my inmost self I wanted to eat him, to possess him, to make him mine.... If I was a little sharp with Roly, it was because I was angry that he had seen what I truly thought I had kept hidden. [13]

Here, then, the complexity of the framing device extends to embrace the commentator on the narrative as well as the narrator himself. Subjective and objective accounts of events become almost hopelessly intertwined and the task of forming some conclusion about the significance of events becomes, for the reader at least, virtually impossible. The idea that a point might be proved with "Ramsay says..." [14] is completely inadequate to the complexity of the situation. Indeed, "subject" and "object" are no longer as clearly distinguished as they have been. Is *World of Wonders* Eisengrim's story about Ingestree or Ingestree's story about Eisengrim? The possibilities are even more complicated when one remembers that Liesl and Ramsay participate in the same way in the modification of the reader's impression of Eisengrim.

The growing complexity of the narrative framing devices is, then, one of the most important ways in which Davies unifies his trilogy with reference to its central theme. But this theme may seem to have worked itself into a corner by the end of *World of Wonders*. Has Davies worked so many variations on the contrast between subjectivity and objectivity that the terms themselves have become meaningless? Is his conclusion one of hopeless relativity with no fixed and stable points of reference possible? The trilogy comes perilously close to this kind of relativity but finally avoids it by emphasizing two ideas that act as stable points of reference for its characters and its readers.

The first of these is the importance of the past as a shaping influence on the present and the future. The town of Deptford embodies this concept in the trilogy, but other motifs emphasize it as well. Ramsay, in *Fifth Business*, insists that history and myth are related and that they contain useful truths for the person who studies them diligently. David Staunton discovers that his present difficulties can be understood only by a careful study of his personal past, a study which relates that past to the mythic patterns which fascinate Ramsay. And in *World of Wonders*, Magnus Eisengrim's reverence for Sir John Tresize and the Romantic theatre contributes materially to his success in the contemporary theatre. Each of these men achieves wholeness because of a recognition of the importance of the past in his present life. In *World of Wonders*, Davies contrasts this acknowledgment of the significance of the past with the frighteningly contemporary attitude of Roland Ingestree, who believes "that there is no time but the present moment, and that everything in the past is diminished by the simple fact that it is irrecoverable."[15] Eisengrim's respect for the past offers a stable and consistent point of reference to save one from a present which is meaningless the moment it becomes the past.

But the most important value which the trilogy asserts is expressed through the concept of egoism. Only through a genuinely humble awareness of the importance of the self can the individual reconcile the conflicting claims of subjectivity and objectivity and achieve the kind of wholeness implied by David Staunton's *esse in anima*. The concept of egoism receives its most explicit statement in *World of Wonders*, where Magnus Eisengrim distinguishes between egotism and egoism.

> An egoist is a self-absorbed creature, delighted with himself and ready to tell the world about his enthralling love affair. But an egoist, like Sir John, is a much more serious being, who makes himself, his instincts, yearnings, and tastes the touchstone of every experience. The world, truly, is his creation.[16]

The genuine egoist avoids the pitfalls of relativity by making the world his own creation and then standing for the values he thus creates. It is unlikely that such a creature will be modest, but he may be humble in exactly the way David Staunton suggests. For the egoist is finally a comic character, and it is no coincidence that "egoist" is the last word of the trilogy, applied with love and humour to Ramsay's vain desire to be quoted as the authority on Boy Staunton's death.

But the central egoism at work binding all three books together is the egoism of Robertson Davies as novelist. Davies is a tangible presence in each of these books and they seem to represent an important assertion of the values he holds dearest. Through these books, Davies has made the world his own creation. In them, he has asserted the importance of humble self-understanding in a world that threatens to crumble into hopeless relativity without the unifying, all-encompassing, vision of the egoist.

# Notes

1  Robertson Davies, *The Manticore* (Toronto: Macmillan, 1972), pp. 242-43.

2  Robertson Davies, *Fifth Business* (Toronto: Macmillan, 1970), p. 9.

3  Davies, *The Manticore*, p. 93.

4  Robertson Davies, *World of Wonders* (Toronto: Macmillan, 1975), p. 294.

5  Davies, *Fifth Business*, p. 155.

6  Davies, *The Manticore*, p. 255.

7  Davies, *Fifth Business*, p. 256.

8  Davies, *The Manticore*, p. 144.

9  Davies, *Fifth Business*, p. 10.

10  *Ibid.*, pp. 230-31.

11  Davies, *World of Wonders*, p. 15.

12  *Ibid.*, pp. 152-53.

13  *Ibid.*, pp. 348.

14  *Ibid.*, pp. 358.

15  *Ibid.*, pp. 197.

16  *Ibid.*, pp. 191-92.

# Robertson Davies and the Ethics
# of Monologue

*Stephen Bonnycastle*

I n *A Voice from the Attic* Robertson Davies has provided an account of reading as a personal art, in which the reader is compared to the Lady of Shalott, enclosed in a private world of fantasy. This is an important aspect of many peoples' experience of literature, and Davies is right to encourage readers to cultivate a deep and solitary relation to books. There are some books, however, which assume a public role as well as a private one. These are often the very successful books which, in addition to feeding the private worlds of millions of readers, make an identifiable contribution to the evolving debate about cultural values, and influence what we admire and try to encourage in the world about us. These books, long after they have ceased to require public commendation, often become the subject of public debate.

*Fifth Business* is one such book, and its success is not due simply to the fact that it is very entertaining. I think most readers would agree that the roots of its power are embedded in moral concerns, and that it is exciting partly because it seems to give access to a new world of the spirit. The book presents its protagonist, Dunstan Ramsay, as a hero of an unconventional, scholarly kind, deeply concerned with what are essentially religious questions: the nature of faith, and the development of the human soul. In a recent issue of this journal, Ramsay was described as a saint, "living a life of wonderment," and proposed as a model of conduct for Canadians.[1] *Fifth Business* and its sequel, *The Manticore*, both contain general moral statements of great intensity. Ramsay is told by a Jesuit priest that the beginning of wisdom is to "forgive yourself for being a human creature," and in the second volume one character asserts, in his final statement, "God is not dead. And I can assure you God is not mocked" (*Fifth*, p. 208; *Manticore*, p. 185).[2] But the force of statements such as these is called into question by the novels themselves, which are concerned with deception, and in particular with the ways in which an artist deceives his audience. Ramsay, the fictional author of *Fifth Business*, is said to be agile at "slipping under the guard of the sceptic with a candour that is brilliantly disingenuous," and the magician Eisengrim is skilful in "misdirecting the attention of his audience, which is the beginning and end of the conjuror's art" (*Fifth*, pp. 247, 248).

Is the morality of *Fifth Business* a substantial contribution to the debate about cultural values, or an illusion, like one of Eisengrim's conjuring tricks? This is not the kind of question that the Lady of Shalott would be inclined to ask; but her isolation from society limits her curiosity and makes her a poor representative for readers in general.[3] It is my view that *Fifth Business* is much more ambiguous than is usually supposed, and that the force of its morality is an illusion created by Davies' remarkable craftsmanship. In supporting this view I hope to shed some light on an interesting novel, and indicate some of the skill involved in a brilliant performance. Not everyone is disappointed to know how the magician saws his beautiful assistant in half without scratching the surface of her delicate skin. For those who have "attained to the sophistication that takes pleasure in being deceived," as Eisengrim says, I would add that a dream which concerns itself with morality is already more than a dream.[4] It has forfeited its innocent, inhuman quality, and its didactic intention encourages a response.

## I

The title of *Fifth Business* refers to a principle which is central to much of the morality of the novels, the principle of relational identity. Near the end of the novel, Dunstan Ramsay is told that throughout his life he has unconsciously been playing the role of "fifth business," a role which regularly appears in the plots of romantic opera. It complements four other roles, those of the hero, the heroine, the confidante, and the villain; "fifth business" appears to be a minor role, but it is always necessary to the functioning of the plot. When this is explained to Ramsay by Liesl Vitzlipützli, the reader recognizes that Ramsay *has* spontaneously adopted this role with other people, and he could not maintain it in isolation. Ramsay's silence shows that this is a revelation to him, and he realizes that if he wants to alter his identity, he must change the way in which he typically relates to others. The general principle of relational identity was clearly stated by Alfred North Whitehead:

> The misconception which has haunted philosophic literature throughout the centuries is the notion of "independent existence." There is no such mode of existence; every entity is to be understood in terms of the way it is interwoven with the rest of the universe.[5]

In psychiatry this principle is often applied to the social life of the patient. Anthony Storr, for instance, points out that "in the absence of relationship with others, men become more alike, not more individual; and isolation leads ultimately to a loss of the distinguishing features of personality, not, as might be supposed, to their intensification."[6] Liesl tells Ramsay that by isolating himself with his work as a teacher and scholar, he is ignoring and leaving to chance what really determines the quality of his life: his relationships with other human beings. She encourages him to break loose from the pattern in which he is caught, and he follows her advice.

Not only Liesl uses the principle of relational identity to change the course of Ramsay's life, but also Padre Blazon, another of his advisors, persuades him that neither saints nor miracles have an objective existence, and that they depend on the faith of the believer and the state of knowledge at a given time. Blazon also suggests that young men and old men need different saviours, and that he is beyond the stage at which Christ can be of much assistance to him (*Fifth*, p. 206). In *The Manticore,* the main lesson that David learns during his course of psychoanalysis is based on the principle of relational identity:

> The absolute nature of things is independent of my senses (which are all I have to perceive with), and what I perceive is an image in my own psyche. (*Manticore*, p. 243)

That is, there is not an objective reality to which a man can gain access, and be certain that he is right. What he sees is inevitably coloured by what he is.

I would like to suggest four objections to the morality of *Fifth Business* and *The Manticore*. The first is that although the principle of relational identity lies behind many of the most forceful moral statements in the two books, the relations between characters suggest that they have absolute identities. This is especially the case in the scenes in which advice or instruction is being given, and so there is a contradiction between what is taught and the manner of teaching which impugns the morality. Secondly, in these books Ramsay is made to appear impressive as a teacher, as a scholar and as a partner for Liesl; but his actions indicate the opposite, and he is much less admirable than has been suggested. My third criticism is that the attitude which the books take to awe, or wonder, is not tenable. There are many statements to the effect that awe is a valuable emotion; I would suggest that its value is not absolute and unconditional. The value of awe depends on what inspires the awe, and the state of the person who is experiencing it. Finally, I submit that the many statements in the two books which exalt feeling over thinking are based on a false antithesis, and that they are misleading and harmful. So my first pair of objections refer to contradictions within the books, and the second pair to views which the books consistently support but which cannot, I think, command our respect. All four of these objections, as I will show later, are significantly related to the distinction between monologue on the one hand, and dialogue or dialectic on the other.

## II

Before discussing these objections to the morality of the novels, it may be helpful to describe their content and structure in some detail.[7] *Fifth Business* is concerned with the growth from childhood to maturity of three men who were born in the same village and who all achieve eminence in their professional lives. Although a summary of the events in the novel would necessarily be long and complicated, it is based on a relatively simple system of confrontations between the characters, and this system accounts for the development of the three men. Growth takes place when a character adopts an appropriate parental figure as a model, and it continues if the character relinquishes that model when it ceases to be useful, and finds another. Dunstan Ramsay, who becomes headmaster of a school and an authority on the psychology of religion, receives his instruction from a series of teachers: his parents, a local saintly woman, an English girl who wants to marry him, a Jesuit priest and finally the Swiss woman, Liesl, who is the driving intelligence behind a troupe of travelling entertainers. Boy Staunton, who becomes a powerful entrepreneur and a cabinet minister, models himself on his father, then on the Prince of Wales and finally submits to the malignant influence of his second wife, who tries to turn him into a statesman. The youngest of the three, Paul Dempster, becomes the celebrated magician Magnus Eisengrim; his models are Ramsay, and then an English actor, and in the end he too is brought under the sway of Liesl, and becomes the chief performer in her troupe.[8] The theme of personal development is also central in *The Manticore*. The bulk of the novel is concerned with the psychoanalysis of David Staunton, the son of Boy Staunton, who dies mysteriously at the end of the first book. In the course of David's analysis we find that his growth has depended on his modelling himself on his father and later on his law tutor at Oxford. Like the three characters in *Fifth Business* he has had a successful professional life, as a criminal lawyer. He has, however, reached an impasse in his personal life, and during his psychoanalysis he models himself on his analyst to a certain extent. Like Ramsay and Eisengrim, he is powerfully attracted to Liesl and greatly influenced by her. The rule that personal growth in the novels is achieved by the adoption of models is emphasized by the failure of Staunton's wife to develop; she is unable to keep pace with his dazzling progress, and she ends her life in a state of apathy and despair, neglected by her husband, bullied by her servants and pitied by Dunstan Ramsay, who was at one time attracted to her:

> Poor Leola did not get better and better because she had no idea of what betterness was. She couldn't conceive what Boy wanted her to be. I don't think I have ever met such a stupid, nice woman (*Fifth*, p. 180).

The inability to learn is a serious disease in this world, and for Leola and Boy Staunton, it proves fatal.

The progress of Boy Staunton and Magnus Eisengrim is easy to follow, because it is a matter of professional advancement and there are appropriate signs to indicate that they are rising in the world.

Staunton's income increases until he is one of the very rich, and he lives in a suitably lavish style. Eisengrim's progress in show business is indicated by his move from Canada to Europe to join a minor troupe there; later he enters Liesl's magnificent entourage and his picture appears on the cover of *Time* as the greatest magician in history. Ramsay's progress is more difficult to chart, partly because his line of work does not lead to spectacular public recognition. He becomes headmaster of his school for a while, but he is demoted from that position, and, in the academic world, the universities seem to tower above him. In addition, however, he enjoys an avocation which lends him some distinction: he is interested in the scholarly study of saints' lives. The aristocracy in this obscure field is a group of Jesuit scholars, and the fact that Ramsay is praised by their director for his good work is the sign of his success, and he is satisfied with it. But the reader's strongest impression of progress in Ramsay's life is related to his spiritual existence; Ramsay, unlike Staunton and Eisengrim, seems to grow in personal stature until the end of the novel. The same is true of David in *The Manticore*.[9]

In novels which are deeply concerned with personal and professional development, it is not surprising that when two individuals confront one another, one of the first matters to be settled is which of them occupies the superior position on the relevant scale of comparison. There is an involving account, for instance, of Ramsay's struggle to free himself from the domination of his powerful Scottish mother:

> I was glad that I did not have to be my mother's own dear laddie any longer, or ever attempt to explain to her what war was, or warp my nature to suit her confident demands. I knew she had eaten my father, and I was glad I did not have to fight any longer to keep her from eating me. Oh, these good, ignorant, confident women! How one grows to hate them! (*Fifth*, p. 90)

Eat, be eaten, or escape: these are the three possibilities in the primitive world of Ramsay's family. A similar situation occurs when Ramsay has his first affair with the English girl who nurses him to consciousness after he is wounded in the First World War:

> What was wrong between Diana and me was that she was too much a mother to me, and as I had had one mother, and lost her, I was not in a hurry to acquire another—not even a young and beautiful

one with whom I could play Oedipus to both our hearts' content. If I could manage it, I had no intention of being anybody's own dear laddie, ever again (*Fifth*, p. 98).

Dominate, be dominated, or escape: the choice between these three possibilities confronts Ramsay several times in his life, and it is no wonder that he is an isolated figure. Although he avoids being devoured by his mother and his mistress, his personal development depends on the fact that he is able to maintain child-like relations with other figures in the novel, such as Mrs. Dempster, Padre Blazon and Liesl. Each of these characters talks to Ramsay as a parent talks to a child, and he drinks in their wisdom and incorporates it in his own person. There is no struggle for precedence with these figures, because Ramsay is willing to be dominated. In *The Manticore*, David submits to Dr. von Haller in a similar fashion; the fact that she is a psychiatrist and he a patient establishes her superiority.

The most amusing character in *Fifth Business* is the Jesuit scholar, Padre Blazon; he is one of Ramsay's most important sources of wisdom. They do not need to engage in a struggle for precedence, because the rules for the exchange of goods and services are worked out clearly in advance. Blazon says to the aspiring scholar:

> I am one of Nature's guests...and if you will take care of the bill I shall be happy to recompense you with information about the saints you will certainly not find in our library. If, on the contrary, you insist that I should take my turn as host, I shall expect you to divert me—and I am not an easy man to amuse, Monsieur Ramezay. As a host, I am exigent, rebarbative, unaccommodating. As a guest—ah, quite another set of false teeth, I assure you (*Fifth*, p. 199).

But Ramsay's return on his investment is not obscure information about saints, but wisdom about life in general, and this shows that Blazon is superior in the relevant hierarchy. Blazon discourses admirably on the place of hero-worship in life, and since Ramsay's life is dominated by his worship of Mrs. Dempster and his desire to discover whether or not she is a saint, he is eager to learn. Blazon suggests that Ramsay should apply the principle of relational identity to the idea of miracles:

> Oh, miracles! They happen everywhere. They are conditional....
> Miracles are things people cannot explain. Your artificial leg
> would have been a miracle in the Middle Ages—probably a Devil's
> miracle. Miracles depend much on time, and place, and what we
> know and do not know.... Look at me, Ramezay. I am something
> of a miracle myself.... To a geneticist, I suppose it is not breath-
> taking that after seven daughters a woman should have a son, but
> to my mother it was a miracle (*Fifth*, p. 203-4).

Blazon advises Ramsay to stop looking for objective evidence that
Mrs. Dempster is a saint, and to concentrate instead on discovering
her role in his own life, the figure she represents in his personal
mythology. Blazon suggests that Ramsay should not think of himself
as merely an appendage to Mrs. Dempster's saintliness, but that he
should pay more attention to himself. In this relationship there is no
logomachia, no war in words for superiority, because Ramsay is
willing to listen gratefully. The sign of Blazon's dominance is his
monologue, which flows uninterrupted for four pages. This shows
that he has the authority to define the world in which their friendship
exists.

There is a more even-handed struggle for power between Ramsay
and Liesl; they appear to be cooperating on the magician's entertainment, and Liesl has a good deal of respect for Ramsay's distinction
as a scholar and a hagiographer. In addition, they have a ferocious
wrestling match in which Ramsay is the victor. But in the end Liesl
is triumphant, as her monologue shows, and she achieves superiority
in the same way that Padre Blazon did: she sees and understands
patterns in Ramsay's life of which he is unaware, and he realizes that
her vocabulary and power of analysis are stronger than his own:

> Even Calvinism can be endured, if you will make some compro-
> mise with yourself. But you—there is a whole great piece of your
> life that is unlived, denied, set aside. That is why at fifty you can't
> bear it any longer and fly all to pieces and pour out your heart to
> the first really intelligent woman you have met—me, that's to
> say—and get into a schoolboy yearning for a girl who is as far from
> you as if she lived on the moon. This is the revenge of the unlived
> life, Ramsay. Suddenly it makes a fool of you. You should take a
> look at this side of your life you have not lived.... You must get
> to know your personal devil (*Fifth*, pp. 265-66).

Liesl has already told Ramsay that he has been so obsessed with the virtue of Mrs. Dempster that he has despised everyone else; she now introduces him to the notion of fifth business, and warns him that he should find out if this is the role he has been playing for fifty years. Ramsay is awed by her power, and rapidly absorbs these new ideas.

I think most readers would agree that Ramsay's relation with Liesl has a fascinating quality, and I believe this is due to the fact that it is basically incestuous. Liesl is presiding over the rebirth of Dunstan Ramsay, and she points out that he has been reduced to the state of a child. Ramsay recognizes that Liesl is talking down to him, and complains that he is being bullied (*Fifth*, pp. 259-60). One sign of the inequality is that Liesl is able to launch into monologue, redefining Ramsay and changing the course of his life. At the same time they appear to be friends, and three pages later we are told that they "took from each other something that could find no requital in presents." What is omitted in this description is the sense of insecurity, approaching terror, that a person being invaded and transformed normally feels, and any awareness that a friendship is likely to be destroyed if one person tries to remake the other. It is part of Davies' brilliance that he can make us feel that Ramsay and Liesl have become friends and equals as well as lovers, but the form of the text at this point—monologue—is entirely against it, as is psychological probability. Ramsay is being eaten alive; it is surprising that he should submit to this, and retain the sympathy of the reader.

*Fifth Business* is a novel about a continuing apprenticeship, and what Ramsay learns from his teachers can best be described as a language. He enjoyed using words to dominate others as a child; this was known, in the argot of his village, as "getting off a good one" (*Fifth*, p. 6). The purpose of getting off a good one is to silence your opponent, and Ramsay achieves a minor victory when the clown in his school tries to taunt him (*Fifth*, p. 29). He also has a good one in reserve to use against Boy Staunton should the need arise: he knows the embarrassingly affectionate pet name which Staunton's mother used of him.

> I knew that I had but once to call him Pidgy Boy-Boy in the schoolyard, and his goose would be cooked; probably suicide would be his only way out. This knowledge gave me a sense of power in reserve (*Fifth*, p. 26).

But Ramsay seeks a repertoire of expressions which do not depend for their efficacy merely on the embarrassment of the victim, and that is one of the reasons he is interested in myth. Myths, he realizes, indicate patterns in human events, and if you can recognize the pattern at the outset, you can predict the final result. He knows, for instance, that if he submitted to the demands of his English mistress, he would be embarking on the same pattern of events as did Oedipus when he married his mother, and Ramsay predicts that the outcome would not be pleasant. With the help of Blazon and Liesl, he develops this skill to the level of a fine art.

Ramsay is particularly successful at seeing patterns in Boy Staunton's life. He says that "it was characteristic of Boy throughout his life that he was always the quintessence of something that somebody else had recognized and defined," and when Staunton begins to have marital problems, Ramsay observes that "the Stauntons rarely escaped cliché in any of the essential matters of life" (*Fifth*, pp. 129, 214). Ramsay sees that Staunton, by showing him pictures of his naked wife, has involved himself in the dangerous pattern defined by the myth of Gyges and King Candaules; and he recognizes, in Staunton's depression at the end of the book, an Arthurian desire for oblivion. Ramsay also predicts Staunton's death when he criticizes his friend's atheism:

> "I'm not surprised," said I. "You created a God in your own image, and when you found out he was no good you abolished him. It's a quite common form of psychological suicide" (*Fifth*, p. 284).

This succession of Ramsay's predictions points to a similarity between cliché and myth. Both words may refer to patterns of behaviour, such as Staunton's infidelity to his wife. Seen from above (from Ramsay's viewpoint, for instance) the configuration of events is defined and predictable, and so he sees it as a cliché. Seen from below, from Staunton's position, the pattern is not evident, and the events in it have the ominous, numinous quality which is still sometimes associated with the word "myth." Whether you call a pattern of events a myth or a cliché is a matter of relational identity: the word you use indicates not merely the events, but the way in which you perceive them. The teacher says to the pupil, "Your myths are clichés to me; listen carefully and I will explain them." This is the attitude of Blazon and Liesl to Ramsay; and Dr. von Haller says to her patient David:

> Mythic pattern is common enough in contemporary life. But of course few people know the myths, and fewer still can see a pattern under a mass of detail (*Fifth*, p. 230).

Ramsay has worked hard to learn to recognize these patterns—*Fifth Business* traces his progress in learning this language—and the penultimate scene, in which Ramsay and Staunton come to their final confrontation, is his reward for his diligence and native wit. As he says when he introduces this involving and powerful scene, Staunton's subsequent suicide was not "really surprising" to anyone who knew the history of his life. Ramsay has recognized the myth which defines the structure behind these events.[10]

The relationship between Dunstan Ramsay and Boy Staunton is unusual in the two novels because neither is willing to submit to the other, and the backbone of *Fifth Business* is their battle with one another for precedence. In the course of the novel they establish a symbiotic relationship: Staunton provides Ramsay with money, food and human contact; Ramsay is a willing listener and he provides an air of intellectual distinction which Staunton savours. Each feels that he deserves the gratitude of the other; each thinks that he has been the benefactor, Staunton with his financial advice, Ramsay with his psychological insight. It is as though each feels that he has been a father to the other, and the conflict between them is ugly. Staunton appears to win in the early rounds of this contest; he marries the girl to whom they are both attracted, and, as chairman of the board of governors of the school in which Ramsay teaches, dismisses his friend from the headmastership. In the face of these defeats, Ramsay naturally feels some satisfaction in learning that Staunton has become bored by success and weary of the world.

The final confrontation between Ramsay and Staunton is an elaborate reconstruction of the opening scene of the book; in both the two compete openly with one another, and in both Ramsay wins easily.[11] Staunton refuses to admit Ramsay's superiority, and he resists the redefinition of his life which Ramsay offers him. In the conflict he receives three blows which, combined with his general depression which he has already admitted to Ramsay, prove fatal.

These blows are a name, a pattern and a myth, and they confront Staunton with the fact that his existence is a cliché. He is reminded that his mother called him Pidgy Boy-Boy, and that he has never grown up; that he has repeatedly masked brutal self-assertion with deceptive friendliness; and that he is following in the footsteps of King Candaules. With Eisengrim's assistance Staunton's subconscious death-wish rises to the surface, and he drives his Cadillac off a pier into Toronto harbour.[12]

I think it is implied that Ramsay is breaking out of his habitual role as fifth business when he asserts himself in this scene; he reverts to an earlier strategy and offers Staunton the same choice which his mother offered him: be eaten, or escape. A more humane compromise does not occur to Ramsay, perhaps because his teachers never offered him one. Although they had a good deal to say about compromise with ideals and shaking hands with the devil, they insisted on teaching by monologue. Ramsay was willing to listen in silence, and his education prepared him for the final battle with Staunton. His weapons are precisely those which Blazon and Liesl had provided: an insistence upon seeing life as a whole which incorporates good and evil, a recognition of the frailty of the human condition and a knowledge of psychological patterns, or myths, which establish the relational identities of individuals. The meaning of Ramsay's final victory in this long battle is that Ramsay has a deeper grasp on life than Boy Staunton; Staunton's involvement with business, politics and women is shown to be unsatisfying and even ignoble in comparison to Ramsay's concern with education, magic and religion. The sign of victory in this full-fledged logomachia is, once again, monologue. In this case the monologue is the whole of *Fifth Business*; the death of Staunton leaves Ramsay with the authority to define reality.

*The Manticore* is strikingly similar to *Fifth Business*. David's progress is very like Ramsay's, and both novels support the same hierarchy of values. Much of David's education has been a matter of learning and unlearning vocabulary. As an adolescent he admired his father and tried to acquire the language appropriate to the son of a "swordsman"; then a priest tried to disillusion him about his father by showing him the tawdry nature of the world described by a swordsman's language. David acquired a powerful legal language from his tutor at Oxford, which brought him success in the world, but a major part of his psychiatrist's effort in *The Manticore* is devoted to showing him that language cannot describe the full range of human experience. David shows some inclination to compete with Dr. von Haller at first, but gradually their relationship is resolved into a teacher-pupil hierarchy, as is Ramsay's with Liesl in *Fifth Business*.

David is no match for Dr. von Haller because he is her patient, but her real advantage, when there is a skirmish for the superior position, lies in the powerful vocabulary which she uses to outflank him and expose his weakness. For instance, David gives a long description of the admiration, verging on madness, which a weak man may feel for a stronger person, and adds:

> I imagine you get it, as an analyst, when people think you can unweave the folly of a lifetime. It's a powerful force in life, yet so far as I know it hasn't even a name—

Dr. von Haller replies:

> Excuse me—yes, it has a name. We call it projection (*Manticore*, p. 52).

This shows the advantage of brief, accurate language. What David fumbles over for a paragraph, Dr. von Haller holds in a single word. In a similar way she is able to sum up areas of David's experience with words such as "shadow," "anima" and "persona," and she redefines "fantasy" and "fanticism" so they have more powerful meanings (*Manticore*, pp. 83, 162, 226, 56, 191). Her superiority depends on the fact that she recognizes patterns in human conduct of which David is ignorant, and she has names for them. The most striking example occurs when David realizes that she has been able to predict that he is going to fall in love with her:

> "Do you sit there and tell me that it is part of my treatment that I should fall in love with you?"
> "It is one of those things that happens now and then, because I am a woman.... Always there comes this period of special union with the doctor. This feeling you have—which I understand and respect, believe me—is because we have been talking a great deal about Judy Wolff [David's first love]" (*Manticore*, p. 157).

Dr. von Haller refrains from naming this process, perhaps for fear of hurting her patient's feelings. She is also careful not to encourage

David's "love" for her; she points out that the feeling has nothing to do with her personally (*Manticore*, p. 164). One of the main differences between this novel and *Fifth Business* is that David and Dr. von Haller's exchanges are less intense and less competitive than many of the exchanges which involve Dunstan Ramsay. Dr. von Haller does not want to dominate her patient or to engage in logomachia; she wants to make him feel strong, and as he learns some of her vocabulary, he gains in real strength.

*The Manticore* concludes not with a battle, but with David's promotion to a more powerful teacher, Liesl. She belittles the psychiatrist and prepares David for a new language and a new range of experience. This is the most powerful example of teaching in the two novels; David is taught the meanings of the words "heroism" and "awe." He says that he is not attracted to the heroic life, and that he does not know what awe is. To convince him of the reality and the importance of these two things, Liesl takes him to an underground cave where prehistoric men worshipped bears. She describes these men as heroes, David recognizes her awe, and he shows a kind of heroism himself in enduring the ordeal of crawling through the narrow passage which leads to the cave. This is instruction at the highest level, and enormous moral force lies behind the words "heroism" and "awe." To fail to learn this language is to be puny and despicable, not merely slow or recalcitrant. This language has an eternal quality, because it is associated with prehistoric men; they experienced awe in their underground shrine, and had the courage to endure life, as Liesl points out:

> We share the great mysteries with these people. We stand where men once came to terms with the facts of death and mortality and continuance.... Does this place give you no sense of the greatness and indomitability and spiritual splendour of man? Man is a noble animal, Davey (*Manticore*, pp. 272-73).

Liesl is using strong words, but she is even more powerful when she stops talking and withdraws into silent prayer.

It is difficult to give an impartial description of this scene, because it may appear either numinous and deeply moving, or simply offensive. Liesl is engaged in a teaching process, which is meant to produce a kind of rebirth for David; she may seem courageous and deeply concerned for him, or brutally self-assertive and arrogant. It is interesting to notice that David resists Liesl in a small way, and that he is embarrassed by her religion rather than immediately converted to it. But later he apologizes, admits that he was too small-minded to understand her meaning or intent, and begs her not to exclude him from her friendship. Liesl replies:

> Apology is the cheapest coin on earth, and I don't value it. But I think you have learned something, and if that is so, I'll do more than be your friend. I'll love you, Davey. I'll take you into my heart, and you shall take me into yours. I don't mean bed-love, though that might happen, if it seemed the right thing. I mean the love that gives all and takes all and knows no bargains (*Manticore*, p. 276).

In this final sequence, *The Manticore* takes on the atmosphere of *Fifth Business*. Once again, Liesl teaches with enormous power and authority, and she reduces her pupil to the condition of a defenceless child in the process of instruction. David can do nothing but acquiesce, and although he makes some statements in the course of this scene, they are ridiculed by Liesl. He might have retained more dignity by remaining silent, as did Ramsay. Liesl seems to be promoting what is basically an incestuous relationship, in which David is jolted from the status of an equal to that of a dependent child at the whim of his teacher. If this is more disturbing than Liesl's similar treatment of Ramsay, that is because we have much less reason to believe that David is independent of her. He is not simply fascinated with her, he is engulfed by her.

Concentrating on matters related to language in the two novels is helpful, I think, in seeing through the clutter of delightful events and in settling on what is essential in them. In saying this, I am using "language" to refer to the verbal habits which reflect the individual's way of thinking and feeling; a character shows us his "reality" by encoding it in a distinctive idiom.[13] The novels, then, are concerned with the learning of languages and with the struggles between different languages. When David learns the meaning of "awe," his whole view of human nature will have changed; and it is implied that his father's suicide might have been avoided if "awe" had been a part of his working vocabulary. Blazon's redefinition of "saint" changes Ramsay's life considerably, as does Liesl's introduction of the term "fifth business." It is interesting to notice that when two characters differ in their language, as do David and Dr. von Haller, they have a great deal to say to each other, whereas two characters who speak the same language can only exchange trivial comments, as Ramsay and Liesl do at the conclusion of *The Manticore*. This conveys a strong feeling that language precedes character, and that "language is not the vehicle of thought but its determining medium."[14] Liesl's confidence could be described as her assurance that she manipulates the most powerful language, and so inevitably encompasses her pupils; she has nothing to learn from them, they have everything to learn from her. Nothing in the two novels suggests that she is wrong.

Liesl's language, which is also taught by other characters in the two books, draws heavily on Jung's analytical psychology.[15] The forceful advice given by Blazon and Dr. von Haller to their respective pupils is drawn from the writings of Jung, and Ramsay acquires a similar body of knowledge and tries to pass elements of it on to Staunton in *Fifth Business* and to David in *The Manticore*. Even minor characters to whom the heroes resort for counsel have read and absorbed Jung's works: Surgeoner, the leader of the Lifeline Mission, and Knopwood, the priest who advises David about his spiritual and sexual life, both speak the same language: and even Pledger-Brown, an official in the College of Arms in England, gives David a Jungian harangue when his stepmother is looking for respectable ancestors (*Manticore*, pp. 233-34). This dispersal of a single language into the mouths of several authoritative characters provides a compelling example of how ideas may be converted into an ideology.

> Ideology is not the product of thought; it is the habit or ritual of showing respect for certain formulas to which, for various reasons having to do with emotional safety, we have very strong ties of whose meaning and consequences in actuality we have no clear understanding.[16]

There is no reason to believe that the teachers in these novels have no clear understanding of the Jungian basis of their thought and language; but, with the exception of Dr. von Haller, they teach as though this were the case. Their pupils are either speechless or divested of authority, and so their morality can be presented in the form of assertion rather than argument. The teacher is not required to reply to objections or to submit evidence in support of his or her opinions; the ideology shields itself from critical scrutiny. A brief description of the two novels which captures, I think, their major intention, is that they make some of Jung's ideas seem "natural," and therefore above criticism.[17]

### III

I would now like to turn to the four objections to the morality of *Fifth Business* and *The Manticore* which were briefly described in the first section. My task is to indicate why the morality of the two novels is not convincing, and to show how it is made to seem attractive, and even inspiring. I think there are two conditions which must be fulfilled if moral statements in a novel are to have force outside it. The first is that the statements must be consistent with the rest of the text. The second is that the world of the novel must be representative *in some way* of the real world.[18] If the reader feels that a novel is unrelated to his own world, he will not be tempted to transpose its morals to his world. They may seem interesting or curious, like the codes of behaviour of distant countries, but they will not seem relevant to his own concerns. I would like to suggest that much of the morality of these two novels is either not consistent with the whole of the text, or convincing only within the confines of the narrow world they define. This is an interesting problem to study, because of the light it sheds on the two novels, and on the techniques of deception which a novelist may use in order to increase his authority. This project is also attractive in general terms because it is liberating. These novels divide the world into the deceivers and the deceived, or the magicians and the rubes. It is satisfying to be able to cross the boundary between these two classes.

The principle of relational identity lies behind many of the most powerful moral statements in the two books, and it is usually advanced by a teacher in order to persuade a pupil to abandon his devotion to a false absolute, which is ruling and impoverishing his life. Blazon and Liesl both try to wean Ramsay from his fanatical devotion to Mrs. Dempster, and Liesl implies that Ramsay is wrong to sever himself emotionally from others, because he only has an identity in relation to them. Similarly, David's psychiatrist encourages him to reduce his devotion to his persona as a criminal lawyer, which he admits he developed to "keep people at bay" (*Manticore*, p. 227). Ramsay criticizes Staunton for creating a God in his own image, and so making his own self an absolute; and Ramsay's Christmas moral to David, "Cherish your bear, and your bear will feed your fire," suggests that a person has several facets, and that it is a mistake to exalt one and ignore another (*Fifth*, p. 284, *Manticore*, p. 279).

The force of the moral statements which are based on the principle of relational identity is undermined by the fact that the two books establish an absolute and rigid hierarchy of spiritual wisdom which is very powerful and never seriously challenged. When two characters form a relationship, this hierarchy determines who will be the teacher and who the pupil; and its absolute quality is suggested by the awe which teachers are able to inspire in their pupils and which allows them to teach by monologue. A notable feature of most examples of teaching in these books is that the teacher learns nothing of importance from the pupil, and this suggests a parallel between teaching and the production of magical entertainments, at which Liesl is such a genius. For she makes it clear that there can be no human relationships between the magician and his audience if the magician is to produce awe (*Fifth*, p. 245), and she is careful to generate awe in her personal pupils, Ramsay and David. It is a measure of Davies' skill that he can make Liesl's relations with these two men seem friendly. A careful investigation, however, shows that the quality of this friendship is thin, and that all the important information flows in a single direction. There is no evidence that Liesl is influenced by either Ramsay or David, although they are reborn through her agency; and at crucial times she treats them both like little boys. Liesl is the unmoved mover of the two novels, and her position precludes friendship.

The summit of the spiritual hierarchy in the two books is shrouded in mystery and exempt from the principle of relational identity. This is particularly evident at the conclusion of *The Manticore*, when David is taken to Liesl's castle high in the Swiss Alps, where Ramsay is a resident scholar and Eisengrim is perfecting his technique in magic. Here life is lived in a finer tone, free of care. The three permanent residents say very little to one another; instead David (who is manifestly their inferior) goes from one to another asking questions and receiving instruction. It is one of the problems which the novel explicitly recognizes that this process will make him seem a spiritual runt (*Manticore*, pp. 263-68); but although much of his instruction is based on the principle of relational identity, it is not suggested that David's runt-like condition is the result of his association with Liesl, who enjoys playing the role of a goddess, nor is it mentioned that a hero is only perceptible when he is surrounded by a chorus of unexceptional men and women. The reason for the book's silence on these matters is clear. Liesl's identity is not relative; it is grounded in absolute value and the trip to the shrine of the bears demonstrates this. The hierarchy in which Liesl occupies the top position, and against which Ramsay's spiritual progress in *Fifth Business* is to be measured, represents an absolute reality.

For the reader interested in morality this shift from relative to absolute standards poses a problem. The principle of relational identity is regularly used to dethrone false absolutes in a pupil's life and revolutionize his thinking. But how are false absolutes to be distinguished from real absolutes? The novels provide no answer to this difficult question. Liesl uses the principle of relational identity at her discretion, and this makes it seem a rhetorical weapon rather than a principle of knowledge. The morality which the books really propose is that psychological might is right, and they suggest that inspiring awe in another person is a useful tactic in achieving superiority over him. It is disturbing, even for an admirer of Jung, to find this old doctrine presented in a deceptive new guise. Davies softens the blow by misdirecting the reader's attention to ethical statements which encourage tolerance, learning and the full development of human beings; this obscures the way in which ideas are imposed on helpless pupils. The value accorded to awe is an important element in this deception. The pupils are supposed to be benefiting from their experience of awe, and David is told that he is suffering from starvation of the soul (*Manticore*, p. 267). But while the soul is being fed, the mind is being programmed, with two sets of contradictory instructions. The content of the instructions is based on the principle of relational identity, and suggests that all values are relative; their form—assertion and monologue—shows the absolute hierarchy in human relations. This makes awe seem like a narcotic used to prevent the pupil from asking questions about a complex and questionable doctrine. Why would Liesl make regular use of this unfair advantage if her morality were as impressive as she claims? It is a weakness in the novels that their doctrine is not tested or questioned by anyone strong enough to present a real challenge.

One of the chief attractions of *Fifth Business* is its protagonist, Dunstan Ramsay. His admirable qualities have been described in an article by Wilfred Cude in the November 1974 issue of the *Journal of Canadian Studies*. Cude says that Davies "has created a character who seems to have a comprehensive grasp of reality," and that Ramsay has "genuine humility."[19] Ramsay himself tells us that he is a good teacher (*Fifth*, p. 133), and he is attractive because he pursues an academic subject single-mindedly with no evident reward beyond his delight in knowledge. He is also engaging because he seems to grow personally for an unusually long time. His story is a variation on that of the ugly duckling, and it is satisfying to see him blossom, later than his contemporaries, but to a fuller humanity and a high degree of power.

Yet Ramsay is much more ambiguous than this description would suggest. Cude says that Ramsay is "quite prepared to come to grips with any mode of thought that passes his way," and quotes the following passage:

> I clung to my notion, ill defined though it was, that a serious study of any important body of knowledge, or theory, or belief, if undertaken with a critical mind, would in the end yield some secret, some valuable permanent insight, into the nature of life and the true end of man (*Fifth*, p. 196).

This is an inspiring statement of faith, but Ramsay does not really believe it. Later in the book, when he says that he is slowly and painstakingly trying to write "a sort of a prologue to a discussion of the nature of faith," he adds:

> Philosophers have tackled this question, of course, and answered it in ways highly satisfactory to themselves; but I never knew a philosopher's answer to make much difference to anyone not in the trade (*Fifth*, p. 234).

Cude does not stress this passage, although he quotes the sentence which immediately follows it. Ramsay's arrogant dismissal of the entire field of philosophy does not suit his image as a polymath, or do credit to the seriousness of a scholar who is hoping to "carry the work of William James a step further" (*Fifth*, p. 187).

Several of Ramsay's actions make us feel that he is humble, and kind to others. But the incident which is the fictional cause of the writing of *Fifth Business* shows that he can be proud and aggressive as well, with little justification. At the beginning of the book we are told that Lorne Packer, a junior teacher at the school where Ramsay taught for forty-five years, wrote a farewell article on Ramsay for the school magazine in which he suggested that serious historians are concerned with "scientific history" rather than mythic speculation. Ramsay is outraged by the article, and he writes a long letter to the headmaster of the school objecting to it. The letter is, in fact, the text of *Fifth Business*. Packer's article is not a particularly attractive piece of writing, but it is difficult to sympathize with Ramsay's hysterical response. The article is not ungenerous, and since very few people will read it, it is insignificant. Ramsay is being pathologically sensitive to launch into prophetic denunciation of Packer. His rage is undirected; it is childish and petulant for him to write to the headmaster of the school to object to it. What galls Ramsay most is:

> The patronizing, dismissive tone of the piece—as if I had never had a life outside the classroom, had never risen to the full stature of a man, had never rejoiced or sorrowed or known love or hate, had never, in short, been anything except what lies within the comprehension of the donkey Packer (*Fifth*, p. 8).

Packer can scarcely be expected to write about something which is beyond his comprehension, and it is well known that editors of school magazines are more often beggars than choosers when they assemble their copy for the press. But Ramsay's suggestion that the *College Chronicle* should reveal the intimate emotional life of a retiring teacher is ludicrous; and for a man who has absorbed the principle of relational identity, Ramsay is curiously intolerant of the need of a younger man to assert himself. What is most significant, however, is the way in which Ramsay dismisses his opponent. We are told almost nothing about Packer, and even less about his "scientific view of history." The man receives a barrage of childish invective and his view of history is not considered.[20]

Ramsay is applying Liesl's teaching methods: he tries to reduce his opponent to the state of a threatened child and enforces silence on him. No character of *Fifth Business* offers an explanation or a reasoned defence of philosophy or of scientific history, and Ramsay's dismissal of both disciplines is based on scorn rather than on understanding. This shows the advantage of monologue: the speaker is able to define the world because he encounters no resistance, and if he is adroit, he can make his stupidity seem like a virtue. Ramsay is very interested in power and he enjoys aggression against defenceless enemies, which he sometimes calls "getting off a good one." Although this is not unusual among scholars, it is not a virtue of the profession.

Some of Ramsay's aggressive tendencies reappear in the final confrontation between himself and Staunton. This is, once again, an instance of teaching, and Ramsay is using Liesl's methods to convey Liesl's wisdom about life. Although Staunton's behaviour is not attractive, he correctly identifies Ramsay's intention to undermine and humiliate him. Ramsay's attempt to teach Staunton some of the "fundamental truths of life" ends in disaster; and the equanimity with which Ramsay accepts Staunton's death shows that his concern for others does not interfere with his competitive instincts. In this book Staunton, Packer, scientific historians and philosophers are made to seem either imbecilic or immoral, and so Ramsay appears admirable in his attempts to slay these dragons. But Ramsay has a dark side to his character. These novels often suggest that the seamy underside of a man's life is fascinating, but this does not seem to be the case with Ramsay. The ignorance and insensitivity which he shows when he is being unnecessarily self-assertive is simply banal. These failings need to be taken into account when he is assessed as a hero.

I would like now to consider briefly the attitudes which *Fifth Business* and *The Manticore* take to awe and to thinking. In the first novel, both Ramsay and Liesl imply that the experience of awe gives dignity to men, and that the tendency of modern civilization is to eradicate this emotion (*Fifth*, pp. 233, 244). The effort they put into the magical entertainment is justified because through it "a hungry part of the [audience's] spirit is fed" (*Fifth*, p. 244). David's main problem at the end of *The Manticore* is that he has not experienced awe, and Liesl says to him, "Awe is a very unfashionable, powerful feeling" (*Manticore*, p. 267). The novels never suggest, however, that it is just as dangerous to feel awe too often and too intensely as to be deprived of the emotion, although there is one minor character who suffers from an abundance of awe. This is Staunton's step-daughter Lorene, who is cheerfully described by Ramsay as being repulsive and uncontrolled (*Fifth*, p. 281); at Eisengrim's entertainment she becomes hysterical and has to leave halfway through. This would indicate why awe might not only be unfashionable, but also an impediment in the development of a full human life. If many people responded to Liesl's magic as Lorene did, the provision of awe for large audiences would not seem as innocent as Liesl claims. In any case it is difficult, especially since the advent of the drug culture, to suppose that awe is as unfashionable as she maintains. Producers, directors, authors and advertisers compete fiercely to provide awe for mass audiences, and receive large rewards when they succeed. Liesl is not a pioneer in this field, although she talks as though she were.

Wordsworth, who was also very concerned with the importance of awe, or wonder, felt it was necessary to distinguish between a false wonder which some playwrights and novelists of his time provided, in order to satisfy their public's "degrading thirst after outrageous stimulation," and the wonder which an "elevated" mind can experience in the face of "ordinary things." The first kind of wonder, Wordsworth felt, blunted "the discriminating powers of the mind" and reduced it "to a state of almost savage torpor."[21] He was aware of the way in which the easy wonder of fantasy can induce an unhealthy state of passivity in a person, and thought it a worthwhile project to combat the effect of what he considered bad, but spectacular, art. This is not a problem which engages Liesl's attention.

The anti-rationalism of *Fifth Business* and of the third part of *The Manticore* is a significant aspect of the two books. This attitude has its roots, it would seem, in Jung's well-known belief that the man who is "chiefly adapted to the world through thinking would be likely to function poorly in matters of feeling."[22] Ideally, there would be a balance between the two, and there is one passage in the novels which suggests this. Dr. Von Haller says to David:

> You are not asked to set your intellect aside, but to find out where it can serve you and where it betrays you. And to offer a little nourishment and polish to that poor Caliban who governs your Feeling at present (*Manticore*, p. 92).

But this moderate view is not representative of the novels, which are on the whole highly antagonistic to thinking. Ramsay's rejection of philosophers and scientific historians is a case in point. Another is

Liesl's outburst at the end of *The Manticore* in which she describes thinking as "the greatest bolt-hole and escape-hatch of our time" (*Manticore*, p. 266). In *Fifth Business*, Father Blazon says reflectively,

> Sometimes I wonder why so few saints were also wise. Some were, of course, but more were down-right pig-headed. Often I wonder if God does not value wisdom as much as heroic virtue (*Fifth*, p. 201).

The vices which are associated with the dominance of the intellect are harshly criticized in the two novels, particularly the arrogant self-confidence of the man who has a scheme for success which is not, ultimately, satisfying in human terms. Boy Staunton is criticized on these grounds, as is his second wife Denyse; and part of David's problem is that the over-development of his intellect at Oxford has left him stunted emotionally. But the antagonism to the intellect is not the accidental result of the presence of these one-sided characters in the novels; it is essential to their fabric, and especially to the dominant figures, Ramsay and Liesl.

Their distaste for reason is evident in their dislike of argument. If we think of rationality as the set of conventions which allows debate to take place between two individuals or two groups, and prevents debate from degenerating into wrangling and aggression, then it is clear why Ramsay and Liesl are against it. They prefer their relations with others to be coloured with awe (on one side), and they like it best if information passes in a single direction. They teach not by giving the pupil equipment to use and the independence to use it, but by overwhelming him with concepts and attitudes which are beyond comprehension. Above all, they dislike systematic thought. This is particularly evident in Ramsay's attitude to religion, and the way in which he opposes it to science and progress (*Fifth*, p. 233). One of the remarkable achievements in *Fifth Business* is that Davies convinces the reader that Ramsay is deeply involved in the psychology of religion. Ramsay says in Mexico that he is writing "a sort of prologue to a discussion of the nature of faith" (*Fifth*, p. 234); by the end of the novel he has published a major book on psychology and religion, and it has been well received. But Ramsay has almost nothing of interest to say about religion beyond his conviction that it is important, and that faith and wonder contribute to psychological health. One reason that Ramsay makes no appreciable progress in this field is that he usually expresses his ideas in either the form of assertion, or that of surmise; he is not interested in connecting his thoughts to form an intelligible argument.

Jung's distinction between the "feeling person" and the "thinking person" is used in these novels to support a polemic in favour of feeling, and particularly awe; and this is achieved partly through the denigration of thinking. It is worth suggesting that there is no necessary antagonism between these two activities; good thinking is based on strong feeling, and feeling gains in force when it is supported by accurate and subtle thinking. Nor is there any necessary opposition between awe and thinking, as the lives of many scientists, philosophers and poets show; it is only the dispositions of Ramsay and Liesl that make this appear to be the case.

The four objections which I have raised to the morality of *Fifth Business* and *The Manticore* are all related to the distinction between monologue and dialogue, and it is this distinction which penetrates the ethos of the novels most deeply. The principle of relational identity cannot be dramatically embodied in a series of monologues arranged in a hierarchical order, with an absolute authority such as Liesl at the top, because the principle itself is subversive of absolute authority; we can imagine a person who achieves his identity by dominating other people and forcing his monologues upon them, but it is difficult to admire this form of cannibalism. Ramsay's shortcomings as a scholar and as a person are the result of his intolerance of the needs of others, and his preference of monologues, given or taken, to more even-handed discussion. The indiscriminate approval accorded to awe serves to make monologue—and magical entertainments—more respectable, and the denigration of thinking prevents pupils from acquiring the tools which would allow them to challenge their own teachers and begin a dialogue. This shows that a dominant form in a novel—monologue in this case—can have a pervasive influence on its doctrines.

One of the most striking consequences of monologue in these novels is the rejection of most forms of social intercourse as possible ideals in life. It is repeatedly asserted in these books that a man must find something or someone greater than himself in order to live a useful and happy life. This is what Liesl tells Ramsay, what Ramsay tries to tell Staunton, and what Liesl tries to show David in the cave of the bears. But when the search for something higher is so intense, the most obvious possibilities—friendship, marriage, participation in the life of a group or of society—are not seriously considered. These novels are set themselves against social institutions, and individuals find the answers to their problems by escaping from society. This is why Ramsay and David are isolated figures, and why neither of them wants to go back to Canada. The religion of these novels proposes a new ideal, something primitive and sublime, in which society and its institutions are insignificant, and dialogue and the reasoning powers of the mind are eliminated.

When thinking, reasoning and dialogue are undervalued, it is significant that chance, or destiny, should take on unusual importance. This is appropriate, because monologue, for the listener, is almost a linguistic equivalent for destiny: you cannot influence what happens, you can only submit to it. The role which chance plays in Ramsay's life is particularly interesting. Dunstan Ramsay is an exciting figure primarily, I think, because his life suggests that Christianity and psychology, myth and magic, can all be combined in such a way that life, although difficult at times, will be filled with wonder and delight. The new range of spiritual possibilities presented by *Fifth Business* is the more intriguing for being based neither on wealth nor on exceptional talent; there is no apparent reason why the quality of Ramsay's life, so admired by Cude in his article, could not be achieved by any intelligent and well-meaning man. Ramsay appears to fill the role of an exemplary figure, an everyman, a hero. But in my opinion Ramsay is not a convincing representative of mankind either as a teacher, or a historian, or a psychologist, or a man of faith, or as all of these together. His distinctive characteristic is his good fortune. This consists primarily in his discovering a new and compelling heroine when he is well past middle age, one who is willing to remake his life and then act as his consort. This in itself is not unusual, and when it does occur the result is not always attractive, although in Ramsay's case it seems to be. At several points Ramsay refers to the importance of collaborating with destiny, and this is a natural reflection for a lucky man. The man who wins the lottery may build a shrine to fortune, but he cannot expect many others to worship at it; his situation is not likely to be considered typical of the human condition, and his triumph is not an inspiring one. Davies is subtle, persuasive and, I think, wrong in suggesting that Dunstan Ramsay—whose life is a freak of fortune—should set a standard for our conduct and our attitudes.

## IV

*World of Wonders*, the third in this series of novels, is strikingly similar to the previous two, and it represents their doctrine in a pure, explicit form. The bulk of the novel is concerned with the development of Magnus Eisengrim, who tells the story of his life in an extended monologue. We are also told something of the adolescence of Liesl. Like Ramsay in *Fifth Business* and David in *The Manticore*, both Eisengrim and Liesl consider as their deepest formative experiences their instruction by mentors who treat them as children, teach them by total domination, and provide them with an experience of rebirth. This is carried to an extreme in the case of Eisengrim, who learned his dignified and impressive manner by modelling himself on a famous English actor, Sir John Tresize. Eisengrim's astonishing success was due to the absence of personality in him; he is described by Sir John's wife as "a sort of charming nothing; a dear, sweet little zero, in which one can paint any face one chooses" (*World*, p. 187). Eisengrim does not merely adopt some of his mentor's ideas. He strives to become identical with him in body and spirit, and he is so successful that in the end the two are indistinguishable on the stage.

As in the two previous novels, the state of wonder is glorified (*World*, pp. 323, 355), and feeling triumphs over thinking: Eisengrim is implicitly praised for having no inclination to think at all (*World*, p. 325). Ramsay shows his hostility to abstract thought by surmising that the Devil was responsible for inventing numbers (*World*, p. 60), and we are told that Sir John's theatre troupe deals in feelings, not in ideas (*World*, p. 261). Criticism of modern systems of education is a recurring theme in the novel; authoritative characters make statements such as "Education is a great shield against experience," "education...is the great modern destroyer of truth and originality" (*World*, pp. 18, 16), and:

> if you're going to be a genius you should try either to avoid education entirely, or else work hard to get rid of any you've been given. Education is for commonplace people and it fortifies their commonplaceness. Makes them useful, of course, in an ordinary sort of way (*World*, p. 305).

The alternative model of education which is proposed is apprenticeship to an exacting master who himself is driven by a single-minded
passion for his art. This is what Eisengrim found in Sir John Tresize:

> Sir John wasn't cruel, or dishonourable or overreaching in common
> ways; but he was all of these things where his own interest as an
> artist was concerned; within that broad realm he was without
> bowels.... He was wholly devoted to an ideal of theatrical art that
> was contained—so far as he was concerned—within himself.... His
> egoism lay in his belief that art, as he embodied it, was worth any
> sacrifice on his part and on the part of people who worked with
> him (*World*, pp. 192-93).

Liesl, in turn, found a similar egoism in Eisengrim, and it introduced
her to what she calls the "Magian World View," taking the name
from Spengler's *Decline of the West*. Here many of the themes of the
novels come together:

> We have paid a terrible price for our education, such as it is. The
> Magian World View, in so far as it exists, has taken flight into
> science, and only the great scientists have it or understand where
> it leads.... We have educated ourselves into a world from which
> wonder, and the fear and dread and splendour and freedom of
> wonder have been banished. Of course wonder is costly.... Wonder
> is marvellous but it is also cruel, cruel, cruel. It is undemocratic,
> discriminatory, and pitiless (*World*, p. 324).

The account of Sir John Tresize and the Magian World View provide
a clear statement of the "might is right" philosophy which lay beneath
the surface of *Fifth Business* and *The Manticore*.

The main difference between *World of Wonders* and the two
earlier novels is that the latter seemed to be concerned with ethics,
with making choices which could be morally right or wrong. They
dealt with education, religion, and psychiatry—fields of human activity in which compassion and concern for the integrity of others are
important and perhaps essential. But these virtues, Davies suggests,
are only a hindrance in show business, and this is the world which the
third novel explores. Compassion is replaced by a thoroughgoing
fatalism in *World of Wonders*; in Liesl's and Eisengrim's Magian
World View morality is insignificant because the things which matter
are predetermined. As Eisengrim says, "part of the glory and terror

of our life is that somehow, at some time, we get all that's coming to us. Everybody gets their lumps and their bouquets and it goes on for quite a while after death." This ultimate justice he finds "rough and tough and deeply satisfying" (*World*, p. 355). Chance was important in *Fifth Business*, but in *World of Wonders* it is glorified. Eisengrim's education is a matter of following his own accidental compulsions, and he is lucky enough to find a master who will accept his servitude. The quality of his life is indicated by his own simple statement:

> We wolves like to possess things, and especially people. We are unappeasably hungry. There is no reason or meaning in the hunger. It just exists, and possesses you (*World*, p. 347).

Certainly there is no room for ethics here. Eisengrim's autobiography is based not on choice, but on chance—the inner chance of his innate, wolf-like character, and the outer chance which is called destiny, fortune, fate, or, at the end of this novel, *weird*. This exaltation of the arbitrary provides a fitting conclusion to a series of novels in which dialectic is overwhelmed by monologue. These novels imply that the elimination of dialectic leads to a view of life in which man is essentially the plaything of chance. This may be true; but I do not share the assumption, which is evident throughout the novels, that monologue need be the dominant way in which men relate to one another. "Eat or be eaten" is not a necessary rule, even between a reader of novels and an author whose work he enjoys.

## V

Does the doctrine of these novels matter? Does it have any public importance? Both the form and the success of the trilogy suggest that the doctrine deserves examination and evaluation. In an essay written five years before *Fifth Business* appeared, Lionel Trilling said:

> Modern literature...is directed toward moral and spiritual renovation; its subject is damnation and salvation. It is a literature of doctrine which, although often concealed, is very aggressive. The occasions are few when criticism has met this doctrine on its own fierce terms. Of modern criticism it can be said that it has instructed us in an intelligent passivity before the beneficent aggression of literature. Attributing to literature virtually angelic powers, it has

passed the word to the readers of literature that one thing you do not do when you meet an angel is wrestle with him.[23]

This is an apt description of the doctrine of the Magian trilogy, and the behaviour it recommends for apprentices, catechumens and readers. These books contain a strong element of an extremely popular form of literature, found in its pure form in "How to" books. But the trilogy is not concerned with acquiring some particular skill. It deals with succeeding in life in a general way, and its doctrine indicates ways for individuals to become happy, satisfied, successful individuals. The Jungian ideology contributes to this in the first two novels, and in the third great stress is laid on Eisengrim's eminence, his lasting achievement and his personal happiness. Each of these books is cast in the form of an autobiography, which traces the growth of one or two characters: this is a process which we all go through, and so ideas about it have an almost universal relevance. Davies has been extremely skilful in blending the "how to succeed" form with fictional autobiography, and in giving an enticing glimpse of a higher life which is very appealing. I think this partially explains the enthusiastic reception of the novels. Davies seems to have realized the dream of every educator: he has the ability to inspire others with a new ideal.

If I concentrate on the inadequacies of this ideal it is not because I feel it has no virtues. The novels themselves speak strongly in its favour, and the embodiment of Jung's ideas is powerful and instructive. But the ideal proposed in these novels—their image of the good life—has serious and interesting flaws which are carefully hidden.

The fundamental message of the trilogy is an inversion of *un sot trouve toujours un plus sot qui l'admire*, based on the story of Sleeping Beauty: "Each man can find a hero who will transform his life."[24] This hero must be a person who is so superior to you that he or she can treat you like a child and drive you mercilessly. The reason why this doctrine is useless if not positively dangerous—and the reason why the general comments on education in the novels are vacuous—is that in most cases, teachers who are tyrants and insist on total submission from their pupils, are inhuman, frustrated and insecure people. They are not rare, and in all but very unusual students, they inspire loathing rather than respect. Usually that is the appropriate response.

I think it is generally accepted that growth during adolescence often takes place through identification with an older person who may be admired with a passionate intensity.[25] In the Magian trilogy, the protagonists go through this process much later in life: Ramsay is in his fifties, David in his forties and Eisengrim is twenty-two. The idea of spiritual growth is an exciting one for many older people, and to represent it Davies has transferred to later life a process which is common in adolescence. But conversion is not always such a pleasant process for older people, and the personal revolutions which Davies describes are often accompanied in real life by nervous breakdowns. Davies gives all his protagonists boundless self-confidence, so they can be reduced to nothing by their teachers and still survive. By leaving out the pain which usually accompanies major psychic upheavals, Davies bases his theory of education on extraordinary cases. This puts its general validity in question.

Not only is the doctrine of the Magian trilogy misleading; it is also, in broad social terms, repugnant. One of the most attractive features of the life of the mind (in which it bears a close relation to the religious life) is that its riches are potentially available to everyone, and one man's gain is not another man's loss. That is why Chaucer's Clerk was glad to learn and glad to teach, and why Matthew Arnold says that culture

> seeks to do away with classes; to make the best that has been
> thought and known in the world current everywhere; to make all
> men live in an atmosphere of sweetness and light....[26]

Northrop Frye echoes these words when he says, "The ethical purpose of a liberal education is to liberate, which can only mean to make one capable of conceiving society as free, classless, and urbane."[27] The Magian trilogy sets itself against these ideals in an uncompromising and clear-eyed way, and promotes a fierce aristocracy of the spirit. This is why the books suggest that real education is a matter of rising into a tiny elite which possesses great authority and power; why Liesl is an heiress and all the important characters are rich and successful; why the world of entertainment consists of the deceivers and the deceived, with a barrier which is both rigid and carefully maintained between them. What is repugnant about this view of the world is not that it claims to be a statement of the facts, but that the people on the top gain their sense of being from their superiority to those at the bottom, and do their best to keep them in their place. These books are about culture and education as private—and jealously guarded—property.

The most serious deception in this trilogy, which is relevant to every life and every day in every life, is that in which form and content come together to suggest that monologue is the summit of human discourse. Throughout the novels monologue is a sign that a character has triumphed: he has turned his companions into an audience, and he holds them because of his acknowledged superiority. Each of the novels is predominantly a monologue, and some of the most impressive writing comes in long, uninterrupted speeches by minor but authoritative characters, such as Blazon and Zingara. But what if monologue is a sign of failure rather than triumph—a sign of isolation, of rigidness, of estrangement from a changing world? Then the attempt to glorify it, by exalting it above dialogue, is mistaken. I see no reason to suppose that an outstanding magical entertainment, a brilliant lecture, or even an entrancing drama, are more wondrous, numinous, or life-enhancing than the ability of two persons, or a group of persons, to communicate with one another, to correct one another's misconceptions, to satisfy one another's needs, and to participate in the dialectical processes of an evolving world. Nor does dialogue demand less skill than does showmanship, or permit less subtle refinements—there are enough, I am sure, to occupy a lifetime. To choose between the two spheres, the two views of the world, the two modes of activity, is of course a personal choice, a choice which we make and remake with every person or group we encounter. It is a choice between having an audience and having a partner.

# Notes

1   Wilfred Cude, "Miracle and Art in *Fifth Business,*" *Journal of Canadian Studies*, Vol. IX, No. 4 (November 1974), pp. 14, 16.
2   References to *Fifth Business* (Toronto: Macmillan, 1970) and *The Manticore* (Toronto: Macmillan, 1972); subsequently referred to in the text as *Fifth* and *Manticore*.

3   The Lady of Shalott represents the reader as pure consumer; she produces nothing as a result of her reading, and so it is often assumed that a hundred such readers all consume the same thing. This is not the case, as every teacher of literature knows, and some interesting contemporary research is concerned with the part which the reader plays in (unavoidably) *interpreting* the text, according to his own inclinations and the strategies of interpretation which have been taught to him. This subject is explored in the chapter entitled "Literary Competence" in Jonathan Culler's *Structural Poetics* (London: Routledge & Kegan Paul, 1975). Roland Barthes proposes a psychoanalytic typology of the pleasures of reading in *Le Plaisir du texte* (Paris: Editions du Seuil, 1973), pp. 99-100; he distinguishes between the reading methods of the fetishist, the obsessional, the paranoiac and the hysteric. My disagreements with Cude about *Fifth Business* could be attributed to the differences between the second and fourth methods; the text itself encourages the first, with its emphasis on magical words and phrases. *Le Plaisir du texte* has been translated by Richard Miller (New York and Toronto: Hill and Wang, 1975).

4   This quotation is taken from the third novel in the series, *World of Wonders* (Toronto: Macmillan, 1975), p. 303. Subsequently referred to in the text as *World*.

5   This passage is quoted in Jonathan Culler's article, "Modernism: Linguistics," *The New Review*, Vol. 1, No. 10 (January 1975), p. 13. This is a short and clear introduction to some of the basic theories of structuralism, and shows how the methods of structural linguistics can be of use in studying how literary works produce meaning. One advantage of these methods is that they allow the critic to go beyond surface beliefs and explicit hierarchies and to describe the structures, or systems of transformation, on which these are based.

6   Anthony Storr, *The Integrity of the Personality* (Harmondsworth: Penguin Books, 1963), p. 35.

7   My description of *Fifth Business* and *The Manticore* is a structural analysis in the sense that I am trying to describe the system which lies behind the novels; similarly Saussure, the founder of structural linguistics, tried to describe the system behind the functioning of a language. This is an interesting exercise because these novels are unusually systematic, and contain a great deal of repetition which is skilfully disguised. Many people feel insulted when a work of art is described as systematic, and Liesl is especially scornful of "system grinders" in the humanities (*World of Wonders*, p. 324); and so it is worth pointing out that the purpose of looking for a system in a novel is not to deny its originality or the spontaneity of its characters, but to locate these qualities by describing the novel as carefully as possible. Similarly, the purpose of looking for systematic patterns in language is not to prove that man is a predictable machine, but to stress his creative powers, as Chomsky makes clear in *Language and Mind* (New York: Harcourt, Brace & World, 1968). My description of the novels is clearly not complete or

definitive; it is like a rough map of a newly discovered island, and stands in need of improvement.

8   In *World of Wonders* we learn that Liesl was domesticated by Eisengrim, rather than the reverse; but their relationship seems to be a case of the tamer tamed, because in the first two novels, Liesl appears to be in command.

9   *World of Wonders* differs from the first two novels in that Eisengrim, whose life the novel recounts, does not grow spiritually. He becomes technically more skilful, and it is asserted that he attains a *Weltanschauung* which is rare and exceptionally valuable, and which allows him to see wonder in the world. This is described at length by Liesl who identifies it as the Magian World View of Spengler (323-24). Whether this outlook is an attractive one, and whether it justifies Liesl's general condemnation of modern education and sensibility, each reader will want to judge for himself; but Magnus is as involved with this world view when he is seduced by Willard the Wizard at the beginning of the book, as he is at the end. This is what we would expect from the description of the *Weltanschauung*, which sets itself against progress, and is closely related to the archaic part of the personality which Freud called the id and which Eric Berne describes as the "child ego state" and the most valuable part of the personality; see his *Transactional Analysis in Psychotherapy* (New York: Grove Press, 1961), pp. 29-36.

10  Dunstan Ramsay's interest in myth as the primary reality of life rather than as a series of pretty stories used for decoration makes him representative of one of the major changes in literary criticism in the twentieth century. Myth is also taken seriously in psychiatry, which has had an obvious impact on criticism. The use of structural analysis and of myths in psychiatry is one of the main subjects in Eric Berne's *What Do You Say After You Say Hello?* (New York: Bantam Books, 1973), and he provides an interesting contrast to Ramsay. Both are interested in identifying the myth behind a man's life, and the script which he is unconsciously following; but Ramsay takes a contemplative attitude to the script (in Staunton's case) because he feels that it is provided by fate or destiny, and observes the violent conclusion with detached interest, while Berne feels that the script is (to a great extent) provided by the family of the child, and can be altered in many cases so the patient can avoid his "payoff" (pp. 110-13).

11  One of the value judgments which is frequently repeated in these two books is that what is old is superior to what is new. Ramsay won the sled race in the opening scene of *Fifth Business* because Staunton's "fine new Christmas sled" would not go as fast as Ramsay's old one (*Fifth*, p. 1); he defeats Staunton in the end partly because he is a student of mythology, partly because he remembers the past and partly because he has kept the stone which Staunton threw at him after he lost the sled race. The theme that age confers value reaches a climax at the end of *The Manticore*, where Liesl reveals the significance of bear worship in caves 75,000 years ago, and Ramsay measures the insignificance of the individual by comparing himself to the age of the granite stone, which is approximately 1,000,000,000 years old (*Manticore*, pp. 273, 262). Repeated assertions of this sort establish an

ideology without calling attention to it; in this way, the ideology can appear "natural" and inevitable instead of the result of a set of value judgments. Collecting the relevant assertions is part of the process of reading, and may occur consciously or unconsciously. Roland Barthes' *S/Z* (Paris: Editions du Seuil, 1970) is a practical treatise on the structure of narrative as well as a sentence-by-sentence commentary on a short story by Balzac, in which he shows how the novelist makes use of, and transmits, an ideology. It has been translated into English by Richard Miller (New York and Toronto: Hill and Wang, 1974).

12  The death of Boy Staunton, and the participation of Ramsay and Eisengrim in it, is the subject of the concluding pages of all three novels; this parody of the detective story becomes a sign that the novel is drawing to a close. One of the unexplained changes in the last volume is that Ramsay becomes fascinated with the facts and wants to find out what actually happened, whereas in *The Manticore* he poured scorn on David's attempt to understand his father's death, and called him a "great clamorous baby-detective" (*Manticore*, p. 261).

13  This subject is discussed in the first chapter of George Steiner's *After Babel* (London: Oxford University Press, 1975), which is entitled "Understanding as Translation."

14  This suggestion was made by Leibniz in 1697, and is reported by Steiner, *op. cit.*, p. 74.

15  The use of Jung's thought in *Fifth Business* is described by Gordon Roper in "Robertson Davies' *Fifth Business* and 'That Old Fantastical Duke of York Corners, C.G. Jung'," *Journal of Canadian Fiction*, Vol. 1, No. 1 (Winter 1972).

16  Lionel Trilling, *The Liberal Imagination* (Harmondsworth: Penguin Books, 1970), p. 285.

17  "Naturalization" is a subject of great interest to structuralists. The word is an ugly one, but so is the process, in which an ideology, which is a human, cultural product, is made to seem an unchangeable part of nature, and so unquestionable. What is concealed is how the ideology came into being; because it is supposed to be natural, it seems eternal. Technology, repetition and parataxis are useful tools for achieving naturalization, because (verbally) they eliminate time. There is an amusing example of naturalization in *Fifth Business* when Staunton dismisses Ramsay as headmaster of Colborne College because his interest in saints is unnatural (*Fifth*, pp. 228-31). Staunton has a single message to convey, which he repeats in a variety of forms; Ramsay's resistance to the explanations makes it clear that naturalization rests on authority and not on truth. Staunton, as Chairman of the board, possesses the necessary authority, and so Ramsay has to acquiesce. This incident is seen in an ironical light, because it is part of the ideological message of the book that what Boy Staunton thinks natural is in fact perverse. The same ambiguity is not evident in the most powerful example of naturalization in the two books, which occurs during David's trip to the cavern of the bears at the end of *The Manticore*. Liesl refuses to

answer David's questions, and the incident is bathed in a timeless, magic light by its association with prehistoric man.

The structuralists make no claim to avoid or eliminate ideology themselves. It is difficult or impossible to live without making assumptions about the nature of the world. Their purpose is to raise consciousness to a higher level by questioning the dominant ideologies, which tend to be shielded from scrutiny by their own success. The structuralist project is itself clearly based on assumptions about what is valuable. Barthes' *Mythologies* (Paris: Editions du Seuil, 1957; English translation Frogmore, Herts.: Paladin, 1973) provides an introduction to this subject and some amusing analyses of French bourgeois ideology in the 1950s.

18 Both allegory and romance can be representative of the world, and have enormous moral force. J.R.R. Tolkien's *The Hobbit* and *The Lord of the Rings* are examples of romance which have had a moral impact on many readers, and these two books are similar in many ways to *Fifth Business* and *The Manticore*. In both a quest is passed on to a younger hero in the second volume, along with a numinous object which needs to be lost, and in both the hero of the first book retires to a distant and magic castle where he does obscure research.

19 Wilfred Cude, *op. cit.*, pp. 3, 4.

20 Ramsay calls Packer a dullard, a donkey and an "ineffable jackass" (*Fifth*, p. 8). He is also indignant at Packer's illiteracy in religious matters, which he shared at a similar age (*Fifth*, pp. 9, 141). Davies seems to be suggesting that Ramsay's anger is directed against his former self.

21 William Wordsworth, "Preface to *Lyrical Ballads*," *The Prose Works of William Wordsworth*, ed. W.J.B. Owen and J.W. Smyser (Oxford: Clarendon Press, 1974), Vol. 1, p. 128.

22 Anthony Storr, *Jung* (London: Fontana, 1973), p. 76. Storr thinks that Jung's typology which opposes thinking to feeling and sensation to intuition is one of his "least satisfactory contributions" to psychological theory, "of little help in grasping how different personalities perceive the world," and that it is little used by Jungian therapists (pp. 76-9).

23 Lionel Trilling, *Beyond Culture* (Harmondsworth: Penguin Books, 1967), pp. 200-1.

24 Eric Berne describes the everyday meaning of the story of Sleeping Beauty in *What Do You Say After You Say Hello?*, pp. 49-51.

25 See the chapters on "Identification and Introjection" and "Identification and Projection" in Anthony Storr's *The Integrity of the Personality* (Harmondsworth: Penguin Books, 1963), especially pp. 107-8.

26 Matthew Arnold, "Sweetness and Light," in *Criticism: The Major Texts*, ed. Walter Jackson Bate (New York: Harcourt Brace Jovanovich, 1970), p. 472.

27 Northrop Frye, *Anatomy of Criticism* (Princeton: Princeton University Press, 1957), p. 347.

# *One Half of Robertson Davies* by
# Robertson Davies

*Joyce Carol Oates*

To understand how a writer of such modest though agreeable gifts as Robertson Davies can be considered Canada's leading man of letters, one must know something of the current literary climate. (It is not I who make this claim for Davies, but others: I would put forth the names of Northrop Frye and George Woodcock if asked to name Canada's "leading" men of letters.)

Not long ago there was no "Canadian literature" as such—writers wrote, and presumably people read them, but not many people read them and rarely with the deep, considered respect they held for the *real* literature, which was that of England; or Europe; or even the United States. Literary journalists as well as academicians professed contempt for the writers and poets of their own country who, writing of native, immediate and often distinctly regional matters, seemed to them obviously inferior to Wordsworth, Dickens, Austen, Shakespeare *et al.* (I note the same, now rather outdated, attitude in Robertson Davies who, in the few literary pieces included in this collection, speaks warmly and knowledgeably about Dickens, Henry James, Graham Greene, Evelyn Waugh, even John Cowper Powys, even the nineteenth-century melodramatist Sheridan Knowles, but who charges the literature of his own time with being excessively "gloomy," godless and Freudian; and who, in a speech with the title "What May Canada Expect From Her Writers?" manages the astonishing feat of mentioning not one Canadian writer at all—the piece is about Solzhenitsyn and Robertson Davies.) Canadian writers were made to feel not only inferior to Great Writers, but unreal: with no critical response, and a very small reading audience, how were they to attain any sort of image of themselves? How were they to feel that their efforts had any value?

In the 60s, however, with the rise of Canadian Nationalism, the situation began to improve. Genuinely gifted writers like Margaret Laurence were "discovered;" neglected works like Sinclair Ross' *As For Me and My House* were recognized as minor masterpieces. Younger poets and writers appeared. And were encouraged by early publication. And by frequent publication. The most influential anthology of the era, and of the present time, is Gary Geddes' *20th-Century Poetry and Poetics*, which boldly—some might say recklessly—sets down poets with the dubious fits of an Al Purdy beside Yeats and Pound and Eliot and Frost. (In fact Purdy has nine poems in the book, to Auden's seven.) One discovers A.M. Klein beside Dylan Thomas, one puzzles over bp nichol, whose concrete poetry is of a sort to give undergraduate poets hope for their own apprentice work. Elsewhere, in critical journals, Canadian writers are discussed with easy reference to "other" twentieth-century writers like Joyce, Lawrence, Mann and Faulkner. Perhaps Canadians are not inferior after all; perhaps they are superior? The Revolution grows fierce, belligerent. An undergraduate English major asked our departmental council why some of us believed English majors should be encouraged to take courses in Shakespeare—after all, doesn't Shakespeare belong to the past, and today we have Earle Birney. In Alberta, Canadian nationalists objected to symphony orchestras in the habit of playing works by Beethoven and Mozart; aren't there, they inquired, Alberta composers whose compositions might mean more? And the other day one of my students remarked that all of the stories in the anthology we are using are "American" (i.e. Chekhov, Mann, Kafka, Joyce, Flaubert, Calvino, *et al.*)—where were the Canadians?

Since it has been decided that Canadian writers are now worthy of those old, enviable adjectives—*great, masterly, brilliant, profound*—literary journalists and critics are in a frenzy to apply them to actual people. The talented Margaret Atwood must endure well-intentioned publicity that places her "in the ranks" of Conrad on the strength of one novel, *Surfacing*, and insists upon her position, at the age of thirty-eight, as the "reigning Queen of Canadian Letters." (And, in the wings, the "next major Canadian woman writer" is already being groomed—a twenty-five-year-old poet of extremely slender and derivative gifts.) In art there is Harold Town, who has gamely imitated, over the years, nearly every school and gimmick to acquire publicity in New York, and imitated it badly: Canada's "outstanding" artist. And there is, of course, Robertson Davies, whose twenty-fourth book we have here.

A former newspaper editor (of the *Peterborough Examiner*), now professor and Master of Massey College at the University of Toronto, Davies has written nine novels, eight plays, three books of criticism, and has collaborated on other books. His best-known work is an informal, and unplanned, trilogy that consists of *Fifth Business, The Manticore*, and *World of Wonders*. (Of his earlier, lesser work I have read only *Leaven of Malice*—and would not quarrel with the judgment that it is lesser.) In Canada the trilogy is considered something of a masterpiece, partly because, as Davies says in one of his speeches, it is clearly a moralist's fiction—"quite often people reap what they have sown"—and because, as Davies also says, it won the enthusiasm of a "large and generous readership in the United States." *Fifth Business* is a winning, likeable, plausible, well-crafted (in a 50s textbook manner) novel, proudly old-fashioned in characterization and style and theme, and while it will not excite many readers it will certainly not disappoint. *The Manticore*, however, reads like an uninspired though rather antic fleshing-out of Part I of Jung's popular *Man and His Symbols* (Davies is a Jungian, and a talkative one—more of that later); the third novel of the trilogy, *World of Wonders*, is painfully weak, a hodgepodge of details and memories that constitute the "autobiography" of a man whom Davies wants us to consider the world's greatest magician, but who is no more than a talking—a perpetual talking—machine. Yet in general these novels received ritual acclaim in Canada: it seems to be the case that very few Canadian critics are willing to take note of the Emperor's exceedingly flimsy new clothes.

No doubt the present volume, which consists of speeches given by Davies over a period of many years, will receive the same sort of ritual response in Canada. Like Goethe and Mann, whom Davies admires greatly, he is not "crippled" by inordinate modesty; he thinks it quite reasonable that occasional speeches, conversational, jocose talks he has given to the girls of Bishop Strachan School, at commencement ceremonies at the University of Calgary, to the Ontario Welfare Council, to Massey College's faculty and students at their yearly Gaudy (a Christmas party), even to a society of industrial accountants, should be preserved. As if apprehensive of the fact that the printed word differs irrevocably from the spoken word, Davies instructs us to try to *hear* the book as we read it. And perhaps this was my problem—I did seem to hear the book, as I read it. And to realize that my cunning in avoiding commencement exercises over the years was no more than instinctive wisdom: those speeches *are* as bad as everyone says. Yet the experience of reading *One Half of Robertson Davies* was enlightening—I was forced to realize how close, how astonishingly close, colossal vanity is to pristine innocence.

Here is Davies on the proper education of women:

> Women are not simply creatures with an undeveloped masculine type of intellect, but the possessors of a type of intellect very much their own, which is complementary to that of the male. Religion, of course, has always recognized this.... Man is good at Civilization, but Woman is good at Life itself. But universities still work on the assumption that a brain is a brain, whatever sort of psychological organism it is hitched to.... Why do universities believe this?

But should one think that Davies prefers men, and resents the girls in his classes, he tells us confidentially in another speech: "Every autumn when I meet my new classes, I look them over to see if there are any pretty girls in them.... A pretty girl is something on which I can rest my eyes while another student is reading a carefully researched but uninspiring paper." He jokes that he is not now, and has never been, a homosexual. In one of the better pieces in the book, "The Conscience of a Writer" (which is, in fact, a low-keyed commentary on Jung's theory of individuation, though the term, for some reason, is never used), Davies states baldly that we all experience a change in the middle of our lives. It is highly important for the writer to recognize this phenomenon:

> In women this change is physiological as well as mental.... But in men the change is an intellectual and spiritual one of profound consequence, and this is something observable in the careers of virtually all writers of the kind we are talking about here—the committed writers, the servants of the writer's conscience.

But what kind of writers *are* we talking about here? They struggle, they endure, they work in solitude, "cheered by no one except perhaps a faithful and long-suffering wife."

Of these twenty-two pieces perhaps five are worth preserving; the others, particularly a "satirical" poem on *Hair*, not to mention a coy, cute animal story written for children but included here because "several people" assured Davies it was really for adults, might have been tossed away without regret. The collection improves as it progresses, though this may be a consequence of Davies' choice of subject matter (Freud, Jung, Trollope, melodrama, ghost stories, Proust, etc.) rather than the actual quality of his writing. We learn, for instance, that Evelyn Waugh, with a powerful Catholic belief in evil, was able to write superior novels because, for one thing, he did not partake of the follies of the Freudian Revolution (under the Freudian flag, in fact, the Devil has gained a good deal of ground. How do we know? Well, the "wallow of sentimentalism that attended the recent abandonment of capital punishment in Canada" is typical of the "kind of thinking" that springs from half-baked Freudian morality. Davies is said to regret that public floggings and hangings have been discarded—they were a good warning to potential evil-doers.) On Dickens he writes knowledgeably, if without any particular genius; on Jung he is disappointingly simplistic, and makes statements I would challenge—"For Jung," Davies says, "God was a fact for which evidence existed in the mind of man." And is it true that "Jungians assert the existence of God?" The Jungian position as I understand it is that a *God-experience* of some kind is possible psychologically. But, as an empiricist, Jung would hardly make the claim that God exists apart from the human psyche.

The collection ends with four conversational lectures on the problems of evil in literature, and one of those essays most Canadian writers have felt compelled to write in recent years, "The Canada of Myth and Reality." In the essay Davies repeats what many have said—that Canada, having a colonial mentality, is apt to feel self-righteous as a consequence of virtual powerlessness, and to blame the United States for its own problems. I am not altogether convinced, however, that Davies knows, or really cares, where Canada is, or who comprises its population. In his speeches he is careful never to mention the name of any distinguished Canadian contemporary of his, out of indifference—or perhaps envy. He speaks as if "the writer" must show Canada to Canadians—as if no writers have yet done so? He will speak learnedly of the supernatural in literature, and confine himself to English writers, ignoring Canadian writers—like Howard O'Hagan, for instance, whose *Tay John* is worth the windy rhetorical conventions of all of Davies' books. In one speech, he calls his nation "somnambulistic"—but what, in terms of present-day Separatist agitation, and a long history of regional resistance to Ottawa, does this mean?

It is grossly misleading to bill Davies as Canada's "leading man of letters," and he should certainly not be taken, by non-Canadians, as a "great" Canadian writer. He is, depending upon your taste, a genial storytelling moralizing conservative; or a pompous but charming Tory; or a narrow, exasperating reactionary; or a curmudgeon of the old school whose spite, anger and vanity have been successfully—or nearly so—hidden behind a persona of bemused old-fashioned courtliness. I read him as possibly the very last image in Canada's collective dream of an older English tradition: a Floating Head whose allegiance is with the Queen (that is, the one who died in 1901), a symbol of all that younger Canadian writers and artists have been struggling to accommodate, or repudiate, or transcend, or forget.

# The Two Voices of *A Mixture of*

# *Frailties*

*Clara Thomas*

The muhd's everything. Get it and you'll get the rest. If you don't
get it, all the *fiorituri* and exercises in agility and *legato* in the
world'll be powerless to make a good singer of you. The muhd's
at the root of all. And that's what I teach my beginners, and my
advanced pupils, and some who've gone out into the world and
made big names, but who come back now and again for a brush-up
with special problems. And mostly it all boils down to the muhd.[1]

Goaded, cajoled and driven by Murtagh Molloy, Monica Gall learned
to "breathe the muhd" and sing. So did her creator, Robertson
Davies—for the difference in quality between *A Mixture of Frailties*
(1958) and *Fifth Business* (1970) is precisely a matter of the mood
and its sustaining. From its first words to its last, the voice of Dunstan
Ramsay in *Fifth Business* is as unremittingly on target as the
trajectory of the fated snowball that begins his story. In contrast, the
third person narrative voice of *A Mixture of Frailties* moves between
two keys which at times clash in discord. The frame story of Salterton
and the Bridgetower Trust is narrated by Davies' early and familiar
voice, that of a social satirist, detached, funny and sharp, but
sometimes also gross and crude. The voice which narrates the story
of Monica Gall is much closer to its subject, still sharp with wit, but
always warm with understanding and sympathy.

Nevertheless, there are many reasons for looking again at *A
Mixture of Frailties*, reasons that range from its own autonomy as a
highly readable novel, to its heightened present interest as a forerunner
and, in some senses, a foreshadower of the Deptford trilogy—*Fifth
Business*, *The Manticore* and *World of Wonders*. The novel's deepest

themes are moral. They are the same concerns about problems of evil, guilt and responsibility that permeate the Ramsay-Staunton-Dempster trilogy. Again, like each one of the latter, the major plot-line concerns the individual's growth to maturity, self-recognition and self-acceptance—in this case the growth as artist and woman of Monica Gall. Furthermore, the portrayal of Monica Gall stands alone in all of Davies' works. She is drawn in depth and with an entirely believable complexity of temperament and motivation so that beside her any of the rest of his women characters, even Liesl Vitzlipützli, seems a cardboard-flat figure from a morality play. The strange alchemy of successful fiction transports Monica from the pages to live in the mind and imagination as surely as do Willa Cather's Thea Kronberg and Margaret Laurence's Morag Gunn, her fellow-fictional developing artists.

The story of Monica Gall is both framed and propelled into action by the terms of the Bridgetower Trust and the dilemma of Solly Bridgetower and his wife, Veronica. Thus, at its beginning *A Mixture of Frailties* is linked with its predecessor *Leaven of Malice*, the story of the miserable, malicious, false engagement announcement—and the true and finally successful romance—of Solly and Veronica (Pearl) Vambrace. The book starts in the same vein of sardonic humour that permeated its predecessor: "She had planned her funeral, as she had planned all her social duties and observances, with care.... Not two hours after her physician had pronounced her dead, her lawyer, Mr. Matthew Snelgrove, had put a fat letter in the hands of her son Solomon, on the envelope of which was written in her firm, large hand, *Directions for my Funeral*" (p. 1).

The humour quickly becomes black and bitter. Mrs. Bridgetower's entire estate is to be devoted to the training and education of "some young woman resident in this city of Salterton, who is desirous of following a career in the arts.... She is to be maintained abroad in order, as your mother says, that she may bring back to Canada some of the tangible treasures of European tradition" (p. 16). The trust, which involves the income from over a million dollars, will only terminate if and when Solly and Veronica have a son. " 'That's what you can really call laying the Dead Hand on the living, isn't it,' said their friend, Molly Cobbler, 'I suppose it's something to be proud of, in a way; not many people have the guts to make a really revengeful will' " (p. 22). Though Solly defends his mother's memory, we are left in no doubt as to the truth of Molly's judgment when the disruptive and demeaning effects of Mrs. Bridgetower's conditions begin to show themselves in the lives of Solly and Veronica.

The movement and the engrossing interest of the novel really begin with the introduction of Monica as an applicant for the Trust and her selection by the committee. Hers is a Cinderella story, with the endless appeal of its ancient motif. She is poor and naive, a typist in the Glue Works with an ineffectual father, a wild, crude and primitive mother, a jealous sister and a fairy godmother. Her gentle Aunt May serves Monica in that capacity until the dead Mrs. Bridgetower assumes that totally incongruous role. Aunt Ellen, a spinster, forever faithful to her dead lover, is the only adult whom Monica knows who is neither cynical, nor coarse, nor a failure. On the contrary, Aunt Ellen is the epitome of the gentle—and genteel— romantic dreamer, and her greatest and most constant dream is music.

> There are a great many musicians in the world who do not live in rooms which speak so decisively of a life given to music as the living room of Miss Ellen Gall. There was no picture which was not musical in theme. Over a piano hung a collotype of an extremely artistic girl with a bird's nest of dark hair, playing the cello to a rapt old man with a white beard; it was called *Träumerei*. Over the bookcase was a picture of Beethoven, much handsomer than life, conducting the Rasumovsky quartet with great spirit. A little plaster bust with a broken nose, said to be Mendelssohn, sat on top of the rosewood upright piano. And everywhere on the walls were little pictures of opera singers, cut out of magazines and framed (p. 64).

In her sentimental and personal museum of music, Aunt Ellen has taught Monica to play the piano, encouraged her to sing, listened with her to the Saturday afternoon opera broadcasts and dreamed with her over the lives of great stars recorded in the Victor Book of the Opera. That and the novel, *The First Violin* by Jessie Fothergill, the very ultimate in the sentimental romance of music, are holy books to them both. Monica's dream of her future is Aunt Ellen's as well.

> You can repay me by being a great artist, dear. And a great artist is always a lovely person, remember that. The really great ones were always simple and fine, and loved everything that was sweet

in life. Keep yourself sweet, Monny, and remember that any gifts you have really belong to God. If you do that, you won't have to worry about me (p. 71).

With such a background, with such a view of art and the artist, with a going-away party that is certainly the most ghastly social occasion to be recorded in Canadian literature, but with a voice judged promising by England's leading conductor, Sir Benedict Domdaniel, Monica is chosen to be a recipient of the Trust and is sent to England to be trained.

In chapter four, a little less than one-quarter of the way through *A Mixture of Frailties*, the story of Monica's growth as a person and artist really begins. This is the story that obviously engrossed Robertson Davies, beside which the frame of Salterton and the Bridgetower Trust soon seems perfunctory. At this point Davies' narrator's voice becomes steady and sure, and, barring the interruptions of the frame story into the text, it continues so to the end. Monica's story is a novel in itself. In it, the Cinderella motif is metamorphosed into the Pygmalion motif. Monica Gall is Canada's Eliza Doolittle and at least once there is a direct and perhaps deliberate echo of Henry Higgins, when Giles Revelstoke, her language coach, finally says, "Got it now, I think," after a long and desperate session with vowels and stresses. Monica is moulded by three men, not one, however: by Murtagh Molloy, her voice coach, who teaches her to act and sing and "breathe the muhd;" by Giles Revelstoke, who teaches her speech and the literature of music and by Sir Benedict, who is the "Chief Magician," her mentor, patron and friend, in charge of her career and responsible for sending her to the other two.

Each of these men helps to "create" Monica Gall and each one of them finally wishes to possess his creation, Murtagh with a clownish and pathetic sincerity and Giles in utter selfishness. Finally, Sir Benedict, who comes to know Monica truly, as adult, woman and artist, asks her to marry him, giving her the dignity of an honest declaration.

I am old enough to be your father; nevertheless you must take my word for it that I am still young enough to be a lover. But I will not deceive you; at my age love is not, and never can be, the whole significance of life.... I do not ask you to love me as you might a young man, but to love me, if you can, for what I am.... At my

age, my work is bound to be the mainspring of my existence. But
if you were with me, my work would have a sweeter savour.
Because it is your work, too, I know that you will understand this,
and not think that I am being either cool or pompous (p. 376).

Monica, however, finally develops into far more than the sum of her
creators' efforts. She becomes her own woman. Her story is essentially a quest romance and its patterns of escape, transcendence and
growth fit the process that Northrop Frye describes in "the Recovery
of Myth," the culminating chapter of *The Secular Scripture*.

> Unconsciously acquired social mythology, the mythology of prej-
> udice and conditioning, is clearly also something to be outgrown:
> it is therapeutic to recognize and reject it, as with other repressed
> material. Lying beyond it is the next level of social mythology, or
> roughly speaking, the area of serious belief...genuine social my-
> thology, whether religious or secular, is also to be transcended,
> but transcendence here does not mean repudiation or getting rid of
> it, except in special cases. It means rather an individual recreation
> of the mythology, a transforming of it from accepted social values
> into the axioms of one's own activity.[2]

This is the path of rejection, assimilation and growth that Monica
must take if she is to mature—and she does take it. In the beginning
she is completely enchained by Salterton, the Glue Works, Pastor
Beamis and the Heart and Hope Quartet and her family, all of whom
epitomize a blind and stifling provincialism, too walled-in to look
beyond its own boundaries and therefore suspicious and cruelly
dismissive of anything alien in an individual or in society. Any kind
of speech other than her own crudity Mrs. Gall calls "a lot of
snottery;" George Medwall, Monica's suitor from the Glue Works,
sums up everything Mrs. Gall most fears in a son-in-law: "He was
not a Thirteener; he was not even a church goer and felt no shame
about saying so. He did not drink, he saved his money, and he was
civil; she gave him all that. But there was in him a quality of ambition
which disquieted her; it prevented him from being what she called
likeable" (p. 62). When Monica and her parents are interviewed by
the executors of the Bridgetower Trust, they bring with them their
minister, Pastor Sidney Beamis of the Thirteenth Apostle Tabernacle.
He argues for Monica with enthusiasm, talking a great deal "about
the opportunities a singer enjoyed to do the Lord's work, by uplifting

people and turning their minds to the finer things of life; in his own work he had been able to observe the splendid harvest of souls which could be reaped through the Ministry of Music" (p. 46). The Galls, however, are almost speechless: "They thought it might be nice if their daughter had a chance to study music abroad, but in their heart of hearts it was a matter of indifference to them" (p. 46). By the time that Monica sailed for England, her family had persuaded themselves that they would never see her again: "The sea-voyage would almost certainly end in shipwreck; the more Mrs. Gall thought of it, the surer she became" (p. 87).

Monica is sustained in her choice and her leaving only by her Aunt and the dream they share, of her development into a great diva melodiously renamed Monique Gallo. She quarrels with George Medwall, who speaks more truth and commonsense to her than any of her family is capable of, when he says, "Nothing could make a fool of you, Monny. But don't call it luck. People only get chances if they are ready for them. It's not luck. It's character" (p. 60). But Monica is furious with him when he seems to slight her parents and obviously is already uncertain of herself and her capacity for remaining the true and loyal daughter she wishes to be.

> I'm proud of my family. Proud!... Now let me tell you something, and don't ever forget it, George, because I mean every word. If there's one thing I hate in this world, it's ingratitude and disloyalty. And nothing, absolutely nothing, is going to make me disloyal and ungrateful (p. 60).

Monica's initiation to adulthood and responsibility and her apprenticeship as a singer go hand in hand, but the former is more a prolonged and painful process than the latter and in its cause she experiences bewildering complexities of feeling that shatter her precious sureties of gratitude and loyalty.

From his first interview with her, Sir Benedict pushes and prods at Monica's opinions on proper appearances, behaviour and speech to find and to make her find the bedrock of strength and ambition that lie behind her facade. "Monica was not, in fact, accustomed to thinking anything which was contrary to the opinion of any older person with whom she was talking," but challenged by Domdaniel she admits to belief in her talent: "I think I have talent. And I want to sing more than anything else in the world." She also admits her romantic dreams of becoming a great diva. "In your heart of hearts you think of singing as a form of power," Domdaniel says, "and you've got more common sense in your heart of hearts than you have on that smarmy little tongue of yours" (p. 106). Their first session in England ends with Domdaniel's own credo, for life and for art.

> There are, the world over, only two important political parties—the people who are for life, and the people who are against it...you know about Eros and Thanatos? No, I didn't really suppose that you did. Well, I'm an Eros man myself, and most people who are good for anything, in the arts or wherever, belong to the Eros party. But there are Thanatossers everywhere—the Permanent Opposition (p. 108).

Monica, he continues, has probably been educated by "crypto-Thanatossers," who pretend to be on the side of life, but who actually live a death-in-life. Her training and even more, her experience of life, must break through her shell, if she is to be any good at all: "there's a chance that you may be on the Eros side; there's something about you now and then which suggests it" (p. 108).

Molloy batters at her to "breathe the muhd" and later, Revelstoke is mocking and infuriating, but he is also perfectly serious about the essentials of his work: "It is the spirit we must work with, and not the mind as such. For the spirit searcheth all things, yea, the deep things of God" (p. 158). Monica's is a hard and humbling training, but long before she can gain confidence in her own talent, strength and determination, the reader sees these qualities increasingly in action—in the early days in London when she has no money and no friends, in the sessions with Molloy and, especially, with Revelstoke, when her pride steels her determination to stand up against his arrogant sneers.

At the same time, through Domdaniel's direction, Monica's range of experience widens immeasurably. Plays and concerts, Paris with Amy Neilson and the Christmas house party in Wales expand her culturally and socially, and her affair with Revelstoke, together with her immersion in his group of hangers-on, force her emotional growth. The first of two climaxes in Monica's maturing comes when she is summoned to Canada by the illness of her mother. In her family's eyes, she is the fortunate one, alien from them now, and they look to her for leadership. In this passage Davies shows us clearly, convincingly and poignantly, the dilemma of a young woman who meant her declaration of loyalty, but whose talents, opportunities—and insecurities—have inexorably pushed her away from her family.

> Loyalty! Monica had not forgotten her protestation of loyalty when George Medwall hinted that she might want to abandon some of the beliefs and attitudes of her family. She had meant it then, and she still meant it. But she had not realized how costly such loyalty might be. She had not foreseen that it could mean keeping two sets of mental and moral books—one for inspection in the light of home, and another to contain her life with Revelstoke, and all the new loyalties and attitudes which had come with Molloy, and particularly with Domdaniel. To close either set of books forever would be a kind of suicide, and yet to keep them both was hypocrisy (p. 266).

In none of Davies' writings up to *A Mixture of Frailties* is there a passage of compassion and charity to compare with his recording of Monica's last days with her mother. Ma Gall is terrified of being taken to the hospital. In her fear, and to the consternation of her doctor, she is giving herself to death; a gall-bladder condition that is operable becomes a mortal illness. Monica is the one who has to make the terrible choice and accept the responsibility for it.

> "You realize that your decision may be bringing about your mother's death?"...
> "My decision *may* do so, Dr. Cobbett, but your decision would do so beyond any doubt. My mother lives by the spirit as well as by the flesh; if I kill the spirit by delivering her, frightened and forsaken, into your hands, what makes you think that you can save the flesh?" (p. 276).

During Monica's vigil of seven nights beside her mother's bed the conversations that they share are moving and entirely believable. So are Monica's internal monologues, as she struggles to reconcile the woman she has become with the daughter she would like to be.

> She was specific in her demands and exhortations to Monica, however. Was Monica a good girl? The question came again and again when she was partly conscious, and thus phrased, from Mrs. Gall, it could have only one meaning. Monica had no intention of

saying that, in her mother's terms, she was not a good girl. But she had to meet the question in her own mind. Was she? To say yes was disloyal to home, to the woman who was in such distress at her side. But there were seven of these weary nights, and before the last Monica was sure of her answer. She was a good girl. Chastity is to have the body in the soul's keeping; Domdaniel had said it, and everything in her own experience supported it (p. 282).

Technically, the emotional authenticity of these scenes rests on Davies' modification of his initial burlesquing of the Gall family. In the first part of the book, Ma Gall is a repulsive grotesque and her husband a whining nonentity. Authorial tact has removed the grotesquerie from a frightened, dying woman and made Alfred Gall's agony and stricken silence a sign of love, not weakness.

Monica cannot be reconciled to her mother or her family on their terms or in their understanding and her acceptance of this is a climax in her maturing. There is some amelioration of her loss in a final exchange with her mother.

"I've got quite an imagination. That's where you're like me, Monny. Always remember that. You got that from me."

Tears came into Monica's eyes; they were tears of happiness, for at last she shared something with her mother. She wept, and laughed a little, as she said—"Yes, Ma, I got that from you. We're very alike, aren't we?" (p. 282).

Furthermore, Monica gradually realizes that this is true:

For in Ma, when she told tall stories, when she rasped her family with rough, sardonic jokes, when she rebelled against the circumstances of her life in coarse abuse, and when she cut through the fog of nonsense with the beam of her insight, was an artist—a spoiled artist, one who had never made anything, who was unaware of the nature or genesis of her own discontent, but who nevertheless possessed the artist's temperament (p. 303).

The recital which the members of the Bridgetower Trust wish Monica to give while she is at home takes on a double purpose: not only will it demonstrate to Salterton the results of Mrs. Bridgetower's bequest, but for Monica, privately—and this is its more important function—it will be a memorial for her mother. The singing of three songs which are her farewell to Ada Gall leaves Monica deeply peaceful. The recital is a great public success and with it, Monica has redeemed the Trust's choice of herself as beneficiary. She is now also, as her inner voice tells her, free: *"You did your best for her, and now you are free. You will never have to worry about what you can tell her, or what would hurt her, again"* (p. 289).

At this point, Davies might well have ended the story of Monica Gall, and had he been writing a naive romance, he would have done so. The public Monica, vindicating her choice in her recital, and the private Monica, reconciled to herself and confident enough to move into further growth—this would have been a conventional closing scene of climax and success. It was obviously not Davies' intention to write a naive romance about the artist apprentice, however; he is interested in a fuller, deeper portrait of Monica Gall and in her further—and painful—growth.

Domdaniel had warned Monica, long before, that in her heart of hearts she thought of singing as a form of power. Back in Salterton, she has been the one in command, first of all forced into that position by her family and then surely and professionally in command of her recital. She has also found herself the recipient of $45,000 which has accrued in the Bridgetower Trust, and this money she determines to give to Giles to finance his opera, *The Golden Asse*. When Veronica Bridgetower appeals to her for a loan of some of that money, she regrets saying no—but she says it. Monica, as the narrator has been careful to let the reader see all along, is now engaged in the pursuit of "love-as-power." She is Giles Revelstoke's mistress and though he does not love her, and actually rejects the word "love," Monica believes in her own powers of transformation:

> He was hers. Though he had spoken coldly to her, and bargained, and said flatly that he did not love her, she was confident. She would win him at last. He should be brought to say it. He would love her, and tell her so (p. 222).

To that end Monica cleans and cooks for Revelstoke; she acts as typist and bookkeeper for his journal, *Lantern*; she bears with the strange group of hangers-on who surround him, even with his former mistress; and finally, she turns over to him all the money she can scrape together from the Trust. She does not think of herself as keeping Giles—she thinks of herself as financing his opera. From being utterly without power, moulded and patronized by everyone she meets, Monica now becomes the patron, and unconsciously, for she sees all this as being done for love of Giles, she enjoys the eminence.

Davies' portrayal of Monica is both subtle and convincing. Even when she is abasing herself and cheating her benefactors she never loses her humanity or the reader's sympathy. For instance, she is shocked with pity when, at a masquerade, Murtagh Molloy clumsily attacks her and declares his love for her. There is no conscious enjoyment in her of power for its own sake:

> He wept, and Monica wept with him, but it cannot be pretended that they understood each other. Two puritanisms were in conflict, and could not meet. But under that, in a realm below the morality which was bred in the bone, they wept for the sadness of all unrequited love, all ill-matched passion (p. 260).

The great moral crisis for Monica comes in an episode of sheer melodrama which shocks the reader, but does not fracture the novel because it is so in keeping with the personalities of Giles and Monica as Davies has built them up. Revelstoke is a brilliant musician, but he is childish, selfish and cruel. His opera, first performed in Venice, conducted by Domdaniel, is a great success, but Revelstoke's one performance as a conductor is a disaster. He cannot accept his failure with grace; he dismisses Monica with brutal words and leaves Venice; she writes a letter breaking off their relationship, regrets it, hastens to London and his flat and finds him ostensibly dead from escaping gas—a suicide.

Under shock, Monica is at first paralysed. When she gains enough courage to look at him more closely she thinks he is dead. As she turns the gas off, she sees that in each hand he holds a piece of paper and that one of these is her letter. Her paralysis gives way to calculating self-preservation: "Danger dispersed her panic. She must behave sensibly now, or God knew what would happen to her. She retreated to the window again, and made her plan" (p. 339). Thankful that she is wearing gloves, she takes the letter and leaves the flat, turning the gas on again before going out. Once out she is almost overcome by confusion and despair, but she is also still in command of herself. This despair is as nothing to what she feels when it is found out that Giles died from suffocation in his own vomit, not from gas-poisoning:

> Monica was left with no course but to face the fact that Giles Revelstoke had not been dead when she took the letter from his hand, and that if she had thought more of him and less of herself he need not have died at all. By her selfishness and littleness of spirit she had killed him (p. 348).

In the last four chapters of the book, Davies' concern is with the same questions of guilt and responsibility that form a major and basic motif in the Deptford Trilogy. Monica has to live with her own ineradicable guilt; at the same time she has to listen to guilty confessions by four others who are convinced of their responsibility in Revelstoke's death. Stanhope Aspinwall, the music critic with whom Revelstoke had feuded, whose sharp comparison of Domdaniel and the composer as conductors of *The Golden Asse* had been in the dead man's hand, is convinced of his responsibility. Bun Eccles, one of the *Lantern* group, is convinced that the death was his fault. He had fixed Revelstoke's gas-meter so that it would run longer with fewer coins. When she goes to see Giles' mother and together they go to the grave, Monica has to listen to her confession of guilt: "You see, my dear, I have a terrible feeling that I failed Giles.... I come back to the feeling that if I hadn't failed him—whenever or however it was—Giles wouldn't be here now.... I sometimes feel I killed Giles" (p. 356). Finally, Domdaniel himself confesses his sense of guilt to Monica: "I committed one of the great follies. I tried to mould somebody else's fate. And you've seen how it ended.... Morally, I killed him" (pp. 361-62).

There is a certain self-indulgence in all these various claims of guilt and Davies makes sure that we see it. Monica's part in Revelstoke's death, however, is a matter of hard and circumstantial facts and actions. She confesses to Domdaniel and he counsels her with the utmost practicality, neither minimizing her part in the death nor allowing her to dramatize it:

> What you did would probably be considered—not murder, most certainly not that—but manslaughter, or criminal neglect, or something of that order. Because, after all, you did turn the gas back on. Nothing can change that. And it's vital that you should clarify

your thoughts on this matter. Whatever deception you may have
to practise on other people, you must not, under any circumstances,
deceive yourself.... You must—you absolutely must—make a
judgement on your own behaviour (pp. 363-64).

From his first meeting with Monica, Domdaniel has been her mentor.
At various points in the text, beginning with his Eros and Thanatos
speech, he has also been Davies' voice of humane wisdom, a civilized
corrective to the processes of prudery, philistinism and proper
appearances which threaten Monica's growth. The Domdaniel voice
is a familiar one in all of Davies' writing and sometimes prejudicial,
in its set didactic passages, to the flow of its narrative. It is close to
the voice of Samuel Marchbanks, though Marchbanks often has a
self-consciously comic tone; it is the voice of the author himself in
*A Voice in the Attic;* it is echoed in the Deptford trilogy by Father
Blazon and, sometimes, by the voice of Dunstan Ramsay himself. It
is an eighteenth century voice of reason and balance, certain of its
moral and ethical standards but broadly and humanely aware of the
complexities involved in translating them into life and action.

The truth is, as we finally see, that everyone in Monica's orbit,
and Monica herself, have been relentlessly manipulative of others.
Monica has been moulded by Salterton and her family, particularly
by her mother; Domdaniel, Molloy and Revelstoke have all tried to
mould her; she has tried to mould Giles—at the end everyone is
inextricably bound up in the process of shaping others and everyone
is "guilty." What Davies is finally saying, however, is that guilt
inhibits and restricts life. It belongs to the Thanatos party. Responsibility, however, which must be recognized and carried, can also be
carried onward—its recognition and acceptance are necessarily a part
of the growth and maturing of one of the Eros party. The Domdaniel
figures in Davies' work already know this lesson—all the others who
choose to be on the side of life must learn it. The Eros figures also
know, and must learn as Monica learns, the truth and wisdom of the
quotation from Lord Halifax that is the epigraph to this novel and the
source of its name.

Nothing softeneth the Arrogance of our Nature like a Mixture of
some Frailties. It is by them we are best told, that we must not
strike too hard upon others because we ourselves do so often

deserve blows. They pull our Rage by the sleeve and whisper Gentleness to us in our censures.

Like much else in this novel, its epigraph also points irresistibly forward to the Deptford Trilogy, whose windings of guilt and responsibility enmesh all the characters in a gradually recognized, revealed and accepted mixture of frailties.

As a novel within a frame, Monica's story is complete and convincing. The Salterton frame story is not entirely compatible to it, however, and this is a question of a split between Davies' narrative voices. The voice of the satirist of small-town Canadian puritanism and provincialism is familiar in the Marchbanks collections, in *Tempest-Tost* and *Leaven of Malice.* Its wit is sharp, but its wisdom is not deep—and sometimes, as in its description of the Gall's going-away party for Monica, it is both crude and cruel.

> "Gotta go, folks," said he, "and when you gotta go, you gotta go." (A whoop from Ma Gall, who found a lavatorial significance in this.) "But seriously, I wish I could stay here with you lovely folks and emcee this affair right through till dawn. But the Mater Dee will be looking for me at the Paraplegics' Ball in just fifteen minutes, and its time to say Goodbye. Before I go, Syd"—here he turned with an affecting boyishness to Pastor Beamis—"would it be too much to hear the Heart and Hope just once again?"...
>
> "Doh," whispered Beamis, and his wife emitted a low moo, upon which the others formed a chord. "Granny" murmured the leader, and slowly, with immense expression, the quartet sang *Eden Must Have Been Like Granny's Garden* (p. 80).

This is itself a confined and provincial voice and its effects are as broad and cheaply-bought as crude burlesque. After Monica leaves Salterton and her story moves strongly into being, the frame story interrupts the action from time to time, to take us back to Salterton, the Bridgetower Trust and the dilemma of Solly and Veronica. Davies usually modulates his earlier tone in these passages and he does build up sympathy for Veronica and Solly. In their story he also skirmishes a little with the problem of evil and its manifestations in the "Dead Hand" and the continuing malign influence of Mrs. Bridgetower. This is another early exercise in a theme which was later to engross him in the Deptford trilogy. The modifications of that broad satiric voice are not consistent in these interruptions, however. The

McCorkills, a Canadian couple whom Monica visits in London, are far too broadly drawn to be compatible with the tone of Monica's story:

> By this time Lorne, with much shaking and measuring, had composed the Canadian Lyric, a cocktail made of equal parts of lemon juice and maple syrup, added to a double portion of rye whisky, and shaken up with cracked ice.
> "The trouble we had getting real maple surrp!" said Lorne. "But I ran it down, finally, in a dump in Soho—a grocery that gets all kinds of outlandish stuff—and here it is, with that real old Canuck flavour! Boys-o-boys! Just pour that over your tonsils and think of home!" (p. 124)

This—and the entire episode with the McCorkills—is a raw caricature, funny enough as a skit for a stand-up comedian, though offensive in its broad contempt for the hick-Canadian, and completely jarring in its context in *A Mixture of Frailties*.

Monica's presence, however, is finally strong enough to transcend the narrative that has contained her. Like all the enduring characters of fiction, her memorable and believable complexity finally pushes her free of the form that has both revealed and confined her, to live independently in the reader's mind and imagination. Davies' final chapter is a successful climax, again in the tradition of romance, and at the same time, a tantalizing, open-ended finish for his novel. After her confession to Domdaniel, Monica has again come home to Salterton. There she agrees to sing at a service in the Cathedral for the fourth annual Bridgetower Trust commemoration. Solly and Veronica have had their baby boy—Monica will no longer be the Trust's beneficiary. She has also received Domdaniel's proposal of marriage. As the service progresses the words of the Dean's sermon and Monica's troubled musings are counterpointed in the text. There are no easy answers for Monica. The voices of Ada Gall and of Giles, she knows will be with her always: "Will I acquire other voices as I go through life? It isn't frightening—not a bit—but it's certainly odd. It is perhaps my substitute for thinking—orders and hints and even jokes from deep down, through the personality of someone I've loved—yes, and feared?" (p. 372)

Monica isn't listening to the Dean's sermon, but it meshes with her own thoughts at the end, when he speaks of the grace of God and she prays for help in words that put her unmistakably in the Eros party: "Oh God, don't let me slip under the surface of all the heavy-handed dullness that seems to claim so many people, even when they struggle and strive to keep their heads above the waves! Help me! Help me!" (p. 379). Then she sings her part in the service, "and when she was finished, she found that her mind was cleared, and she knew what she should do" (p. 379). It is impossible for the reader to decide with any assurance which decision Monica will make, however, and it is a measure of the power and complexity of her character that this is so.

Monica's growth, as artist and woman, is compounded of unremitting hard work, experience in living and the distillation of that experience into her personality and her art. She stands well beside Morag Gunn and Thea Kronberg and she also stands well beside Dunstan Ramsay, even though the voices of her narrator by no means achieve the harmony of tone and effect of *Fifth Business*.

"How do I know that I've any talent myself?" she asks Domdaniel, and he replies, "you don't, but you're industrious."

> So get on with the job. Stop fretting because you're not worldly-wise and chock-full of Beethovenian *Sturm und Drang* at twenty. That's not your type at all. Stop fussing that comfort is going to knock the props from under your genius. Develop what you've got: make it possible for your emotions to grow. Get on with the job. Work, work, work (p. 137).

Domdaniel's voice seems to be Davies' voice as well. There are no magic, mystical success routes for his artist. There is talent, but never the surety of talent; there is work; and there is experience:

> It isn't what happens to you that really counts: it's what you are able to do with it.... Art's distillation; experience is wine, and art is the brandy we distill from it (p. 137).

Like the career of Monica Gall, Robertson Davies' expanding skill as a novelist has proved his point.

# Notes

1 Robertson Davies, *A Mixture of Frailties* (Toronto: Macmillan, 1958), p. 113. All subsequent page references are from this edition.
2 Northrop Frye, *The Secular Scripture* (Cambridge: Harvard University Press, 1976), p. 170.

# A Mixture of Frailties and "Romance"

*W.J. Keith*

The word "romance," along with its cognates, resonates throughout Robertson Davies' third novel; indeed, it is possible to claim that, on one level, *A Mixture of Frailties* is a probing inquiry into the various meanings that gather around this word, and the ways in which romantic attitudes relate to the conditions of everyday experience. Furthermore, the novel itself is clearly influenced to a considerable extent by the traditional form or genre of the romance, a circumstance highlighted within the text by an intriguing and, I would argue, highly illuminating reference to Jessie Fothergill's Victorian romance novel *The First Violin* (1877). In the following pages, I propose to follow up these references and indicate how the process can lead to a firmer appreciation of *A Mixture of Frailties* as a work of literary art.

The opening part of the novel, involving the Bridgetower Trust and its efforts to find a beneficiary under the terms of Mrs. Bridgetower's idiosyncratic will, continues in the comedy-of-manners style that has characterized the earlier Salterton novels, *Tempest-Tost* and *Leaven of Malice*. At the beginning of the second part, however, this third novel takes an interesting if, from an artistic viewpoint, a rather abrupt change of direction as Davies focuses our attention on the character and development of Monica Gall. It is here that "romance" and "romantic" become prominent and significant words. The first usage occurs in a conversation between Monica and her boy friend George Medwall, in which she claims that "realistic" is his "favourite word."[1] George's characterization of Monica is very different: "You're what's called a romantic. You see everything in full Technicolor all the time. Feelings before facts, that's you" (*Mixture*, p. 59). What he means becomes clearer in the next section, where we are introduced to Monica's "great dream of life" (*Mixture*, p. 63). We learn that, through the influence of her Aunt Ellen, who is described as "a specialist in romance and dreams" (*Mixture*, p. 68) and has herself been a participant in a sad and abortive romantic attachment, Monica has developed a fantasy of escaping her prosaic occupation in the Salterton Glue Works and entering the mysterious and glittering world of music and opera. She is unsettled because the Bridgetower Trust now appears to have opened for her the door to this "great, glorious, foreign world" (*Mixture*, p. 65). It seems just possible that "romance and dreams" are going to turn into reality.

At this point, Davies introduces his reference to Jessie Fothergill's novel, which Monica and her aunt "had both read with deep enjoyment more than once" (*Mixture*, p. 66). The passage needs to be quoted in full:

> In it, a humble English girl with a lovely voice was engaged as companion to a wealthy old lady who took her to Germany to study; and there she had learned to sing from the magnetic—but daemonic and sardonic—von Francius, and had engaged in a long and sweetly agonizing romance with one Courvoisier, who was first violin in the orchestra, a man of mystery, and, in the end (for this was an English novel and such a dénouement was inevitable) had proved to be a German nobleman, disguised as a musician for reasons highly creditable to himself and shaming to everybody else (*Mixture*, p. 66).

The romantically inclined Monica, whose audition with Sir Benedict Domdaniel has just been described as "the most elevating and releasing experience of her life" (*Mixture*, p. 63), now begins to daydream and to apply this romance pattern to the new life that is opening up before her:

> Domdaniel would do very well as von Francius, though he was rather too affable for a genuinely daemonic genius, and showed quite ordinary braces when he took off his coat. And who was to be the First Violin; who was to be Courvoisier? (*Mixture*, p. 66)

Davies' strategy should now be clear. He has given us in the summary of *The First Violin* a typical instance of the popular romance.

Monica's speculations about its applicability to her own life indicate that Davies is going to use Fothergill's book as a kind of romantic yardstick against which to present his account of Monica's own progress. As Michael Peterman has pointed out (without elaboration, however), *The First Violin* "provides a mythic pattern for her story."[2] It will be instructive to follow this clue further and see how Davies relates the romantic pattern to the actualities of Monica's subsequent experience, an experience that will not exclude "romance" but will reveal the existence of a "world of wonder" within the ordinary and the quotidian.

Certain basic parallels will already be evident. Both May Wedderburn, Fothergill's heroine, and Monica Gall derive their opportunities for advanced musical training from old and dying women, though Miss Hallam, the invalid whom May serves as companion, is much pleasanter and more supportive than Davies' Mrs. Bridgetower. At the same time, Davies carefully provides information that qualifies any simple conclusion that Monica's success is purely a matter of romantic good fortune. She has demonstrated a noteworthy determination and resourcefulness in agreeing to pay her own expenses for the audition with Domdaniel, and George Medwall has underlined the point by insisting that she shouldn't regard her opportunity as mere luck: "[D]on't call it luck. People only get chances if they're ready for them. It's not luck. It's character" (*Mixture*, p. 60). By contrast, Miss Hallam's choice of May to accompany her to Germany is much closer to the traditional flick of the fairy godmother's wand.

Similarly, both heroines have to leave their provincial homes to be educated—in the art of living as well as of music—in the larger world outside. But, and the difference is crucial for a proper understanding of Davies' position, Monica goes for her training to the country that May had to leave in order to obtain hers. I want to insist on this point because Davies has been subjected to criticism for transporting his heroine to England rather than to the United States or continental Europe or (since nationalism becomes involved here) keeping her in Canada. This matter tends to get snagged with complaints about Davies' alleged Anglophilia. Thus the *Montreal Star* reviewer asserted that "most of the London narrative...is tinged uncomfortably with awe."[3] More recently, Peterman has claimed that Davies "makes it clear that she couldn't receive an education of such quality except at the centre—in England."[4] T.D. MacLulich makes a similar remark: "She must first be transported away from her provincial Canadian environment in order to find the proper climate in which to nurture her talents."[5] Such interpretations, I believe, underestimate Davies' complexity, his irony, and even his realism.

First of all, it is still highly desirable for any serious music student from any country to go abroad not only to encounter expert teachers but to experience different styles and traditions of music making. Moreover, in the 1950s, when *A Mixture of Frailties* is set, study outside Canada was virtually essential. The terms of Mrs. Bridgetower's will, however, preclude study in the United States, since (typically) she wants the beneficiary to "bring back to Canada some of the intangible treasures of European tradition" (*Mixture*, p. 16). While it is true that study in continental Europe might have been more desirable, in Monica's case it would be impracticable, since she is obviously unilingual at this time and would hardly benefit from immediate residence elsewhere. (Later, of course, she gains different kinds of experience in Paris and Venice). Besides, the Bridgetower Trust—especially Puss Pottinger—are unlikely to have considered anywhere except England as suitable. Davies' irony at the expense of Salterton Anglophilia is surely in evidence here, and it is unobtrusively accentuated by the contrast with May Wedderburn's move from England to Germany. Coming from a small village in the north of England where her father is a country clergyman, May is as much a victim of "cultural malnutrition" (*Mixture*, p. 54) as Monica. It is made absolutely clear in *The First Violin* that she would not have "the means, or the chance, or the possibility of getting that [i.e., the requisite] training in England."[6] Moreover, Monica's response to the setting of *The First Violin* includes the observation that late nineteenth-century Germans "were terribly musical and cultured and even more romantic than the French" (*Mixture*, p. 66). While Davies obviously wants to continue his recurrent debate about English Canada and its relation to the mother country, he also wants to contrast the hothouse romanticism of Fothergill's novel with a presentation of England that is realist and even drab.

From the outset of Monica's journey, Davies stresses its realist aspects. On shipboard she had "anticipated the sea voyage as an exciting and perhaps even a romantic introduction to her new life" (*Mixture*, p. 86), but it becomes no more than a prosaic ordeal of homesickness. As for her arrival in England, once again a comparison with Fothergill's novel throws light on Davies' effects. In *The First Violin*, May has a romantic adventure before she even arrives at Elberthal. She manages to miss her train connection at Cologne, and is befriended by a mysterious stranger (who turns out, of course, to be Courvoisier). They spend a touchingly—and, by Victorian standards, daringly—intimate afternoon together, during which they visit the cathedral, where May is overcome by part of Bach's *St. Matthew Passion* played on the organ—a scene that Davies draws upon much later in *A Mixture of Frailties*. In his presentation of what we might call "real romance," Davies in his novel again emphasizes the drab. Monica expects England to be "fun," a country which "was to transform her" (*Mixture*, pp. 88-89), but initially there are no romantic adventures, just loneliness and "the smell of Marylebone Road" (*Mixture*, p. 92). The reviewer who found uncomfortable "awe" here was not reading attentively. The opening sections of the fourth part are clearly designed to challenge Monica's naive illusions about the unremitting romance and glamour of the musical life.

When Monica's musical education begins in earnest, she is subjected to an interrogation from Domdaniel, and later a lecture in which he questions many of her basic attitudes. It is typical of Davies' procedures that Domdaniel challenges these preconceptions of romantic glamour first by insisting that a singer's life is "a dog's life" (*Mixture*, p. 105), but then by immediately acknowledging that this is itself another kind of romantic simplification. At the same time, he warns her against the narrowness of refinement. He refers quite specifically to "Romanticism," not dismissing it but setting himself against "the people who think that Romanticism is all there is of music" (*Mixture*, p. 107). His intention, clearly, is to encourage her to think about her art as a totality and in relation to other aspects of her life. He realizes that her training must not be confined to musical technique but must extend to the cultural, the social and the emotional. Above all, he feels the need to counter various attitudes she has picked up from Aunt Ellen and from the ethos of Salterton: "You really must shake off these fat-headed nineteenth-century notions you have about musicians being romantic characters who starve in garrets, doing immense moral good to the world through the medium of their art" (*Mixture*, pp. 135-36). This comment bolsters Monica's growing awareness of the difference between romance and reality. Once again,

Fothergill's novel is used as a point of reference. At her first lesson with the voice coach, Murtagh Molloy, she realizes that he "was a long way from the daemonic von Francius in *The First Violin*" (*Mixture*, p. 110).

At the end of her first year in England, after her unconventional initial encounter with Giles Revelstoke (seemingly a "daemonic genius"—but can he be her Courvoisier?), Monica is invited down to a Christmas in Wales, a setting frequently employed by Davies to represent a land of romance—what in his later fiction will be designated a world of wonder. Various meanings of "romance" come together here. Her fellow guest, the American John Ripon, represents literary romanticism, while the Griffiths family is associated with a potential romanticism of history and ancestral tradition. The unexpected appearance of Giles propels what might be exploited by another novelist as a specifically erotic romanticism. Indeed, there is a faint analogue (within the moral limits imposed by Victorian respectability) to be found in *The First Violin* where, thanks to a most unlikely skating accident, hero and heroine are temporarily brought together at the same festive season. This is, however, a typically chaste love scene linked with adventure and spiced with the *frisson* of danger. It is typical of Davies that Monica's introduction to love should be sudden, physical, unconventional and conspicuously lacking in romantic atmosphere. (It happens when she goes to the bathroom to brush her teeth). This "maiden no more" scene (*Mixture*, p. 178), with its comically allusive reference to Thomas Hardy's *Tess*, is a witty parody of the expectations of conventional romance.

With the entry of Giles Revelstoke, the comparisons and contrasts between the two novels become more intricate. Clearly, and by his own acknowledgment in Monica's day dreaming scene already quoted, Davies is following Fothergill in the basic pattern of having a heroine flanked by two characters representing different kinds of romantic male figure. But Davies' inventiveness goes well beyond Fothergill in terms of plot ingenuity. In *The First Violin*, as we have seen, von Francius is the "daemonic and sardonic" mentor-figure, while the love-interest is centred upon Courvoisier. Yet, as we have also seen, Monica has asked herself: "Who was to be Courvoisier" (*Mixture*, p. 66)? In Fothergill, von Francius is never presented as anything more than the exacting but appreciative "Musik-direktor." His concern is always focused on May's artistic development. Thus, like Domdaniel in Monica's case, he gives May her first solo role because he "wants to accustom [her] to appearing in public" (*Mixture*, p. 80). Coincidentally, after Miss Hallam's return to England, he finds lodgings for May opposite Courvoisier's boarding house, and so, like Domdaniel who arranged for Monica's invitation to Wales, played his part in bringing the lovers into close proximity. But there is no rivalry between the two men for May's favours. Perhaps significantly, in *The First Violin* it is May's sister Adelaide who deserts her husband to live with von Francius. A moral question is certainly posed here: "Isn't it possible that sometimes it may be right to do wrong?" she asks (*Mixture*, p. 285), but the heroine herself must naturally be left virtuous. Davies ultimately shatters the propriety by having Monica emotionally involved with both men; her half comic, half disturbing meeting with Giles when he appears naked (*Mixture*, p. 145), is Davies' deliberate jolt to the conventions. For Fothergill, chastity could never be defined as "having the body in the soul's keeping" (*Mixture*, p. 242)!

Davies creates his own special effect, indeed, by skilfully rearranging the various qualities of Fothergill's two romantic heroes into more appropriate combinations. Giles, like von Francius, is composer as well as performer, but it is Domdaniel who takes over von Francius' capacity as "a conductor of the first rank" (*Mixture*, p. 216). Fothergill describes von Francius as "rather Jewish-looking" (*Violin*, p. 57), an ancestry which Davies carries over to Domdaniel. On the other hand, while Courvoisier's aristocratic background may be parallelled by Domdaniel's knighthood, the latter is an honour awarded in recognition of merit, not inherited by birth. Davies' shrewd and plausible blending of realism and romanticism is again in evidence here; although Domdaniel admits to being born "with a very good weight of silver spoon in [his] mouth" (*Mixture*, p. 135), he also acknowledges that he is "not really out of the top drawer," citing "a large grandpaternal pop-shop in Birmingham" which it would be ungrateful of him to deny (*Mixture*, p. 213). Davies' "romanticism" consists of an acceptance of the element of wonder as a not uncommon ingredient even in comparatively drab lives, but he is careful to avoid the exaggerations and absurdities of the conventional romance.

Another example of the distinction is to be found in his transformation of Fothergill's Carnival Ball. In *The First Violin*, May and her sister Adelaide go undisguised as Elsa and Ortrud, heroine and villainess respectively of Wagner's *Lohengrin*—and von Francius even appears as Lohengrin himself! The stage is clearly set for emotional climax and romantic intrigue. In a particularly melodramatic scene, Adelaide's husband (also, of course, in disguise) overhears her declaration of love for von Francius. This is the very stuff of operatic plot-contrivance that becomes part of the never-never-land of Fothergill's romance story. Davies, by contrast, takes over the possibilities of fancy-dress complications, and even allows his theatrical enthusiasms full measure, but converts melodrama into rollicking and *just* plausible farce. His Vic-Wells Ball is characterized less by high passion and evil in high places than by grotesquerie and bathos. Far from responding to any romantic glitter, Monica (who has been invited by the incorrigibly romantic Ripon) finds it "dull" (*Mixture*, p. 257). Moreover, at a time when she is abjectly in love with Giles, and the rapport between herself and Domdaniel is gradually becoming evident, she is subjected to a ridiculous (and, later, comically violent) declaration from Murtagh Molloy, who is ultimately exposed and taken home in disgrace by his wife. This is certainly contrived, but it is clearly offered as a parody of high-romantic contrivance. Davies is at pains to show that, when attempts are made to introduce the excesses of "romance" into "real life," the results are likely to be ludicrous rather than sublime.

It would be unfair, however, to deny any serious artistic concern to Jessie Fothergill's novel. From time to time, May expresses a clear determination to be a serious artist, even if this theme tends to get sidetracked by the stronger imperatives of romantic convention. But once again, the subject of artistic seriousness is communicated in essentially conventional terms. Here, for instance, is von Francius' exhortation to May:

> You have in you the materials of a great artist; whether you have the Spartan courage and perseverance requisite to attain the position, I can hardly tell. If you choose to become an artist, *eine volkommene Künstlerin,* you must give everything else up—love and marriage and all that interferes with your art, for, *liebes Fräulein,* you cannot pursue two things at once. (*Violin,* p. 279)

He goes on to articulate the standard romantic notion that "no artist is possible without sorrow and suffering and renunciation." Davies, of course, is second to none in his insistence on the rigour of the artistic calling, but he will have nothing to do with the simplistic dichotomies of romantic cliché. Domdaniel's advice is, in many respects, the opposite of von Francius': he argues that, as an artist, Monica cannot fulfil her potential unless she has gained emotional experience and maturity in her own life. Once again, Davies tempers romantic attitudes with a more sober wisdom without in any way denying the kernel of truth that lies at the heart of the concept of romantic aspiration.

Ultimately, when he comes to elaborate on his main theme, that is, the many ingredients that go into the training and development of a serious artist, Davies leaves Fothergill far behind. May's training as a singer is presented within delicately circumscribed limits. In true Victorian fashion, she is initially as shocked as Miss Hallam, her invalid employer, at the prospect of her appearing on the professional stage, and, once she is married to Courvoisier, we hear no more of a singing career of any kind. Davies has shaken up the whole situation, and has integrated the music plot and the love plot as Fothergill never does. Monica's training in *A Mixture of Frailties* is far more varied and technical than what we hear of May's in *The First Violin*. Moreover, it is presented in greater detail and at greater length. Commentators temperamentally unsympathetic to overt didacticism have criticized various passages in the book where Monica learns from her mentors, but these scenes have an essential function within the whole. It is important, for instance, that Giles should persuade her "to give up her determination to learn like a parrot, and to imitate her masters without really understanding what they did"; part of his own function as teacher is to bring her to "a point where she could feel a little, and understand, respect and cherish her own feeling" (*Mixture*, p. 158). Significantly, we hear nothing like this in Fothergill's novel. Even more significantly, the last reference to *The First Violin* within Davies' text comes at the point when it eventually becomes clear to Monica that the "intense, genteelly romantic world of *The First Violin*" was an illusion and that Aunt Ellen "had hold of the wrong end of the stick" (*Mixture*, p. 267).

But the serious didactic element in *A Mixture of Frailties* extends far beyond music education. One of the main lessons that Monica has to learn has nothing directly to do with musical ability but rather with the toughness and even ruthlessness that is essential for success in a demanding profession. Monica, in the middle of her rather shabby love affair with Giles, is ironically but perhaps appropriately cast as False Witness, and her début as soloist in the *St. Matthew Passion* sparks off a personal crisis. She must learn first to subsume her own personal concerns to the demands of her profession and of the work of art. She also learns a useful lesson from Domdaniel on the relation between the physical and the emotional life.

Later, the moral crises she must face become subtler, less conventional and more controversial. In supporting her mother's refusal to go to hospital, even when it means hastening her death, she repays, in a curious sort of way, the debt she owes to her mother for her determination and obstinacy that she has inherited from her and desperately needs in her life as an artist. Immediately following upon this, Monica must be strong enough to refuse Veronica's request for a loan even when it makes her seem hard, unfeeling and ungenerous. But Giles' opera is at stake, she has promised the money, and the development of her own career is also involved. Once again, her motives are snagged, but her emotional ties to Giles and her loyalty to art prove paramount, and she knows that she must be firm.

But the greatest test comes, of course, at the moment when she finds Giles apparently dead from asphyxiation. His gesture of attempting suicide with Monica's letter in his hand is an exaggeratedly romantic one, and at this point Monica realizes instinctively that even her relation with her lover cannot come between herself and her artistic career. Her actions in appropriating the letter and turning on the gas once more are technically criminal, but she is obeying a higher imperative. By contriving the situation so that Giles revives but then dies of suffocation, Davies does not spare her. She has to "face the fact...that if she had thought more of him and less of herself he need not have died at all. By her selfishness and littleness of spirit she had killed him" (*Mixture*, p. 348). Yet this judgment is itself tempered (though by no means cancelled) by Molloy's reiteration that "a public performer's first duty is to himself" (*Mixture*, p. 357).

As Fothergill's novel fades from *A Mixture of Frailties*, its function as subtext is taken over by Apuleius' *The Golden Asse*, the subject for Giles' opera. Davies characterizes the Roman classic within his novel as the "story of the unfortunate Lucius, whose meddling in magic caused him to be transformed into an ass, from which unhappy metamorphosis he was delivered only after he had achieved new wisdom" (*Mixture*, p. 316). Davies is not a formal allegorist, but a number of rough parallels can be discerned here between subtext and text. (It is not coincidental, for example, that in Giles' opera Monica plays the role of Fotis, the servant girl responsible for turning Lucius into an ass.) *The Golden Asse*, however, contrasts false magic with the true religion of the goddess Isis, and in one sense we can see Monica's story as another transformation: from the vulgarity and spiritual shoddiness of the Thirteeners and the Heart and Hope Gospel Quartet, via Aunt Ellen's simplistic romanticism, to the complex and demanding world of art. While I would not push the analogy too far, I do believe that *The Golden Asse* references allow Davies to allude to a noteworthy psychological/mythic pattern beneath his novel.

Be that as it may, although specific allusions to *The First Violin* disappear from the closing chapters of *A Mixture of Frailties*, the continuing debate about what constitutes romanticism does not. The whole section devoted to the group associated with *Lantern* looks critically at the "garret" side of Romanticism. Monica thinks of them, conventionally, as "Bohemians, though they would have hooted at so romantic and unfashionable a word" (*Mixture*, p. 204). Eventually, thanks to Domdaniel (*Mixture*, p. 210) and Ripon (*Mixture*, p. 237), she learns to see them in a more mature perspective. Later, of course, Davies transfers his main characters to Venice, the most "romantic" of all cities, yet again uses the situation to qualify the term. Monica makes several trips in a gondola, "which might have been romantic if she had not always been accompanied by her portable typewriter, or the very heavy suitcase which contained the orchestra parts for *The Golden Asse*, or Giles himself in his anti-Venetian mood" (*Mixture*, p. 314). According to Giles, the romance of Venice was "spurious." Davies, however, distinguishes between romanticisms here. Just before the first night, Monica thinks: "To be here, in a dressingroom all her own, in the celebrated Teatro della Fenice—was that not romance enough, without common, touristy sightseeing?" (*Mixture*, p. 318). Similarly, later that evening, after the performance, Domdaniel takes her back to the hotel by gondola, yet the night is chilly, and all that we are told is that, for Monica, "it was romantic and moonlit enough" (*Mixture*, p. 323). What happens is that Domdaniel, instead of initiating a formal love scene, follows old-fashioned formality and gallantly kisses her hand. Yet, as he does so, he provides the artistic equivalent of a scene of high romance by announcing that he now thinks of her as "a fellow artist."

"Romance" and "romantic" occur regularly in the last pages of the novel to reinforce Davies' basic concern, and almost invariably either the word or the idea is invoked in complicating circumstances. The jury that sits on Giles' inquest "were not of a romantic turn of mind" (*Mixture*, p. 344), so they bring in the conventional, diplomatic—and, though they do not know it, ironically accurate—verdict of death by misadventure. In what may be the most traditionally romantic scene in the novel (but it is Monica half-consciously acting out a romantic role), Monica brings Giles' ring to her lips as her London-bound train passes within sight of his grave (*Mixture*, p. 357). When Davies resolves the plot in something close to romantic fashion by having Veronica give birth to the necessary male heir, she is "unromantic" enough to announce a desperate hunger (*Mixture*, p. 370). And finally, of course, Monica receives Domdaniel's proposal—the standard romantic finale, except that he is old enough to be her father. He offers maturity rather than passion and (above all) proposes a union between independent artists that von Francius would have considered impossible. The final appearance of the word "romantic" occurs at the end of the penultimate chapter when Monica hears Giles' disembodied voice and suspects that it will help to keep "her romanticism from running away with her" (*Mixture*, p. 371).

*A Mixture of Frailties*, then, explores the nature of romance and its place within the everyday world and the world of art. While most of his readers will not have read *The First Violin*, it served a necessary function for Davies, who seems to have set himself the task of rewriting the story, of transforming it through his own brand of metamorphosis, so that it might be fitted to the circumstances of modern experience. *The First Violin* may read absurdly today, but this does not mean that "romance" in itself is to be denied. Domdaniel is careful to insist that he is not protesting against romanticism but only against those who confine themselves to the romantic element in music. Monica is encouraged to retain her romantic vision, but she must learn to control it. That casual phrase about the need to keep "her romanticism from running away from her" contains the (possibly romantic) kernel of the whole novel.

The phrase may also contain the (possibly romantic) kernel of Davies' whole *oeuvre*. *A Mixture of Frailties*, besides being a considerable achievement in its own right, is an important transitional novel, one to which many of his previous and later works are closely related. Davies has always been interested in the relation between romance and everyday reality. Indeed, his early one-act play, *Overlaid*, had already employed the world of opera, in the form of the Met broadcasts, as an emblem of imaginative possibility. Similarly, in his first novel, *Tempest-Tost*, Davies had moulded his narrative around a literary text, Shakespeare's *The Tempest*, and shown the lives of his actor-characters in relation to the dramatic roles they play.

The inter-connections of romance, art and reality become much more complex in his later work. *A Mixture of Frailties* shows the development and transformation of Monica Gall, but it also shows how her life and career are moulded by external forces in the forms of Murtagh, Giles and Domdaniel. In a related process, Dunstan Ramsay in *Fifth Business* comes to realize how an individual life plays over certain basic patterns that are recorded in history and myth. (As Wilfred Cude has noted, Dunstan's own life reflects incidents in the life and times of his saintly namesake.)[7] In *The Manticore*, David Staunton is taught by Dr. von Haller and Liesl to recognize basic psychological patterns in his own make-up. Magnus Eisengrim, in *World of Wonders*, tells the story of his own evolution as a kind of artist and shows how his future skills were prepared for by a series of individuals including Dunstan, Willard, the Tresizes and Liesl. Besides, as I have demonstrated elsewhere, Davies not only explores the relation of text and sub-text in this novel but also employs Robert-Houdin's memoirs in much the same way as he uses in *The First Violin* in *A Mixture of Frailties*.[8]

The Cornish Trilogy develops this principle still further. In *What's Bred in the Bone* and especially in *The Lyre of Orpheus*, the lives of twentieth-century characters are seen to relate to the age-old patterns of Arthurian romance. Furthermore, in these novels, Davies suggests that the patterns of individual lives may well be moulded and controlled not merely by external forces within this world but by more remote influences. From the other-worldly perspectives of his personal Daemon and the Angel of Biography, we see how Francis Cornish's early life is controlled in order to prepare him for his unique destiny as idiosyncratic painter and successful art critic and collector. And in *The Lyre of Orpheus* Davies even introduces a Romantic artist-figure, E.T.A. Hoffmann, in a story involving another music student given an opportunity to enter the world of opera and romance, a student whose life and attitudes create an extreme contrast to Monica's. *A Mixture of Frailties* is, in some respects, an angular novel. As Davies himself has admitted,[9] the change of gear from the zany world of Salterton and Mrs. Bridgetower's will to the more serious concerns of Monica's artistic and emotional development is not achieved without a certain awkwardness. But there is exhilaration to be found in Davies' increasingly confident awareness of his new powers. It is not too much to claim that, in *A Mixture of Frailties*, we see him achieving his artistic maturity.

# Notes

1  Robertson Davies, *A Mixture of Frailties* (Toronto: Macmillan, 1958), p. 58. All subsequent references in the text are to this edition. (The Laurentian Library reprint has identical pagination.)

2  Michael Peterman, *Robertson Davies* (Boston: Twayne, 1986), p. 105.

3  W[alter] O'H[earn], "New Davies Novel—Cinderella in London," *Montreal Star* (August 16, 1958), p. 24 as quoted in John Ryrie, "Robertson Davies: An Annotated Bibliography," in Robert Lecker and Jack David, eds., *The Annotated Bibliography of Canada's Major Authors,* Vol. 3 (Downsview: ECW Press, 1981), p. 224.

4  Peterman, p. 112.

5  T.D. MacLulich, *Between Europe and America: The Canadian Tradition in Fiction* (Toronto: ECW Press, 1988), p. 115.

6  Jessie Fothergill, *The First Violin* (New York: Hurst, n.d.), p. 100. All subsequent references in the text are to this edition. The novel first appeared, anonymously, in England in 1877.

7  See Wilfred Cude, *A Due Sense of Differences: An Evaluative Approach to Canadian Literature* (Lanham, MD: University Press of America, 1980), pp. 77-78.

8  See W.J. Keith, "Text and Sub-Text: Davies' *World of Wonders* and Robert-Houdin's *Memoirs*," *Canadian Literature*, No. 104 (Spring 1985), pp. 176-78.

9  See J. Madison Davis, ed., *Conversations with Robertson Davies* (Jackson: University Press of Mississippi, 1989), p. 40.

# Cultural Redemption in the Work
# of Robertson Davies

*Richard Plant*

C entral to the lives of Canadians is the experience of a journey in search of a new home. Over the years, the nature of the journey has changed so that what was once actual and represented literally is now psychological and treated metaphorically, giving to present-day literature a depth that early-Canadian writing did not possess.

Among the most probing of present-day works are those of Robertson Davies whose sophisticated treatment of the theme provides special insight into Canadian life. For that reason, I propose to examine in this essay a selection of his writing. While I shall concern myself chiefly with five of his plays, I shall explore one novel, *A Mixture of Frailties*, and make passing references to others, to show that the theme is not exclusive to either his drama or novels. For in some respects, there is a gap between Davies' narrative and dramatic voices. The novels, especially the Deptford Trilogy, contain a more complex expression of ideas, and have met with greater critical acclaim than the plays. In many ways that is not surprising. Narrative fiction is a more contemplative form not passing us by in a momentary living picture as stage drama does. Then too, over the years Canadians have taken the novel more seriously than drama so that acclaim is more readily accessible to that form than stage plays. Whatever the case, having raised this spectre of the gap between Davies' novels and drama, I shall confront it again later on in my discussion.

Just as much of our earlier literature depended heavily on narrative accounts of the authors' own journeys, so many of Robertson Davies' works, while not autobiographical, reflect the shape of his life. Simply stated, a pattern for the lives of his characters can be seen in Davies' own experience. He was born in small-town Canada, grew aware of its cultural deficiencies and moral repressiveness, and sought learning outside its boundaries. Much of this learning took place in the British Isles, the home of his ancestors, "presumably since the time of the Dawn Man," as he says in the introduction to *A Jig for the Gypsy*.[1] He returned to find Canada as ill-favoured as when he left it, although he himself had changed. Since then it appears to have been his desire to reshape small-town Canada through the exercise of his cosmopolitan understanding and immense talent. For although Davies travelled outside his small town, Canadians generally have not and consequently have found their sensibilities blunted by the parochial nature of the area in which they live.

This same life pattern, really made up of two aspects found in everyday Canadian life—one in which a talented but repressed Canadian is forced to travel abroad, the other in which a specially gifted foreigner comes to an inferior Canada and tries to alter it—has shaped many of Davies' works. For instance, *Hope Deferred*, performed in 1948, has relatively straightforward examples of both travellers. Count Frontenac is an enlightened French governor who, in his plan to stage *Tartuffe*, tries to bring cultural activity to a barren country. He is successfully opposed by well-meaning clerics who fear that the play will confuse the innocent Hurons about the nature of Christian devotion.

> FRONTENAC: Why is *Tartuffe* evil?
> SAINT VALLIER: It presents piety in an unfavourable light.
> FRONTENAC: False piety.
> SAINT VALLIER: Not everyone is capable of making that distinction.[2]

The Canadian who travels abroad and then returns enlightened is Chimène, a young Huron whom Frontenac has sent to France to be schooled: "Five years ago you [Chimène] were a charming child—an orphan; but your hair reeked of fish and your eyes were red from the smoke of the longhouse." As Frontenac observes, "The sisters [Chimène's tutors] have made a good job of you." (p. 178) Chimène has acquired a sophistication which raises her above the other Hurons. Her former ambition, typical of her fellows—"to grow fat so that some young Huron would love you and let you carry his pack for him" (p. 177)—has been replaced by higher aspirations which show greater discernment.

But as Frontenac is unsuccessful in staging *Tartuffe*, Chimène knows she will be unsuccessful in bringing any cultural awareness to Canada: "I do not have to remain here where I am not wanted, and where I will be treated as an oddity and a laughing stock. [Michel] Baron has promised me an engagement in Paris.... I shall return: my own land does not want me: I shall go where I am wanted" (p. 190).

Chimène's decision reflects the way Robertson Davies saw Canada at this time—as a puritanical, parochial backwater governed by the "tyranny...of organized virtue" (p. 190). In his Introduction to the play he gives examples of this "tyranny":

> I recall the uproar that followed the showing at the Canadian National Exhibition of a female nude; the model wore green slippers, revealing that she was not meant to be a classic subject, and she had pubic hair, which several outraged women's groups regarded as a gross affront to their sex. There was a dispute over the importation and sale in Canada of Edmund Wilson's *Memoirs of Hecate County*, which our Customs authorities refused to pass.... I myself ran into trouble with the United Church, which was still faithful to ideas about what was permissible in literature that stemmed from the Methodist Church, in which it had its roots.... These are a few instances, of action that was restrictive on the growth of art and literature in Canada; organized virtue was unfriendly to freedom of expression.[3]

The picture of a graceless Canada, a kind of fallen Eden in need of cultural redemption, pervades Davies' work from these early years.

This broad concern for Canada's cultural climate is viewed in *At My Heart's Core* through the narrower window of an individual artistic self and its relationship to the Canadian environment. One of the most serious implications of the journey in search of a new home is often the psychological dislocation that occurs from the traveller's being caught between two worlds: he is separated from the old and not yet reconciled to the new. The three women on whom the play centres—Catherine Parr Traill, Susanna Moodie and Frances Stewart—have completed actual journeys into the Canadian wilderness and have built homes there. While on the surface the women appear at ease, at their hearts' core they harbour discontent. As the author himself says, they "were transplanted English and Irish people, grappling courageously with a new country, but they had brought their intellectual furniture with them, and they never changed it."[4] Edmund Cantwell's temptation, which carries the play's main dramatic action, brings the roots of this discontent into the open with disruptive results.

Of the three, Frances Stewart appears the most comfortable. She and her husband, Thomas, a Member of the Legislative Council, live on a less-impoverished farm than those of the Moodies and Traills. However, Frances Stewart's is, in at least one sense, an insecure home, part of a "tight, snug, unapproachable little society" (p. 79) within which she has garrisoned herself against intrusions from the outside and the past, and within which she is unable to keep repressed her inner discontent. As Davies explains, "Mrs. Stewart...never ceased to be an Irish lady of the upper class...it never occurred to her to think that in a new land social values might be different" (p. 112). But she falls prey to the devilish Cantwell:

> You [Mrs. Stewart] are beautiful, highly born, witty, and possessed of that wonderful generosity of spirit...which raises beauty and charm to the level of great and holy virtues. What need has the backwoods of these great things? You should not be here (p. 44).

Because he is acquainted with her past, Cantwell is able to evoke the memory of her former lover in England who momentarily appears before her in a romantic vision exaggerating, by contrast, the harsh realities of her pioneer life. Fortunately, the humbleness and depth of her husband's love allow Frances to see eventually that "that was where Cantwell was so clever and so cruel; from something which was past he created, only for a few moments, something which had never been. What he aroused in me was not regret, but discontent, disguised as respect" (p. 85). As a result, the play ends on a scene of happiness for the Stewarts:

> *She [Frances] is now sitting on the floor beside his chair and they are both looking into the fire. A happy pause.*
> MRS. STEWART: I should be getting tea and calling Susanna and Catherine.

MR. STEWART: Do not be hasty my dear. Let us enjoy our victory a little longer (pp. 85-86).

Catherine Traill and Susanna Moodie are less fortunate than Frances. Unlike the Stewarts, neither the Traills nor Moodies are successful farmers: "Mr. Traill is an estimable gentleman, but it is no secret that he is one of the least capable settlers here about" (p. 47). Susanna's response to the news that her husband is to be given a government post betrays how she feels about their situation: "Giving up his farm? Giving up his backwoods life? Giving up uncertainty and poverty and debt? Oh, God! (*She bursts into tears*)" (p. 82).

Their husbands' "blighted hopes" intensify the women's inner turmoil which they consciously or unconsciously hide behind veneers of exaggerated modesty, duty to their husbands or time-consuming farm labours. Susanna's overbearing manner and her pompous air of respectability render her, in particular, a humorous target for Cantwell's praise which fills both women with delusions about their creative talents and reinforces their regrets about living in Canada. Cantwell claims that Catherine is "a remarkable woman pretending to be an unremarkable one" (p. 48), and that she is "gifted with the power to see into the very heart of Nature herself and to reveal the mysteries of Nature to mankind" (p. 59). Susanna, he asserts, might be as successful a writer as Maria Edgeworth if only she did not "play second fiddle to the incompetence of Lieutenant Moodie" (p. 53). There is truth in what he says. Both ladies do possess talent, but they have compromised it: "Mrs. Traill, for instance, disliked anything that was 'ugly or disgusting,' and so her observations of nature excluded all insect and reptile life" (p. 112). Susanna stooped to writing trivial, patriotic verses: "Huzza for England! May she claim/ Our fond devotion ever;/ And by the glory of her name/ Our brave forefathers' honest fame/ We swear—no foe shall sever/ Her children from the parent's side" (p. 10). Phelim Brady refers to her work as the "thin and bitter squeezings from the weary fancy of a heartsore woman" (p. 24). In reality, Cantwell has only given "words to the pain they have long felt" and revealed to us, as well as to themselves, private, hidden desires "which can never be fulfilled and which are cherished all the more closely for that reason" (p. 75).

Phelim Brady who adds comedy to the action deserves a brief comment. Like Count Frontenac in *Hope Deferred*, Brady is a man of special gifts who has come to Canada where his talent is not wanted. In his own Bohemian way, "that of a storyteller and singer of old songs—the shabby fag-end of a long bardic tradition" (p. 114), the irreverent Brady serves as a foil to Susanna and Catherine, representing living proof that the creative impulse need not be compromised or smothered in Canada no matter how inhospitable the climate.

Although there are no actual journeys in the play, underlying the action are the Britishers' persistent dreams of journeying back to England. What Cantwell says of Lieutenants Moodie and Traill is also true of the three women: "I have watched some of those officers here in Upper Canada following the plough, and whenever they rest...they always come to a halt facing east. I think that without knowing it they are looking toward England" (p. 78). But Cantwell makes the women aware of their fanciful trips "home" and forces them to embark on psychological journeys into their respective selves. They discover that an artist must not only have a climate that is friendly to freedom of expression, but be aware of who and what he is, conscious of what is at his heart's core and how that relates to the world around him. As Robert Rogers later says in *Pontiac and The Green Man*, "a new land has a soul...—perhaps a very old soul—and those who would find what is best in the new land must find this soul, and humbly embrace that soul."[5]

Like *At My Heart's Core*, *Fortune, My Foe* has at its centre an immigrant artist, Franz Szabo, a marionette master who has come to Canada in search of a new home. Before long, Szabo learns, as did the three women pioneers, that the country is inhospitable to his artistry: "But that's Canada, Szabo.... It will freeze your heart with folly and ignorance."[6] So says Irdis Rowlands, a university professor arrived from Wales years before and who has himself very nearly been "overlaid" (to use a word from the Davies' canon) by Canadian spiritual iciness:

> God, how I tried to love this country! How I tried to forget the paradise of Wales, and the quick wits of Oxford! I have given all I have to Canada—my love, then my hate, and now my bitter indifference. This raw, frost-bitten country has worn me out, and its raw, frostbitten people have numbed my heart (p. 112).

A younger man at the same university, Nicholas Haywood, has also fallen victim to his native land's indifference to intellectual and artistic concerns. As a result he has decided to go to the United States where greater opportunity exists.

In contrast to these two professors, and the three ladies in *At My Heart's Core*, Szabo refuses to allow the negative feelings associated with his encounter with the new land to dominate his optimistic vision. Instead, with an artist's strength he reconciles himself to his new home determined to make it better than it was when he arrived:

> I am an artist, you know, and a real artist is very, very tough. This is my country now, and I am not afraid of it. There may be some bad times; there may be some misunderstandings. But I shall be all right. So long as I keep the image of my work clear in my heart. I shall not fail (p. 153).

Szabo's courage arouses the previously apathetic Rowlands, and Haywood too draws strength from the marionette master and resolves to remain in Canada. The new home he seeks will be in an enlightened Canada which he will help build, a Canada over which the "frostbitten" people will not rule.

Again we have a play which comments forthrightly on the plight of artists and intellectuals amid Canada's "spiritual iciness." In contrast to *Hope Deferred*, however, the main characters are not forced to flee the country in search of a home elsewhere. Instead, following the pattern of *At My Heart's Core*, they journey within and with the self-awareness and concomitant courage so acquired they resolve to remain in Canada and seek a new home here. It is worth speculating that these were the same activities and decisions Robertson Davies undertook in his own life. Surely his decision in 1940 to leave the Old Vic theatre company and his work with Tyrone Guthrie, and to return to a Canada like the one his writings reflect, required the same soul-searching journey and courage we see dramatized in *Fortune, My Foe*.

In *A Mixture of Frailties*, a novel published in 1958, nine years after *Fortune, My Foe*, a similar kind of spiritual journey is the author's chief concern where an actual voyage abroad forms the framework for its expression. Here again an artist who is inhibited by the constraints of a culturally impoverished Canada is the central figure. That character's attempts to deal with her background, while transcending it, are the substance of the novel.

Monica Gall is the naive but gifted daughter of a narrow-minded, poorly educated couple from Salterton, a fictional town in southern Ontario. Her creative talents have been held back by the standards of her parents whose life is controlled by a repressive fundamentalism. For them pleasure is sinful, and the unknown fearful. Serious intellectual or artistic endeavours, because they are pleasurable as well as unknown, are rejected. Hence, Monica's only "cultural" activity is singing with the "Heart and Hope" Quartet at her parents' church, the Thirteenth Apostle Tabernacle.

Luckily, Monica is awarded a scholarship to study voice in England and Europe. She accepts, goes abroad, and becomes a celebrated young opera star before returning to Salterton. Her travels allow her to discover the unknown world outside Salterton and those aspects of herself which would surely have remained hidden or, even worse, have turned sour had she stayed in the little town all her life. As already intimated, Monica's actual journey is also a metaphorical one into her inner being which results in new understanding. Through her travels she acquires not only professional skill and worldliness, but finds she possesses a selfless love capable of giving without asking anything in return. She discovers within her self depths of passion and pleasure she had no idea existed. Most importantly, she learns to enjoy these sensuous experiences without the guilt her Salterton upbringing had taught her to feel.

In contrast, Alice, her older sister and a foil for Monica's character, acquires none of Monica's grace as she grows older. In more than one sense Alice goes nowhere. She marries a local boy and remains in Salterton living by a set of pinched principles inherited from her parents. Her goals are those shared by other Saltertonites— "get some money, get a wife, get a house, get some children, get a bigger house, get some more money."[7] They represent an unflattering picture of a part of Canada inhabited by the "half-educated" for whom Franz Szabo says "we can only pray" (*Fortune*, p. 153). It is not surprising that Monica would want to flee from such cultural squalor.

However, flee as one might, home ties are binding, as we saw in the case of the three pioneer women. And they prove equally binding for Canadians going abroad. Instead of the sense of exile and longing for greener pastures commonly experienced by immigrants to Canada,

Monica experiences guilt which arises from an underlying belief that her new way of life betrays her old one. Yet she desperately desires her new experiences.

Caught between two worlds. It is the same split in the psyche I mentioned earlier. For Monica it means:

> Keeping two sets of mental and moral books—one for inspection in the light of home [Salterton] and another to contain her life with Revelstoke, [her lover] and the new loyalties and attitudes which had come with Molloy [her singing master] and particularly with Domdaniel [her guardian]. To close either set of books forever would be a kind of spiritual suicide, and yet to keep them both was hypocrisy (p. 266).

The only way to resolve the tension, she discovers, is to return to Salterton to seek a reconciliation with her past. This entails two trips, the first occasioned when Ma Gall becomes ill.

When she first returns, Monica, in an act of supplication and forgiveness, assumes the responsibility of nursing her mother. Ma is not only physically ill; she is facing a moral crisis as well. Heavily drugged, she is troubled by matters she can ordinarily keep repressed: "She was convinced that she had sinned unforgivably, and that her sins were sexual in their nature...yet she could not confess her transgression or give a clear expression to her remorse. Instead, she accused herself vaguely, and suffered in the tormented images of her morphia dreams" (p. 281). Certain that she had been a "bad girl," Ma looks to her daughter for comfort, unintentionally forcing Monica to face her own inner conflict:

> Was Monica a good girl? The question came again and again...and thus phrased, from Mrs. Gall, it could have only one meaning. Monica had no intention of saying that, in her mother's terms, she was not a good girl. But she had to meet the question in her own mind (p. 281).

After a significant "seven weary nights" of nursing and contemplation, Monica meets the question: "She was a good girl. Chastity is to have the body in the soul's keeping...and everything in her own experience supported it." Moreover, a reconciliation, albeit an oblique and ironic one since Monica is aware of its limitations, finally takes place:

> Mrs. Gall opened her eyes, and looked at her daughter more clearly than she had done since her homecoming.... "I've got quite an imagination. That's where you're like me Monny. Always remember you got that from me." Tears came into Monica's eyes; they were tears of happiness, for at last she shared something with her mother. She wept, and laughed a little, as she said—"Yes Ma, I got that from you. We're really very alike, aren't we?" (p. 282)

To the best of her ability, Ma comes to understand that Monica's new life is right and necessary. As a result, at her mother's funeral, Monica's inner voice tells her: "You are free. You did your best for her, and now you are free" (p. 289). With that firmly in mind, she returns to London to continue her studies.

But life does not suddenly become easy because she has resolved some of the differences with her mother. Before long, serious complications in her European life make a second return necessary. First, Giles Revelstoke, her lover and the composer of the opera in which she starred, commits suicide. Because Monica believes she had provoked his action by breaking off their relationship, his death arouses enormous guilt feelings in her. Even more serious, she had refused to turn off the gas in his apartment when she found him apparently dead—later it was revealed that he had only been unconscious. In addition, Domdaniel, her guardian, had proposed marriage. To complicate matters further, her scholarship is due to end soon. She has to sort things out and Salterton seems like a logical place to do it.

On the voyage back, Monica begins to face her problems. Fearfully seasick, she finds that "her distress of body was paralleled by a marked improvement in her state of mind" (p. 364). By the time she reaches Canada, she has come to terms with her guilt over Giles' death:

> When she got off the boat...it was with the sensation of a widow, but not of a murderess. She was still sure that she had killed Giles, and that it was through grievous faults in her character that she had done so. But, somehow, she had accepted the fact. To that extent, at least, she had clarified her thinking (p. 356).

In Salterton this time, she discovers that although she had been born and raised in the small town, and still carries some of it with her, she has grown beyond it. She can now understand its influence in a broader perspective.

She will not remain in Salterton to become, in Edmund Cantwell's phrase, "a Pegasus at the plough." She will sail to England to find a new home (in a literal sense) if she marries Domdaniel. Whether she marries him or not, she will re-enter the international world of culture continuing her quest, in an abstract sense, for a home of the self that does not deny its past, its natural desires and emotions, however dark they might be.

Monica's adventures show us how the "intellectual furniture" of a Canadian forced to go abroad conditions his or her life; they suggest what might have happened to Nicholas Haywood of *At My Heart's Core* had he decided not to remain in Canada. Clearly, guilt engendered by the influence of Canadian puritanism and the "maggot of respectability" is the traveller's most serious hindrance, and can be assuaged only when the individual returns to confront it at its source—small-town Canada. In this novel, the journey home is both physical and metaphorical—an exploration of the traveller's self. This pattern, which re-appears in a highly sophisticated and illuminating fashion in the later novels, *Fifth Business*, *The Manticore* and *World of Wonders*, was in evidence in an earlier play, *Hunting Stuart* (1955), which dramatized the subject in a more fanciful way than it appeared in Monica's narrative.

*Hunting Stuart* reveals the liberating effect on a quiet, unambitious Ottawa civil servant, Henry Benedict Stuart, of a journey back to the land of his forefathers. Stuart is discovered by a pair of extraordinary scientists to be the oldest living male descendant of the Royal House of Stuart, which makes him, they claim, King of Great Britain, Ireland and the Commonwealth. Through a drug they have invented to test their theory, the scientists vault Stuart back in time where he becomes his ancestor, Bonnie Prince Charlie. In Stuart's assumption of this persona—a cantankerous womanizer and heavy drinker with a caustic tongue—we see the lethargy of middle-class Canada thrown off and are made aware of the detrimental aspects of small-town life. Again material acquisitiveness, petty social ambitions and mindless puritanism come under Davies' attack.

The discoveries Stuart makes about himself indicate, as Davies points out in *Stage Voices*, that "what we are is to a great extent what we believe ourselves to be." [8] While this insight is hardly superficial,

Stuart's character change from being a meek civil servant to becoming
an undaunted hero relates more to his assuming Prince Charles'
identity than to his acquiring spiritual self knowledge. *Question Time*,
written twenty years after *Hunting Stuart* and in the same year as the
complex *World of Wonders*, is openly concerned with spiritual inquiry.

Peter Macadam, the itinerant hero of *Question Time*, is both
representative of Canadians, since he is their Prime Minister, and
someone who stands, a bit less convincingly, for all mankind, as his
name implies. When his aircraft crashes on les Montagnes de Glace
in the Canadian Arctic, he alone survives, but is lost and forced to
wait until help arrives. In the meantime, scenes showing us how
Canadians—Macadam's fellow parliamentarians, government bureau-
crats, his wife, a young couple representing the Canadian public—
react to his apparent death are interspersed with others which
dramatize Macadam's personal adventures in the Arctic.

An "Eskimo shaman," an unusual fellow with a medical degree
and an Edinburgh accent, discovers the Prime Minister. He examines
Macadam and pronounces, "He's not just the picture of health, but
he'll do.... My Edinburgh medicine provides no answer but my Arctic
medicine does. He's gone inside himself."[9] Living or dying is
obviously more than a physical matter, which becomes clear when we
learn that the wilderness in which Macadam is wandering is "not just
the Arctic of geography books...but more of a personal Arctic, you
might say. Your Terra Incognita" (p. 8). In this light, Macadam's
journey, with its Jungian flavour, is really psychological, as is the
home he seeks. The characters that appear are creatures of his
imagination, like Arnak, an Inuit woman synonymous with his
intelligence, and an old Herald who represents the wisdom of the past,
"the continuance of history" (p. 54). Like other characters in Davies'
works, Macadam is a "stranger to his inner world" (p. 36) who must
journey inward to find himself. Just how much of a stranger he is, is
revealed when he proudly and foolishly chooses a bear as his totem
animal, a painful, symbolic experience which leaves Macadam terrified. Suffering from a "want of understanding of himself" (p. 69),
Macadam would have been better to have chosen the beaver. As the
Herald points out, the beaver is an industrious animal which, when
frightened, bites off his testicles and offers them to the foe as a token

of appeasement. The result is a price not worth the paying: "When the orbs are gone, the sceptre is unavailing" (p. 61).

But Macadam need not remain in his state of confusion, of "beaverness." In the second act, the Parliament of the Terra Incognita, made up of figures representing aspects of Macadam's psyche and people from his life as Prime Minister, sits to advise him about his future. In order to do so, the Leader of the Opposition interrogates him: "I asked the Prime Minister who he was and he gave me an unsatisfactory answer. I asked what sort of country this was, and the answer was no better. Let me ask a third question: Why does anybody want to be Prime Minister?" (p. 62) Even that draws only a superficial and politic reply from Macadam which evades any real truth about himself. A further evasion, "Do you serve Peter Macadam?" provokes the following: "A mad answer! A lunatic answer! You describe a man without a core! An empty man.... You represent millions, and you have lost your hold on the one man who is all you have and all you can ever know of life" (p. 65). Immediately before this, Macadam's wife has said to him: "Are you so stupid, so besotted with public concerns, that you don't know that everything—everything in the world—comes at last from what you call the personal level?... What is a man that other men should exalt him if he is not someone whose life on the personal level—on the deepest bedrock of the personal level—is of worth, and colour and substance and splendour that makes him a man in whom other men see something of what is best in themselves?" (p. 64)

Even with this wisdom staring him in the face, Macadam avoids the truth until a confrontation with the Queen of the Terra Incognita, a palpable *dea ex machina*, forces him into submission. He recognizes that she is "the final reality...ourselves, our forebears, and our children; she is this land—so old it makes all monarchies seem like passing shadows on her face, and all forms of power like games children tire of," Macadam promises that he will "Never turn his face from her again" (p. 67). With that, the scene shifts to a national television announcement that the Prime Minister has been found alive and well.

*Question Time* brings together in a dramatic form many of the ideas mentioned in this study, collecting them around two interwoven concerns: "the relationship of the Canadian people to their soil, and...the relationship of man to his soul" (p. *xiii*). Incidentally, this binocular vision, at least in part and quite understandably, made the play confusing in performance. Audiences found that Macadam's dual role as representative of Canadians and of mankind at large was overpowered by the political implications of his office and his nominal resemblance to Pierre Trudeau. What is primarily a metaphysical drama became a political character play.

In any case, as in all three of the Deptford novels, and in *A Mixture of Frailties*, *Question Time* presents a native-born Canadian who goes on an actual journey to an old land which reveals "what a man must do to make himself a completed human being, and the pathetic gaps and holes that appear in his life when he has failed to do so."[10] His travels force him to acknowledge his true self which he had previously hidden behind a veneer of middle-class respectability and shallow public concerns. Since the old land is ironically an unexplored part of Canada, his journey gives him an understanding of his Canadian heritage, and his own place in the "continuance of history;" in effect, what Robert Rogers explains in *Pontiac and the Green Man* about embracing the soul of a land.

These discoveries permit Macadam a vision of a better world and the personal integrity to carry it out. At the end of the play, Macadam is about to return to Ottawa where his special office and enlightened outlook will force him to try to change the ill-favoured world of everyday Canada. Here again, notably in Tim and Marge, the cretinous couple of "ordinary" Canadians, we see a picture of a Canada that is in need of enlightenment. But Davies' viewpoint seems to have changed from that of his early works. Macadam, the gifted individual, does not flee his inhospitable home as Chimène does in *Hope Deferred*, nor does he speak conditionally about the future— "Perhaps you'll succeed where I have failed" (*Fortune*, p. 156). His anticipated return to Ottawa offers a positive statement about the possibility of a better world akin to the "Golden World" in *World of Wonders*.

Earlier I raised the spectre of the gap between the complexity of Davies' novels and the more open didacticism of his plays. The matter may at first appear wholly unconnected with the discussion at hand, but that is not so. Robertson Davies has spoken on occasion about his dissatisfaction with the reception afforded his plays. Concerning *A Jig for the Gypsy*, for instance, he has written, "Nobody wanted to produce it, although several people were kind enough to say they liked it" (*Jig*, p. *vi*). In a speech, "Ham and Tongue," he makes the following revealing statements:

> What I really wanted to do was to write plays. And I did. And most of them have been acted, and some of them have been acted several times. But until quite recently, being a playwright in Canada was uphill work, and there was no money in it whatever. Like most persistent playwrights, I eventually achieved some production abroad, and even joined the gray, inglorious army of those who have failed on Broadway, but I knew that there must be some other, more effective way of grabbing the public by the windpipe and making it listen to what I had to say. So I tried my hand at writing a novel, and lo! it worked.[11]

His early experiences as a playwright led him, rightly or wrongly, to form an attitude of distrust concerning our theatrical resources and the theatre-going public in small-town Canada. We have an opportunity to see that attitude on display in his depiction of the carnival audiences in *World of Wonders*. In drama, we have seen it in *Question Time*'s Tim and Marge and in the Philistine response afforded Franz Szabo in *Fortune, My Foe*. Tyrone Guthrie, introducing Davies' early collection *Eros at Breakfast and Other Plays*, commented as follows about *Overlaid*:

> It says something universally true about spiritual starvation; and at the same time something specifically true about the starvation of rural areas, and, more particularly of rural Canada.... There are two jobs to be done. First to discredit the legend of Rural Paradise; second to make rural life more interesting, rich and varied.[12]

Davies' distrust is often directly stated in his instructions to the people producing his plays. Scene designers seem singled out for especially cryptic comments. In *Fortune, My Foe* he writes: "let no scene painter carelessly represent this scene by the usual huddle of flat roofs and false fronts" (p. 3). In *Hunting Stuart* a similar caution is expressed: "Here is a challenge, then, for the scene designer" (p. 4). In short, what we see at work again is the image of an ill-favoured Canada, of audiences and theatres which are inferior to the playwright's standards, but which he hopes to urge to higher achievement. For them technical matters must be spelled out; thematic implications that would remain the province of the reader's private contemplation in a novel are explained in the plays so that nothing is missed. Davies implicitly says as much about his dramaturgy when he writes in the "Preface in the Form of an Examination" in *Question Time*:

> The content of a play is not simple, but it should, in its unfolding follow a simpler line than the plot of most novels, which may have ramifications and by-concerns that would muddle the action of a play. This is why dramatizations of novels such as *Don Quixote* and *David Copperfield* deal only with a few incidents from the whole work, and often leave us unsatisfied (p. *viii*).

In light of this highly critical stance, one need not wonder that Davies has his Canadian detractors. Someone who tells you that you are not only a moral and cultural Philistine, but ignorant of yourself as well, is unlikely to garner favour. And that is what Davies told his audiences. The inferior nature of the late 1940s theatre was but part of what he saw as a broader cultural and moral inferiority throughout the nation. Canada was, and to some extent still is (as his recent works demonstrate), a kind of cultural and moral hell in need of redemption. Whence cometh the redeemer?

Davies seems to answer in two ways, basing his view on personal experience as well as on an understanding of Canadian history in the context of western civilization. On one hand, gifted and visionary foreigners like Franz Szabo or Tyrone Guthrie can help transform the country, provided they know spiritually who they are, understand the soul of the land, and possess the strength to overcome feelings of estrangement and loneliness. On the other hand, gifted and visionary Canadians like Peter Macadam, Magnus Eisengrim (and Robertson Davies) can acquire spiritual knowledge of themselves and their country and become redeemers. These Canadians, it appears, find it imperative to journey away from their parochial homes in both a literal and metaphorical sense. The guilt they face abroad, in place of the immigrant's sense of exile and estrangement, is engendered by a feeling that their new way of life, less morally restrictive and culturally more enlightened, violates the principles of their small-town Canada upbringing. To resolve this guilt means a reconciliation with their immediate and ancestral past where they become acquainted with the archetypal figures and mythic patterns that give life meaning and shape.

# Notes

1   Robertson Davies, *A Jig for the Gypsy* (Toronto: Clarke, Irwin, 1954), p. v.

2   Robertson Davies, *Hope Deferred* in Anton Wagner, ed., *Canada's Lost Plays*, Vol. 3 (Downsview: CTR, 1980), p. 184. All further references to this play are to this edition and are given in parentheses within the text.

3   *Ibid.*, p. 175.

4   Robertson Davies, *At My Heart's Core and Overlaid* (Toronto: Clarke, Irwin, 1966), p. 112. All further references to these plays are to this edition and are given in parentheses within the text.

5   Robertson Davies, *Pontiac and the Green Man*, unpublished script, performed at the University of Toronto in 1977, p. 66

6   Robertson Davies, *Fortune, My Foe* in *Four Favourite Plays* (Toronto: Clarke, Irwin, 1968), p. 153. All further references to this play are to this edition and are given in parentheses within the text.

7   Robertson Davies, *A Mixture of Frailties* (New York: Scribners, 1958), p. 377. All further references to this novel are to this edition and are given in parentheses within the text.

8   "Robertson Davies" in Geraldine Anthony, ed., *Stage Voices* (Toronto, New York: Doubleday, 1978), p. 70.

9   Robertson Davies, *Question Time* (Toronto: Macmillan, 1975), p. 5. All further references to this play are to this edition and are given in parentheses within the text.

10  *Stage Voices*, p. 77.

11  Robertson Davies, *One Half of Robertson Davies* (Toronto: Viking, 1978), p. 15.

12  Robertson Davies, *Eros at Breakfast and Other Plays* (Toronto: Clarke, Irwin, 1949), p. xiv.

# Writing Paradox,
# the Paradox of Writing:
# Robertson Davies

*Barbara Godard*

Culture in itself seeks only its own identity, not an enemy," writes Northrop Frye, arguing that cultural development takes place not through polemic and dialectic but, in a "vegetative" way, by taking root. Culture is created in an intensive engagement with one's locality, not with others or with centres of power in a national or international space. The language of creativity is thus "a language that cannot argue; it is not based on propositions that do battle with their implied opposites. What it does is to create a vision that becomes a focus for community."[1] "Culture as interpenetration," is how Frye characterizes identity.

"Interpenetration," however, is a term that has been used by the Russian theorist Mikhail Bakhtin for another model of cultural development which is, in contrast, oriented to diversity and transformation. Culture is seen as a process of interchange or debate among differing groups in a particular social and historical instance of conflictual relations.[2] Robertson Davies' fiction, exhibiting a constant concern with the relationship to another wor(l)d, reflects this second theory of culture. Grouped as triptychs, each novel functions as a parallax for another, producing a shift in angle of vision on the issues under examination. Each interpretation of incidents is qualified by a different one; meaning is not singular but produced through an encounter with alterity. This clash of discourses is staged in different modes within Robertson Davies' work. One of the most prevalent of these stagings is his carnivalesque imagery, characterized by oscillation between two polarized perceptions, focused on the point where one moves into the other. The clash of discourses is also staged in the forms of fiction where a "theme of becoming" develops from autobiographical and biographical genres and clashes with a "theme of testing," which is a legacy of the Sophist and the baroque novel.[3] These are terms used by Bakhtin in outlining the poetics of the novel as genre. Bakhtin's theory that the novel is characterized by "a diversity of social speech types…of languages" exemplifying the internal stratification in language at a given historical moment,[4] and his interest in the carnivalesque as one specific mode of the "mutual interaction"[5] of social speech types, has stimulated contemporary re-examination of the novel.

As a genre, according to Bakhtin, the novel emerged in periods of a clash of cultures, of an intersection of languages. The privileged moments of this interrelatedness of languages were periods of bilingual culture when meaning was produced "through another's eyes," as, for example, when Rome saw through Greek eyes or the Renaissance looked out through classical eyes. By extension, I would suggest, contemporary Canadians, post-colonialists, have viewed their geopolitical terrain through Europeans' eyes. This produces a word with " 'a sideways glance' a stylized word enclosing itself, as it were, in its own piously stylized quotation marks."[6] Such interanimation of languages "objectifies"[7] the axiological systems inhering in words: fiction is produced by the translation and reworking of others' works.[8] "A word, discourse, language, or culture undergoes 'dialogization' when it becomes relativized, de-privileged, aware of competing definitions for the same thing."[9] "Dialogism," though, is not dialectic, which is abstract and synthetic.[10] Through its practice of direct and indirect speech, the novel as genre stages the clash of discourses. As such, the novel is, for Bakhtin, the preeminent genre of modelling cultural production through an encounter with alterity. As I shall show, Davies' understanding of the dialogue owes as much to his reading of the literary masterpieces of the dialogic tradition identified by Bakhtin—Rabelais' carnivalesque and Dostoevsky's dialogism—as it does to his investigation of anglo-Ontarian folk ritual. The local and the regional ironically become most visible when refracted through the comparative lenses of a European tradition of the novel, which Bakhtin traces from the Greeks and Romans through Rabelais.

For Bakhtin, the novel is a hodge-podge of alien discourses, but it is also a finished, unique and unrepeatable enunciation. In this, it is preeminently a relational genre. Working at the interface of signification and communication, Bakhtin elaborates a theoretical model of textual exchange wherein discourses are displaced and established. Interdiscursive or intertextual relations are played out in the connections within and between texts, genres and practices. These are contradictory movements of and between discursive sites within what is a "structural model of *uneven* development."[11] The discursive field of an epoch is conceptualized as "contradictions and conflicts" among competing social groups; there is not one but rather several mutually contradictory truths, a situation of "heteroglossia."[12] Within this "plurality of languages and of ideology," the "interchange" is stated in the "superimposition" of different types of significance. Such "dialogism" is resolutely opposed to a "one-sided absorption" in the mechanical substitution of one type of significance for another that functions in dissymmetrical or "monologic" relations.[13]

Bakhtin advances an open-ended poetics, one that would rethink claims to a mastery of knowledge (or knowledge of mastery) and "formulates the conflictual dimension as the realm of the social determination of the weight and value of discursive elements."[14] He sets out a materialist theory of discourse in which ideological creation, that is, the production of meanings and values, is realized only in "some definite semiotic material" (things and actions) which are part of "practical reality." Every ideologeme (ideological product) is "a part of the material social reality surrounding man, an aspect of the materialized ideological horizon."[15] The individual act of creation of the ideologeme cannot be studied in isolation from the social processes that give it meaning, for it is an inseparable part of social interconnection. Speech genres, literary genres, are consequently understood not as a product but as a process, a set of multifunctional relationships. Genre is a text-type, a set of protocols, of modes of address, a contract ratified by a specific social community which contextualizes in a metagrammatical way the discourses, narratives, dialogic positionings operative in that community into the linguistic and semantic patterns that constitute text grammars in such a way as to make meaning for that community.

Bakhtin examined the genres of reported speech in fiction to establish a typology of dialogic strategies. Intersecting within a basic double-voiced discourse that he identified are two or more voices, accents, socially distinct practices. These voices may be subjected to reevaluation when introduced into the first discourse, or even clash with hostility. Sometimes, the other's word is not incorporated into the discourse, but remains outside even as it is taken into account. Bakhtin calls this a "hidden polemic" in which a "polemical blow is struck at the other's discourse on the same theme, at the other's statement about the same object." The word of the other is treated agonistically; this process, no less than the topic under discussion, "determines the author's discourse." Literary discourse, consequently, not only anticipates in advance the objections of its readers and critics, but reacts to a preceding literary style as an "anti-stylization" of it. As well, there is "internally polemical discourse—the word with a sideward glance at someone else's word."[16] Together, these relational positionings of utterances and speaking subjects establish discourse as a network of intersecting texts and discourses.

These theories of Bakhtin's are particularly useful for examining Davies' fictional forms. But before turning to the range of dialogic strategies in his work, I want to remark on the prominence of carnivalesque imagery in his fiction which constitutes a virtual encyclopedia of contemporary Canadian carnival types.[17]

What interested Bakhtin was not the carnival itself, but its transposition into the language of artistic images which he called "the carnivalization of literature."[18] Characterized by the motion between two polarized perceptions of the world, the carnivalesque produces an ambivalent dynamism and affirms the text's critical function. According to Bakhtin,

> Carnivalization made possible the creation of the *open* structure of the great dialogue and allowed people's social interaction to be carried over into the sphere of the spirit and the intellect, which had always been primarily the sphere of a single, unified and monological consciousness or of a unified and indivisible spirit.[19]

The "double-voiced" nature of carnival treats laughter as serious. It is related generically to the most ancient form of ritual laughter which was directed toward a higher order (the gods or an earthly authority), disparaging and ridiculing them to force their renewal in crisis. Mockery was fused with rejoicing. The elevated status of its targets bestowed privileges on such laughter in antiquity which survived into the Middle Ages, as Bakhtin writes, in the form of the "parodia sacra" (i.e., parody of sacred texts) and in the laughter of carnival. This folk humour manifests itself in a variety of forms: in carnival pageants, "comic rites and cults,...clowns and fools, giants, dwarfs and jugglers;" in comic verbal compositions, the "literature of parody" and in curses, oaths, and other forms of billingsgate. In contrast to formal ecclesiastical and feudal ceremonies, the carnival implicitly criticized and/or subverted such ceremonies. Popular feasting was related to the superior goals of human existence—resurrection and renewal—by "the peculiar logic of 'inside out' (*à l'envers*), of the 'turnabout,' of a continual shifting from top to bottom, from front to rear, of numerous parodies and travesties, humiliations, profanations, comic crownings and uncrownings." "As opposed to the official feast," writes Bakhtin,

> one might say that carnival celebrated liberation from the prevailing truth and from the established order; it marked the suspension of all hierarchical rank, privileges, norms and prohibitions. Carnival was the true feast of time, the feast of becoming, change, and renewal. It was hostile to all that was immortalized and completed.[20]

Davies' theme too is paradox: creation through destruction or debasement. Here is played out the conflict between European authority, manifested in the formalism and imperialism of ecclesiastical and political orders, and North American energy and vitality, expressed in the popular folk traditions of the carnival. In what Bakhtin calls the "carnivalization of literature," the authority of tradition is exposed and made strange through the recontextualization that occurs within the Ontario carnival. Paradoxically, though, the authority for this transgression is conferred by the contested tradition. Here in the crowning and uncrowning of the carnival spirit, authority is acknowledged through ritual and tradition even as their force as norm is challenged and displaced. This is the characteristic one-within-the-other, an ambiguity central to the "*open* structure of the great dialogue" which, according to Bakhtin, prevents the establishment of a unified truth.[21]

In studying Rabelais and other Renaissance masters, Davies learned lessons other than characterization. From Shakespeare, about whom he wrote a thesis, and whom he parodied in *Tempest-Tost*, he learned the function of the mask and the profundity of the wisdom of the fool and clown. From Cervantes, whose *Don Quixote* provides the story for the puppet play-within-the-play in *Fortune My Foe*, Davies absorbed his main concern with the plight of the imagination in an inhospitable cultural climate and a theoretical preoccupation with illusion and representation.[22] From Rabelais, he took his attack on idealism and a love for those feasts such as "the country people at the feast where Gargantua is born, chatting and joking over their drinks."[23] Parties, banquets of all sorts are common scenes in Davies' fiction.

Though Bakhtin's theory of the novel is helpful in analyzing Davies' fiction, it should be noted that Davies' approach to the carnivalesque is an independent one, coincidentally developed from the same fictional tradition elaborated by Bakhtin. Indeed, Davies' theory of carnival diverges from that of Bakhtin. Whereas the Russian critic takes an optimistic view of this process of regeneration through destruction, because he views carnival as liberation from the hegemony of ideology, Davies developed a much darker view of carnival. Though he began in the Salterton Trilogy with carnival scenes of parties, banquets and local festivals such as fall fairs and Hallowe'en which are optimistic and emphasize regeneration, the Deptford novels are much blacker in their depictions of dismemberment and death in the circus world. *The Rebel Angels* takes carnival to new depths with the murder of Urquhart McVarish, which involves a literal disembowelling. The later volumes of the Cornish Trilogy suggest that carnival releases the productive force of creative energy through the emergence of works of art from this process of debasement.[24]

While the Salterton novels feature the gaping mouth open for food, drink and song, the bursting and violated nether orifices of the later works are at the centre of proliferating images of debasement. It should not be forgotten, after all, that at the heart of the Saturnalia is the father's devouring of the son. There is violence here, as well as the return of the golden age. Davies' introduction of the incestuous absorption of child by parent is presented in the guise of twentieth-century psychoanalytic terms as the Oedipal and Electra complexes in *Leaven of Malice* and *A Mixture of Frailties*, the latter novel almost entirely structured around scenes from the ancient Saturnalia from the opening funeral wake to the closing feast of the golden ass. In the former scene, allusion to pagan fertility rites, playful unbridled gluttony, costumes evoking the mummers' masquerade—all the elements of the rustic orgy except sexual licence are present, even the illicit brandy.

Festive laughter is trivialized in Ontario where Eros is contained by Thanatos. As we see in *Tempest-Tost*, Rabelais is reduced to child's play, serving as word-hoard, an arsenal of abuse and invective, for the sibling rivalry of young Freddy Webster. Acts of eating replace acts of procreation in the regenerative process. As Bakhtin informs us: "The banquet had the power of liberating the word from the shackles of piousness and fear of God. Everything became open to play and merriment."[25] Music too produces the "free familiar contact"[26] of the carnival, overturning seemingly immutable social hierarchies. In *A Mixture of Frailties*, Davies identifies carnival laughter with the bohemian life of the musician and the revolutionary power of music through the disruptive force of Revelstoke with his upending erotic "catches" and the "anarchy" and "chaos" of his opera.[27]

At the heart of this novel, as in *Tempest-Tost* and the Deptford Trilogy, is an exploration of the relations between imperial power and colony. These are foregrounded in the village festival which celebrates the return of Ramsay to Deptford in *Fifth Business*. There the ideological implications of carnival are played out in the figure of the war hero. Ramsay, as resurrected-from-the-dead winner of the Victoria Cross, goes through two ritual acknowledgements of his bravery: the first in England before the king, when the role of public icon quells his inner awareness of base cowardice; the second in Canada where he is wrenched out of his stasis as symbol into the world of time where he feels "a fool and a fake." Colonial imitations of imperial hierarchies become an uncrowning, focusing on change and becoming as in the thrashing and mockery of the mob around the bonfire at the "antimasque."[28] Carnival laughter this is, for in the ensuing doubled scene, everything is turned upside down: a Red Cross nurse lights the fires of execution as the mob hang and burn the Kaiser in effigy. Deptford's travestying of European powers and wars is at its height in the Roman triumph with which the bonfire begins, when household implements mockingly sound the strains of victory. Everyone except Ramsay, who has experienced the war, takes part in the overthrow of kings and heroes. In his retreat from the North American carnival mob, Ramsay links himself with Boy Staunton, an admirer of kings and colonial imitation of ritual, leaving the role of underworld king in the trilogy to Magnus Eisengrim.

Boy Staunton, who has modelled his life on that of the Prince of Wales and who has become the titular head of the province, is uncrowned in his death in an act of symbolic decapitation when his face is lost in dental plastic in the attempt to make his death mask. (This procedure would detach his head and preserve it as an inanimate object, a monument to the past Boy represents, in violation of the living and becoming body.) As his son David puns, what has happened is "fool-play" not "foul-play,"[29] connecting the circus imagery of the clown to the associations of this travesty of regeneration and under-lining the ominous significance of disguises and masking. The un-crowning of Boy's pretensions, developed through his imitation of British aristocracy and appropriation of a coat of arms, is also played out through David's genealogical research that foregrounds the bas-tardy of the family and produces an alternate family crest that is termed "bum-wipe."[30] Boy has forgotten his nether end, but his son consigns him to the dung heap, reconnecting the family with the living and changing carnivalesque body.

Excrement is associated with all phases of David's becoming in *The Manticore*, most literally in his immersion in the bowels of the earth in the mountain caves where he defecates in his pants. Symbol-ically, however, he also repeats the devil's fart when, at the close of his *amanesis*, he dreams of the father archetype with his trousers down. His opposition to his father, activating "instincts of revolt,"[31] compounds the carnival inversion as in the medieval diableries when the devil's fart, in a travesty of reproduction inverting top and bottom, brought forth more devils. This incident repeats and reinforces the uncrowning of crowned heads carried out by the magician Eisengrim.[32] While he does not actually anoint Boy Staunton with urine, he does besmirch the Crown's representative when he sends him to his muddy death with a stone in his mouth. Significantly, in both these novels, the scatological imagery is introduced through quotations from the Bible[33] which emphasize the necessity of humil-iation for salvation. Davies' enthroning of excrement reaches its apogee in *The Rebel Angels* where Professor Ozy Froats, of the children's nonsense song, is awarded the Nobel Prize for his typology of the human personality according to the composition of its shit. In his burlesque of academic research, Davies expands on his notion of

Holy Shit. Human and divine organs are interwoven into one indissoluble grotesque whole. The limits of the sacred and the profane, of the devouring and the devoured body, are blurred in carnival ambivalence.

The circus is the preeminent carnival site for interweaving imagery of excrement, of sodomy, of hell—the underworld junction where the main lines of the carnival system of images converge. As Bakhtin writes:

> Hell is a banquet and a gay carnival. We find here all the familiar debasing ambivalent images of drenching in urine, beating, travesty, abuse, the downward thrust, inherent in all Rabelaisian images, brings us to underworld, but the underworld also symbolizes this descent.[34]

In Davies' circus underworld are found ambivalent king/slave images of the ancient Saturnalia reworked in the oppressive relationship of Willard and Paul in *The World of Wonders*. This is a world populated by ambivalent carnival figures, such as Paul as Abdullah confounding automaton with human, or Willard as geek blending animal and human. Davies' rich bestiary includes Magnus Eisengrim, as the human being more beastly than the beast, combining the duplicity of the fox as master of ruse with the "unappeasable hunger" of the wolf. The theme of the devourer devoured is inverted when one wolf meets another; Eisengrim, who has acknowledged his wolfish streak, meets Boy Staunton who has masked his.[35] Through Eisengrim's earlier manifestation as Faustus Legrand, the bestiary is connected to the metamorphoses of alchemy and to the demonic pact. Also embodying the ambivalence of the carnival figure are the various hermaphrodites found in the circus, whether gaffed, like Andro in Wanless' World of Wonders, or not, like the Bearded Lady in Le Grand Cirque Forain de St. Vite. Ramsay's discovery of this figure while on a pilgrimage to the shrines of St. Uncumber or Wilgefortis leads to explanations drawing on both the pre-Christian hermaphrodite Great Mother and medical evidence of emotional disturbances producing beards. Both are central to his thesis about the miracle as something that exceeds the powers of understanding: the potential for the sacred is everywhere in the profane and lowly. Paradoxical and excessive, carnivalesque imagery continually disturbs the reader's fixed ideas and hierarchical binaries, preventing the formation of a single, meaning. Through this restructuring potential of the Ontario carnival, Davies wages his struggle against the death-in-life structures of power and propriety.

Bakhtin views such carnivalesque imagery, where ambivalence is sustained in tension even as opposites run into one another exploding boundaries, as only one area where the double-voiced discourse is manifest. More important is the way in which, at the level of artistic representation, the rupture of monological consciousness translates itself into genre poetics. An exploration of this process in Davies' work will lead to a reflection on the conflict in the explicit appropriation of another's discourse and on the evolution of the novel as genre. For Bakhtin, the novel is the preeminent genre because of its open structure. Because the novel is capable of "polyphonic" form, it is in a strategic position to express social and ideological struggles. As such, the novel enfolds within it the discourses of many others, the boundary lines between different languages being flexible and ambiguous. In such "intralanguage heteroglossia," any sense of a unified world view in relation to language—its mythical claims to uniqueness and unity—disappears.

On a macro-level, Bakhtin describes this polyphony in terms of a poetics of quotation, texts being "constructed like mosaics out of the texts of others."[36] Literary history is "the history of the appropriation, re-working and imitation of someone else's property," a history of recontextualizing and refunctioning literary forms; in other words, a history of parody. A prime instance of the explicit appropriation of another's discourse and language is the use made in Euro-American literature of the authoritative and sanctified word of the Bible. This sacred presence raises questions about how the new context relates to it and what sort of intonational frame enfolds it. There is a whole scale of possible relationships, ranging from the isolation of the quotation in a reverential way to the most disrespectful inversion of it. Flexibility and ambiguity of response are more common, however, for the co-presence of two discourses requires the reader to reflect on their potential divergences.

Davies' fiction raises such questions of appropriation through its procedures of embedding and doubling. In *The Rebel Angels*, for example, where there are four scholars in hot pursuit of a manuscript by Rabelais, the reader is forced to reflect on who would make the best use of it. Further questions are raised when Rabelais is quoted in a journal-cum-novel narrated by Simon Darcourt. Would the Rabelais quotations fit more appropriately within the prose of the gypsy girl, Maria, or of her supervisor, the priest Hollier? Or does the thief McVarish, through his ancestor who translated Rabelais, have best claim to him? And what do we make of the transformation of Rabelais from object of study to inspirer of fantasy? *The Rebel Angels* explores the diversity of constructions of academic (intellectual?) desire. There is no doubt that the Rabelais we encounter through each of these perspectives, in dialogue with each of the other perspectives within the novel, is a vastly different one. Similarly, in *A Mixture of Frailties,* the reader is forced to debate the relative claims of Domdaniel and Revelstoke to the opera, *The Golden Asse.* Is it the composer's recontextualization of Apuleius' story that has the greatest validity? Or the interpreter's? Is the cacophony of the former to be preferred to the harmony of the latter? And what about the Salterton Little Theatre version of *The Tempest*? There the drama is played out in the characters' lives, which blurs the barriers between actors and audiences. In each case, the reader of Davies' work must compare the new context given in the fiction to the appropriated text. Davies' fictions contain several such dialogic readings of a classical text within them. By exploring these in light of Bakhtin's theory of the evolution of the novel, we gain insight into Davies' position in the world of Canadian letters, where his mode of "satiric romance" is considered an anomaly.

Contrary to many theorists, Bakhtin roots the modern novel not in the epic, but in Menippean satire. This fictional mode is most fully developed in *The Rebel Angels.* Here we find the short form of the anatomy—the dialogue or the colloquy—used for many of the scenes, especially for the guest nights of the senior common room at Ploughwright College (a fictionalized version of Massey College); the picture on the dust jacket of the published book, however, represents the "angel's roost" at Trinity College. Indeed, an excellent sense of the dialogic mode in Davies' writing may be grasped by comparing that occasion around the banqueting table—which, as Simon Darcourt describes it in "The New Aubrey IV," part 2,[37] accentuates the diversity of academic and secular discourses—with another banquet at the close of the novel, when Maria Theotoky marries Arthur Cornish.[38] No two occasions could be more dissimilar. The first presents its participants with their separate jargons and interests: McVarish and Roberta Burns going at it "hammer and tongs" on the question of love; male and female; literary scholar and zoologist are utterly opposed in their visions of relationships. The second feast presents a heterogeneously mixed crowd attending the wedding of a gypsy with a member of the financial establishment. Social decorum is broken on the second occasion even by the mingling of the sexes. The novel strategically ends with a second guest night colloquy, in order to help us cast our eye backwards, and reflect on the relative collegiality and conviviality of the first banquet. Darcourt reports this last night to be especially "genial." At this point, Roberta and another female academic evoke the memory of the debate of the previous fall. They have the last word against McVarish, who "thought women were lovely creatures whose sexual coals could be blown into warmth by raunchy academic chit-chat. Well, well; one down and a few score around this campus still to go." The male hegemony of the university has been effectively challenged, yet the final words of the evening champion McVarish's "wrenching originality" which seems to be necessary to do "real scholarship." Even as McVarish the man is condemned, McVarish the legend comes to life. For the university has gained two manuscripts from the episode, Rabelais' historic manuscript and the manuscript of Parlabane's novel, rumoured to be nominated for the Nobel Prize. Through both the colloquy form of these scenes and Davies' method of doubling them through repetition, we see the dialogic potential of this fictional mode.

To follow up Davies' many literary allusions is to encounter a veritable catalogue of the genres which Bakhtin describes as coalescing in the formation of Menippean satire. A collection of Davies' early newspaper columns, for example, was organized into sections according to the courses of a dinner and offered to the reader as *The Table Talk of Samuel Marchbanks*: a strategy that recalls one of the oral genres of Roman literature through which were conveyed a number of *contre-partie*, comic fragments to complete a form. These include what Bakhtin calls "parodic-travestying forms: they provided the matter of mimes, satires, epigrams, *table talk*, rhetorical genres, letters."[39] Written as a letter to the headmaster, *Fifth Business* falls within this definition too. One classical model is the Socratic dialogue with its abolition of distance among participants and its dialogic presentation of thought and truth.[40] Davies adapts this form to contemporary philosophical modes in *The Manticore* in the psycho-analytic dialogue which alternates between patient and psychiatrist. Here we find the characteristic testing of an idea and its bearer, central to the Menippean tradition, framed by two traditions, the Classical and the Christian. From the Classical tradition, too, comes Apuleius' *The Golden Asse* in *A Mixture of Frailties*, a model which provides the matter of the opera-within-the-novel and a work which Bakhtin identifies as an embryonic form of "double-voiced" prose.[41] Ancient Christian narrative forms furnish other models. Davies quotes at length from the scenes of crowning and uncrowning in the canonical gospels, especially in *World of Wonders* and *The Rebel Angels*. He also draws on early forms of biography and autobiography, especially on the many classical autobiographical works which arise from the funeral encomium, a civic speech about the inner life. It is undoubtedly St. Augustine's *Confessions*, quoted at length by Davies in *The Rebel Angels*, which is responsible for the confessional mode of the Deptford Trilogy. The three novels share an emphasis on public confession—Ramsay to his headmaster, David to his psychiatrist, Paul to Liesl, Ramsay and Ingestree—which involves each in seeing his/her life from the perspective of a third person, in the double-voiced form of the Menippea. As we have seen in the study of its imagery, the trilogy also focuses on the theme of death which plays a key role in an individual's autobiographical self-consciousness. Certain varieties of hagiography, in which the focus is on the temptation or testing of the saint, on his martyrdom, or on his metamorphosis,[42] were aspects of the Menippea. This tradition actively shapes *Fifth Business*, which is Ramsay's record of the trials of the fool-saint, Mary Dempster, as well as the record of his own metamorphosis into St. Dunstan. Moreover, Davies embeds a number of saints' legends within Ramsay's longer narrative, self-reflexively commenting on this narrative subgenre. I have previously noted the key influence of Rabelais in Davies' work. Then, too, there is his redeployment of the Commedia dell'Arte in the melodrama discussed at length in *World of Wonders*. These models are central to the development of the Menippea in a more recent historical period. Nor does Davies neglect to pay homage to the writer who for Bakhtin most completely embodies this genre in modern times; namely, the great Russian novelist Dostoevsky, to whom Davies' alludes in *World of Wonders* and in *The Rebel Angels*.

But to provide a list of the modes of the Menippea that have shaped Davies' fiction by bringing to it the particular blend of satiric diatribe and romantic focus on becoming, is not to reveal and freeze into literary history the Menippean essence which, according to Bakhtin, resolutely refuses to attach itself to a canonical genre. He writes that "the life of a genre consists of its constantly being reborn and renewed in *original* works."[43] One of the reasons for the vitality of the Menippea is its tendency to self-parody. Indeed, for Bakhtin, this is a most important feature of the modern novel; it is able to incorporate other genres and to criticize them as genres. This contributes to the "destruction of all barriers between genres, between self-enclosed systems of thought, between various styles, etc.,"[44] which is the open structure of carnivalization resulting in the polyphonic novel. An important element of Davies' fiction is the way it parodies other literary genres and—through its recontextualizing and refunctionalizing of them as genres—even parodies the novel itself. Like Stephen Leacock, whom he admires, Davies writes admirable literary parodies; unlike him, however, he also writes serious fiction which expands its own boundaries by incorporating these parodies.

The question of Davies' literary parodies might best be approached through Bakhtin's discussion of quotation, a specific form of allusion. Here the word is appropriated in another's discourse and language, infiltrating the new text which offers a renewed context for it. With a whole spectrum of possible intertextual relationships, the question becomes: "Is the author quoting with reverence or on the contrary with irony, with a smirk?"[45] Is the word set up as an icon, or is it a travestying double entendre? Davies' appropriation of other genres or words conveys the whole range of possibilities at once. We have already explored the complex use of allusion in *A Mixture of Frailties*, with respect to Rabelais' Lantern Land, where the words quoted give a meaning opposed to their literal content, but where the contextual meaning of *Lantern*—the activities of its editors—continues the original meaning. But the impact of such activity is defamiliarization: to make us aware of the word from the outside and to question, rather than automatically accept, its meaning. It is in just this way that Davies' parody of genres opens up the accepted meaning of a genre to new possibilities.

Nowhere is this clearer than in his rewriting of Shakespeare's *The Tempest*, which transports the play from distant England and the

Renaissance to involvement with the here and now (twentieth-century Ontario), moving it from the stage to the carnival. In casting his characters, Davies plays on both similarities and differences to take the play off the stage and into the characters' lives. Prospero and Miranda, when transferred in time and place, are real father and daughter, but Prospero's omnipotence is cast in a more malignant light under the shadow of the Oedipal complex. Similarly, the Canadian Ariel is not an ethereal and dutiful spirit, but the independent, down-to-earth, local heiress, Griselda. Hector is chosen for the role of Gonzalo, the councillor, because he is perceived to be very serious and reliable. Instead, he becomes a fool in love and lets the play down with his attempted suicide. Davies' version of *The Tempest*, moreover, is narrative, not poetry or drama, which constitutes a veritable challenge to the established literary tradition. The word from the past is no icon, but it nonetheless illuminates and adds stature to the present by pointing out the preeminent role of fiction in our time.

In like fashion, Davies travesties other genres and opens them up for our active scrutiny and for new development. Apuleius' romance *The Golden Asse* is translated into an opera in *A Mixture of Frailties*, a metamorphosis which underlines its basis in romance. Almost none of the action is conveyed to us: as audience we are again involved in behind-the-scenes activity and distance from the stage is abolished. However, we are made all the more conscious of the opera's reliance on the beauty of voices when such sounds are absent. That they are burlesqued makes the distant music somewhat audible. We are not duped by the critics' enthusiasm for the tenor's braying throughout the entire second act; however, we hear the words through this double focus. This opera resonates as a double entendre throughout the novel, whose plot follows a mode of evolution similar to Apuleius' with the descent of its centre section.

I could elaborate at length on such connections and reversals in Davies' work that draw attention to the characteristics of both the appropriated genre and the fictional envelope. Ramsay's letter to the headmaster in *Fifth Business* is one example: it disrupts our notions of fragmentary form by its excessive length, even as it enfolds the letter into the fiction. In *The Rebel Angels*, such self-referentiality becomes increasingly complex with the intersection of several fictional genres. Davies' novel builds on Aubrey's *Brief Lives*, which is Darcourt's model for writing biographies and gossiping about his colleagues. It also develops in the direction of Parlabane's lengthy "roman philosophique," though it is not boring, being enlivened by the input of Rabelais. As well, through Parlabane's murder of McTavish, the novel travesties Dostoevsky's preoccupation with crime in a world that Davies qualifies as "topsy-turveydom."[46] Transformed by their superimposition, the whole is greater than any of these parts. In *World of Wonders*, nineteenth-century melodrama functions in similar double fashion. Throughout Davies' fiction, the bawdy songs which seem to be folklore open the novels in this direction.

Davies is very much aware of the difficulty of saying anything new in the face of tradition and authority. Drawing on the writers of the past, he is engaged in an originating act of parricide, both killing them off, to make way for something new, and enthroning the figure of authority. His awareness of this paradox is most forcefully stated in the case of Lawyer Snelgrove in *Leaven of Malice*, a case "in which Nature imitates Art":

> In the nineteenth century it appears that many lawyers were dry and fusty men, of formal manner and formal dress, who carried much of the deportment of the courtroom into private life. Novelists and playwrights, observing this fact, put many such lawyers into their books and upon the stage. Actors deficient in observation and resource adopted this stock character of the Lawyer, and he was to be seen in hundreds of plays. And Matthew Snelgrove, whose professional and personal character was being formed about the turn of the century, seized upon this lawyer-like shell eagerly, and made it his own. Through the years he perfected his impersonation until, as he confronted Professor Vambrace, he was not only a lawyer in reality, but also a lawyer in a score of stagey mannerisms.[47]

In this character, Davies parodies his own use of stock figures through an interesting twist that makes us aware of the stereotype, even as it renews its implications by inverting the usual pattern of life shaping art into art moulding life. This seems to be a direction taken by his own creative imagination.

A parody which probes deeper into the creative act is Davies' burlesque of the autobiographical genre, "The Double Life of Robertson Davies," purportedly written by his persona, Samuel

Marchbanks. Again, fiction precedes life: the novelist does not set up his mirror to nature but works from literary conventions. Here too, Davies is exposing the ways in which these opposing poles of experience merge within the individual creative mind. For while Marchbanks is a mask for Davies, Davies, it would appear from this autobiography, is a stand-in for Marchbanks, someone who will take his place on the scaffold or public arena at risk of being attacked, should the occasion warrant. Public versus private, youth versus age, a number of oppositions are conveyed through this double:

> He was born in Western Ontario, in the village of Thamesville, on August 28, 1913. I am a good deal older than this, and do not mind being mistaken for one so much my junior. It must be said, however, that Davies looks older than his years, and the fact that some of my sayings and doings are attributed to him may account for his gray hair and occasional air of fatigue.[48]

Renewing autobiography through this use of the *Doppelgänger*, Davies emphasizes the shared elements of the characters, the way one pole moves toward the other in what is clearly the other within the self. Making the mask explicit, instead of hiding behind it, Davies draws attention to a feature of his technique of characterization. All the characters are at some level or another his doubles: the distance between author and character is abolished in favour of a continually shifting relationship. In its emphasis on the one and the other—the one in the other—the theme of the double reinforces the carnival theme of the mask.

Doubling is important in another aspect of Davies' characterization. Many of his characters are doubles of each other. The ideal character is the one who contains the oppositions within himself, like that reprobate guide to the old man's God, Padre Blazon. He is, as his name suggests, a blazon: that is "a continuous praise or constant abuse of the object to be blazoned...both the hideous and beautiful, the bad and the good can be equally well blazoned."[49] When the carnivalesque duality is not yet present in the characters, opposing values may be distributed among two or more of them arranged in a triangular relationship. An example of this is the opposition of Dunstan Ramsay and Boy Staunton, private and public, spirit and body, who are involved with the same woman, Leola. Davies underlines the closeness of their ties and the way in which one identity merges with another. A similar triangle develops in *A Mixture of Frailties* involving Monica, Domdaniel and Revelstoke, oppositions of serenity and chaos, sacred and profane, age and youth. The development of parallels, as we noted, led Davies to repeat sections of the text or create look-alike scenes. Consequently, the plotting of his novel breaks sequence, as his fictions double back on themselves.

This characteristic is an important technical feature of carnivalization. As Julia Kristeva interprets it, the "dialogue" is encountered in symbolic and analogical relationships rather than in those of "substance-causalité." Such structural principles have become the organizing features of much modernist fiction exhibiting the carnivalesque, especially the works of Joyce. Even a superficial comparison of Davies' fiction with these works reveals a wide gap between their abrupt juxtapositions in the manner of collage and his more traditional causal linking of sentences, incidents and chapters. While Davies' fiction does exhibit the characteristics Kristeva identifies with the Bakhtinian term "dialogic," namely the double, language and a different logic, they are mainly evident in the imagery and characterization of his works and not in the broader frame of their internal construction, though the intertextual dialogue of parody moves towards the polyphonic novel.[50]

Indeed, the term "monologue" has been attached to Davies' work by Stephen Bonnycastle. Though he is not using it in the precise Bakhtinian sense, Bonnycastle equates monologue with the creation of absolutes and the establishment of hierarchies which, he argues, is what Davies is doing in *Fifth Business* and *The Manticore*, despite claims for openness and ambiguity. As Bonnycastle aptly remarks, the title *Fifth Business* introduces "the principle of relational identity" in morality, and with it that of "dialogue or dialectic" as the appropriate manner of instruction to convey it. He believes, however, that the extended letter of the teacher, Ramsay, is a monologue that does not overturn the established hierarchies, but sets up new ones:

> For the reader interested in morality this shift from relative to absolute standards poses a problem. The principle of relational identity is regularly used to dethrone false absolutes in a pupil's life and revolutionize his thinking, but how are false absolutes to be distinguished from real absolutes? The novels provide no answer to this difficult question. Liesl uses the principle of relational

identity at her discretion, and this makes it seem a rhetorical
weapon rather than a principle of knowledge.

The key issues here are the question of the teacher's monologue
as a principle of instruction and the role of magic, not reason, in
conveying it. These are important knots in the argument, which can
be unravelled, even while recognizing that there is validity in
Bonnycastle's conclusion that "monologue is a sign that a character
has triumphed: he has turned his companions into an audience."[51]
What Davies does is to develop the pattern of ambivalence in the
carnivalized imagery and the contradictions and ambiguities within
his characters, to guide the reader to the very critique of the monologue that Bonnycastle provides.

Although the characters are long-winded, the contexts in which
they deliver their monologues establish the desirability of a response.
Silence is an effective critique of monologue; indeed, it constitutes an
opening for the other through which his view may make itself felt.
Witness the way in which Solly Bridgetower's extended monologue,
a parody of a formal university lecture, is received. While delivering
it, he is sharing a bed with Humphrey Cobbler and his wife, talking
and drinking. This is a decidedly innovative context for such a lecture,
and it serves the purpose of isolating the specificities and limitations
of the academic mode. Solly's words are greeted with silence as his
audience falls asleep. The context establishes the norm of exchange:
when Solly violates it, his audience abandons him.

In similar fashion, the fact that Boy Staunton is dead and doesn't
have the opportunity to add the last word to *Fifth Business* is not a
problem: the reader fills in the missing text that is Staunton's version
of the story. Indeed, we are invited to do so by the epistolary form,
which presupposes an answer. Then again, the audience is directly
addressed as "you" throughout the novel, enjoined to abandon habitual
readerly distance and participate in the creation of the text. Although
the "you" of the apostrophe is specifically attached to the headmaster
by the opening introduction, the reader forgets this as the novel
unfolds, responding to the direct address in his/her own person.
Moreover, the later volumes of the trilogy specifically provide other
perspectives against which we can judge Ramsay's version, and not
the whole story. It is merely a fragment in a greater whole that is in
constant flux and therefore open to new interpretations. This principle

is explicitly explored in *World of Wonders*, when Eisengrim's story of the film of the life of Houdini is presented as subtext to text. Davies' own novel is obviously a rewriting of Robert-Houdin's *Confidences d'un prestidigitateur* which, in incorporating it, raises questions about the novelist's sleights of hand that dazzle us with their illusions.

The question of the relational principle of dialogue, is raised also in the direct confrontations between Liesl and Eisengrim regarding their meeting. Here Liesl jumps into the discussion and gives her version of the events, just as both Ingestree and Eisengrim present us with their stories. The authority of the narrator is undermined by their opposing versions of Eisengrim. In the one he toadies to Sir John, while in the other he emulates him.[52] As Eisengrim sums up the situation in a clear enunciation of the carnivalesque: "There are double words for everything." Davies' use of intercutting limited points of view gives perspective and objectivity while remaining myopic and self-centered. In *The Rebel Angels* he uses this narrative principle again, reflecting events sometimes from the world view of Darcourt, a priest, at other times from that of gypsy Maria, a student of the Renaissance and the alchemists, and both of these are seen from the position of authority and that of popular carnival. In doing so, he opens up the interpretations of incidents to many possibilities. As the reader becomes aware, in considering, for example, conflicting views about Froats' research, oppositions cancel each other out but the book contains them both. There is no single authoritative vision of truth. The author becomes a liar, through self-referential paradox, or else becomes an arranger and organizer of conflicting positions. In either case, the artifice of fiction is unmasked, the realistic illusion destroyed.

The other issues Bonnycastle addresses are those of magic and the power of deception which seem to reside in Eisengrim and by extension in any creative authority. This is a very complex issue, for Eisengrim explicitly mentions that he must have power over his audience in order to effect the hypnosis that will make us all believe he is really sawing the lady in half. "I can't see my audience, and what I can't see I can't dominate. And what I can't dominate I can't enchant, and humour, and make partners in their own deceptions."[53] Yet the last phrase, with the word "partners," suggests a relationship of equals, not one of hierarchies. This contradictory view is expanded in a passage where Zingara teaches Eisengrim how to hypnotize. She stresses the need to be a friend and not to look "domineering hard." The "real art" occurs when you "look at them as if it was a long time since you met an equal.... You got to be wide open to them, or else they won't be wide open to you."[54] Ramsay tells us, though, that Eisengrim hypnotizes without "robbing of...professional dignity." In the talk about hypnotism Eisengrim gives at Ramsay's school, he emphasizes "the fact that nobody can be made to do anything under hypnotism that is contrary to his wishes."[55] One must be a participant in the illusion, or it cannot take place. And it is in this way that the actor/spectator relationship is broken down in the circus, though the actor maintains some extra dimension to himself that simultaneously establishes distance.

By implication, specifically in *World of Wonders*, the illusions of cinema and literature are sustained in similar fashion. The audience must participate willingly, be invited into the book as a friend, or the dialogue will not take place. Eisengrim suggests several ways in which such friendly intercourse may be established. And the two trilogies effectively provide models of such interactions between author and reader. The first is established by convention: when we go to a magic show, we expect to see illusions. We go to be enchanted. Literary conventions also provide us with expectations for enchantment. In the case of *Tempest-Tost*, these conventions are explicitly involved because the text parodied is one that features a master of illusion: Prospero. This knowledge on the part of the audience is what Eisengrim imparts to schoolboys, paying them "the compliment of treating them seriously."[56] The direct address to the audience, the laying bare of the tricks of his trade, including the creation of his masks and disguises—these are all means by which Davies takes the reader into his confidence and instructs him/her how to read his books. Indeed, by focusing his narrative directly on the nature of illusion, as he has in the Deptford Trilogy, Davies exposes his fictional world for what it is—fiction. This self-reflexivity implicitly erects frames around the art object, and allows us to speculate on its meaning in other contexts.

The ability to be both inside and outside the frame, both represented and representing, is central to the functioning of the dialogic imagination. In the novel it may be located in language, where the images of another's outlook and world may be represented simultaneously. There is no unitary language within the dialogic novel, but rather a system of languages of "intersecting planes." As Bakhtin writes: the "novel breaks down into images of languages that are connected to one another and with the author via their own character-istic dialogical relationships. These languages are, in the main, the period-bound, generic and common everyday varieties of the epoch's literary language." "Represented precisely as a living mix of varied and opposing voices...developing and renewing itself," drawing from the "crudely obvious, vulgar contradictions between folk and other languages, literary language seeks to overcome moribund 'literariness'."[57] We have seen how Davies exploits such intersecting planes with the "blasphemous" way in which he uses biblical lan-guage. When taken out of its original context, meaning shifts and opens new possibilities. Foreign languages have the same potential for renewing language, a fact of which Davies is very much aware. In *World of Wonders*, for example, he includes a passage where Paul Dempster, alias Jules Legrand, talks about the way in which the Bible is defamiliarized and prompts new interpretations when he reads it in French.

> That was a surprise for me! Like so many English-speaking people I could not conceive of the words of Christ in any language but my own, but as we worked through *Le Nouveau Testament* in her chunky old Geneva Bible, there they were, coloured quite differ-ently. *Je suis le chemin, la vérité, la vie; nul ne vient au Père sinon par moi* sounded curiously frivolous, but nothing to *Bienheureux sont les débonnaires: car ils hériteront la terre*. I thought I concealed the surprise in my voice at that one, but Milady heard it (she heard everything) and explained that I must think of *débonnaire* as meaning *clément*, or perhaps *les doux*. But of course we all interpret Holy Writ to suit ourselves as much as we dare.[58]

Any language filtered through an ideolect takes on new resonances of meaning, and disrupts the clichés of authority.

Davies makes relatively little use of foreign languages to disrupt our perception—a bit of medieval Latin in *The Rebel Angels* and *The Manticore* for different colouring, but he continually plays with the novel's possibilities for developing intersecting planes in the special-ized languages of professions, occupations, and classes. *The Rebel Angels*, for instance, through quotation and illusion simultaneously represents the language of the alchemists, the Bible, the university—

with all its divergent disciplines—and the gypsy; while *World of Wonders* includes the specialized jargon of the theatre, the cinema and the clockmaker. Individual characters also speak with forked tongues, as we see in the case of Professor Spencer, whose speech on social Darwinism includes a mispronounced French word—"Cream Passional"[59]—from another social level, a slip which lays bare his pretensions and the hidden agenda of the position he is advocating. Paul Dempster's language is "illiterate carnival slang" with a sprinkling of "Biblical turn[s] of speech."[60] *Fifth Business* mixes the language of politics, fundamental Christianity, and the hagiographer—including the detail of the Bollandists' purple ink—and of the circus. Indeed it is the richness and variety, the incongruities of the juxtapositions, that characterize the heterogeneity of Davies' novels. *The Manticore* explores the gaps between the intellectual world of the legal institutions and the intuitive world of the psyche by employing the very specific terminology of Jungian psychoanalysis. The result is undoubtedly Davies' most thorough investigation of the manifold world perspectives opened up through specialized jargons.

The dialogism is most prominent in the Deptford Trilogy, where the incongruities are greater. Nonetheless, in Davies' earlier writing we find great attention paid to the specialized language of music and a superficial contrast between Canadian speech and English speech in *A Mixture of Frailties*. The jargons of journalism, academic literary criticism and the law coexist in *Leaven of Malice*. In these two novels as well, we find a careful study of the linguistic differences between classes in the delineation of Mrs. Gall and Mrs. Little, whose reported dialogue is filtered through an ear attentive to the nuances of the lower middle class.

For Bakhtin, this attention paid to the speech of the people and to its vulgarities is a prime means of renewing literary discourse. Davies might have extended his fictional treatment of these features, for although the bawdy joke or innuendo is everywhere reported to have occurred in his fiction, in relatively few cases is it actually quoted. Rabelaisian obscenities are censored on the tongues of Freddy Webster and Giles Revelstoke. Indeed the crudest expression in Davies' work is the benign "What balls!"[61] from the tongue of Ingestree. More frequently, Davies relies on innuendo and context for his effect, much of which occurs in song, where it appears to have passed the censors' ears more easily than their eyes. Here we strike at the heart of Davies' interest in parody and innuendo. His censors are not political, like Bakhtin's or Rabelais, but moral—Ontario philistines. There is nothing explicit in the version of the hymn sung to the Fat Woman, Hannah:

> Wash me in the water
> > That you washed the baby in,
> And I shall be whiter
> > Than the whitewash on the wall.[62]

The reader must work on the intersection of words and context to fill in the crude sexual jibe. However, this call on the co-operative interpretive powers of the reader restores dialogism on another level, in the interaction of the other (the you) within the text of the writing "I."

In this regard, Davies' extensive use of punning is an example of the dialogic imagination at work. Occurring throughout his work, the puns range from the carefully explained "Hoor yuh today, Paul?"[63]— an insult hurled by the village children to the young Paul Dempster—to the carefully hidden "furbelow" of Revelstoke's "Catch."[64] Here the bawdy enters in covert fashion, though in keeping with the carnival logic of inversion and the principle of the one within the other. For Davies, words have several coexisting meanings, some of praise and some of abuse. The aim of his writing is to point out the way in which the one meaning is constantly running into the other.

The very language of his fiction is shaped by his aesthetic of ambivalence, of paradox. Decorum, though, weighs more heavily on language than on imagery, limiting the extent of formal dislocation in Davies' work. Under the highlighting eye of the dialogic imagination, which brings together within the same text the intersecting planes of the French Renaissance, of Marxist Russia and of Calvinist Ontario, a carnivalesque element of Davies' writing emerges. The shifting horizon offered by such a multiplicity of perspectives illuminates the heterogeneity that is a characteristic of Robertson Davies' fictional world.

# Notes

1 Northrop Frye, *Divisions on a Ground: Essays on Canadian Culture* (Toronto: Anansi, 1982), p. 24

2 Mikhail M. Bakhtin, *The Formal Method in Literary Scholarship*. Trans. Albert J. Wehrle. Foreword by Wlad Godzich (Cambridge: Harvard University Press, 1985), p. 128.

3 Mikhail M. Bakhtin, *The Dialogic Imagination: Four Essays*. Trans. Caryl Emerson and Michael Holquist; ed. Michael Holquist (Austin: University of Texas Press, 1981), p. 393.

4 *Ibid.*, p. 263.

5 Bakhtin, *Formal*, p. 159.

6 Bakhtin, *Dialogic*, p. 61.

7 *Ibid.*, p. 62.

8 *Ibid.*, p. 377.

9 *Ibid.*, p. 427.

10 Mikhail M. Bakhtin, *Speech Genres and Other Late Essays*. Trans. Vern W. McGee (Austin: University of Texas Press, 1986), p. 147.

11 Peter Stallybrass and Allon White, *The Politics and Poetics of Transgression* (Ithaca: Cornell University Press, 1986), p. 196.

12 Bakhtin, *Dialogic*, pp. 67, 430: "Within a language...the problem of internal differentiation, the stratification characteristic of any national language." "Polyglossia" is the co-presence within a culture of multiple languages.

13 Bakhtin, *Formal*, pp. 3, 95, 154.

14 *Ibid.*, p. xiii.

15 *Ibid.*, pp. 7-8.

16 Mikhail M. Bakhtin, *Problems of Dostoevsky's Poetics*. Trans. R.W. Rotsel (Ann Arbor: Ardis, 1973), p. 195-96.

17 For a more lengthy treatment of carnivalesque, see my "World of Wonders: Robertson Davies Carnival," *Essays in Canadian Writing* 30 (Winter 1985-85), pp. 239-86.

18 Bakhtin, *Dostoevsky*, p. 100.

19 *Ibid.*, pp. 148-49.

20 Mikhail M. Bakhtin, *Rabelais and His World*. Trans. Helen Iswolsky (Cambridge: MIT Press, 1965), pp. 4-5, 9, 11.

21 Bakhtin, *Dostoevsky*, pp. 100, 148-49.

22 Davies' interest in the construction of "psychological" masks or personae, the representation of the self to another, is what Bakhtin terms a testing of the protagonist's discourse. (See Bakhtin, *Dialogic* p. 388.) The novels put on trial a variety of forms used in life and art to represent events or emotions. Bakhtin's comment on this self-reflexive element in fiction is instructive:

"The language of the novel is not merely represented, it serves in turn as an object of representation. The word of the novel is always self-critical." See Bakhtin, *Aesthétique et théorie du roman* (Paris: Seuil, 1978), p. 409.

23 Bakhtin, *Rabelais*, p. 169.

24 For a detailed study of doubling in this trilogy, see Cecilia Coulas, "Doubles and Doubling in the Novels of Robertson Davies," Ph.D. Dissertation, York University, 1989.

25 Bakhtin, *Rabelais*, p. 28.

26 Bakhtin, *Dostoevsky*, p. 100.

27 Robertson Davies, *A Mixture of Frailties* (Harmondsworth: Penguin, 1980), p. 327.

28 Robertson Davies, *Fifth Business* (New York: Signet, 1974), pp. 91-92.

29 Robertson Davies, *The Manticore* (New York: Viking, 1972), p. 36.

30 *Ibid.*, p.214.

31 *Ibid.*, p. 237.

32 Robertson Davies, *World of Wonders* (Toronto: Macmillan, 1975), p. 121.

33 *Ibid.*, p. 102; *Manticore*, p. 237.

34 Bakhtin, *Rabelais*, p. 39.

35 Davies, *Manticore*, pp. 347, 349.

36 Bakhtin, *Dialogic*, p. 69.

37 Robertson Davies, *The Rebel Angels* (Toronto: Macmillan, 1981), p. 167-90.

38 *Ibid.*, pp. 315-25.

39 Bakhtin, *Dialogic*, p. 58, emphasis added.

40 Bakhtin, *Dostoevsky*, p. 109.

41 *Ibid.*, p. 371.

42 *Ibid.*, pp. 11, 112.

43 *Ibid.*, p. 117, emphasis added.

44 *Ibid.*, p. 111.

45 Bakhtin, *Dialogic*, p. 69.

46 Davies, *Rebel*, p. 57.

47 Robertson Davies, *Leaven of Malice* (Toronto: Clarke Irwin, 1964), p. 72.

48 Robertson Davies, "The Double Life of Robertson Davies, " *Canadian Anthology*. Eds. Carl F. Klink and Reginald E. Watters (Toronto: Gage, 1966), P. 394.

49 Bakhtin, *Rabelais*, p. 487.

50 Julia Kristeva, "Bakhtine, le mot, le dialogue, et le roman," *Critique*, 23-239 (1967), p. 447.

51 Stephen Bonnycastle, "Robertson Davies and the Ethics of Monologue," *Journal of Canadian Studies*, Vol. 12, No. 1 (1977), pp. 20, 22, 31, 39.

52  Davies, *World*, p. 237.

53  *Ibid.*, p. 5.

54  *Ibid.*, p. 128.

55  Davies, *Fifth Business*, p. 227.

56  *Ibid.*

57  Bakhtin, *Dialogic*, pp. 47-49.

58  Davies, *World*, p. 58.

59  *Ibid.*, p. 134.

60  *Ibid.*, p. 139.

61  *Ibid.*, p. 268.

62  *Ibid.*, p. 78.

63  Davies, *Fifth Business*, p. 96.

64  Davies, *Mixture*, p. 317.

# The Liar of Orpheus: Framing Devices and Narrative Structure in Robertson Davies' Cornish Trilogy

*Ian Munro*

"Look here; it is, as you see, a triptych, an altarpiece of fair size in three panels.... Clean it, right down to the wood, and go to work."[1]

## I

There is a tendency among critics of Canadian literature to consider Robertson Davies as a sort of literary anachronism, a traditionalist determined to preserve a late nineteenth century perspective in his writing. As Janice Kulyk-Keefer remarked in *Books in Canada* upon the publication of *The Lyre of Orpheus*, "to compare Robertson Davies to the Victorians rather than to the Moderns is appropriate enough, given his affection for nineteenth-century melodrama."[2] David Lodge has in fact used Davies as a stick with which to beat the "postmodern" aesthetic:

> Certainly there is at present a lull, indicating either exhaustion or disillusionment, in the polemical and creative struggles of postmodernism, and a literary climate, therefore, receptive to the old-fashioned pleasures of texts like *What's Bred in the Bone* and *The Lyre of Orpheus*.[3]

This opinion of Davies is widespread; he is seen primarily as a popular but old-fashioned writer, cranking out entertaining yet conventional novels which display not only a Victorian morality but also a Victorian transparency of literary motive.

It is true that the novels encourage such a misreading, but I disagree strongly with Lodge's assertion that Davies' writing "is all done in a style hallowed by traditional literary convention, and does not in any way subvert or challenge ways of reading derived from the classic realist text." When one analyzes the techniques and devices through which Davies constructs his work, a different writer emerges, one whose writing thrives on the ambivalence and incompleteness which characterize the postmodern text.

My analysis will focus on Davies' recently completed work, the Cornish Trilogy. This trilogy seems to derive its title from two sources. On the one hand, it is the name of two of the trilogy's protagonists, Francis and Arthur Cornish. However, it is also very close to the word "cornice" (Tancred Saraceni addresses Francis as "Corniche," which is French for "cornice"). One meaning of "cornice" is "frame," as in a picture frame, and it is Davies' use of framing devices that I would like to explore.

The framing device I wish to focus on is Francis Cornish's painting, "The Marriage at Cana," which acts as a paradigm for the entire work. This painting is not introduced until the second book, *What's Bred in the Bone,* which reflects the spatial form of the trilogy. In fact, the trilogy is mimetic of "The Marriage at Cana;" it is structured as a triptych, with the side panels (*The Rebel Angels* and *The Lyre of Orpheus*) acting as supplements to the focal panel *What's Bred in the Bone*), thus allowing a reading from the middle outwards, examining the formal relationships among the three novels.

*What's Bred in the Bone* is the retelling of the life story of Francis Cornish, wealthy art collector and connoisseur. At the beginning of the novel, Simon Darcourt's inability to complete a biography of Francis Cornish draws the attention of two celestial beings, Zadkiel and Maimas. Zadkiel is the Angel of Biography, an assistant to the Recording Angel who preserves the history of the world. Maimas is a daimon, a supernatural entity whose task it is to shape the lives of those marked for a special destiny, such as Francis. Prompted by Darcourt's frustration, the two decide to review the life of Francis, beginning before his birth with his family in Blairlogie, Ontario and ending with his death. Much of their narrative concerns Francis' time in the German castle of Düsterstein, where he worked as an apprentice to the great art restorer Tancred Saraceni, and where he created the work which demonstrated his special destiny.

"The Marriage at Cana" is Francis Cornish's masterpiece, in the literal sense of the word: it signifies the end of his apprenticeship to Tancred Saraceni. The painting is an allegorically rich rendering of the biblical marriage at which Christ turned water into wine (also his masterpiece, in a way, it being his first miracle). Francis populates the painting with all the people who have been important in his life, all the people, in fact, who have played significant roles in the novel. At this point the novel and the painting become one; the relationships between Francis and the rest of the characters are formalized in paint as well as ink. This transformation is more easily comprehended if one keeps in mind that we are already dealing with a formal artifact within this novel; we are being read something from the back files of the Recording Angel. Thus the story of Francis' life is complete before it is related to the reader, thereby emphasizing the atemporal aspect of the novel, and increasing the artificiality of the narrative.

"The Marriage at Cana" acts as a framing device, drawing all the significant threads of the novel into one cohesive tapestry. The painting furthermore allegorizes Cornish, creating his character through an aesthetic construct. Francis Cornish has the people of "The Marriage at Cana" inside him; they are the ones who have formed his life and soul. As his name suggests, Cornish is the frame of the trilogy, and his myth (concretized in "The Marriage at Cana") is the root of the trilogy, spreading outwards into both *The Rebel Angels* and *The Lyre of Orpheus*.

However, *What's Bred in the Bone* ends on a decidedly unfinished note. Francis Cornish is dead, descended into the Realm of the Mothers, but he is not yet remarkable or famous, and Maimas states at the end of the novel, "my task is not yet finished."[4] It is for the other two novels, both working inwards, to simultaneously finish and undermine the work of the Daimon.

The other two novels in the trilogy draw their existence from *What's Bred in the Bone* through the notoriously eclectic collection of Francis Cornish, which has two significant offspring: the "Gryphius MS" of Rabelais and the incomplete score of E.T.A. Hoffmann's Arthurian opera. These two artifacts inform *The Rebel Angels* and *The Lyre of Orpheus* respectively. These side panels of the triptych (trilogy) are ranged along the axis of the most embedded opposition in the trilogy: completion and unravelling. Though elements of both occur in all three novels, at one level the purpose of *The Lyre of Orpheus* is to complete the myth of Francis Cornish, while the purpose of *The Rebel Angels*, paradoxically (or significantly) placed at the beginning of the trilogy, is to undercut it, to unravel the mythic tapestry the trilogy produces. The confusion of this dynamic can be minimized if one keeps in mind the spatial and atemporal form of the trilogy. The trilogy works as a synchronic whole; *The Rebel Angels* is not privileged because of its position, and it is not paradoxical that it unravels something which it precedes diachronically. These ideas are worked out in detail below. For now, I will continue my analysis with *The Lyre of Orpheus*, examining the ways in which it completes the myth of Francis Cornish, yet at the same time remembering the unravelling energy of *The Rebel Angels*.

There are two main plots, distinct but not completely separate, at work in *The Lyre of Orpheus*. The first concerns Hoffmann's opera, *Arthur of Britain, or The Magnanimous Cuckold*. Hulda Schnackenburg is attempting to complete the opera in order to earn her doctorate (her own masterpiece, which therefore on a formal level imitates "The Marriage at Cana"). Furthermore, Hoffmann himself also wants Hulda to complete it, unbeknownst to her, for its completion will allow him to leave Limbo. Finally, the plot of the opera closely parallels the mythical adultery of Maria Cornish (wife of Arthur Cornish) with Geraint Powell (best friend of Arthur Cornish), a situation whose successful resolution is ultimately dependent on the euphonic libretto Darcourt pastiches for the opera.

The second plot concerns Darcourt's biography of Francis Cornish, which is commissioned by the Cornish Foundation. Darcourt's search for information is energized by a tarot reading done for him by Maria's mother, which delineates not only his quest, but also the quest of the opera, implicating many of the important characters in the novel. This tarot reading and the opera (with its libretto) act as framing devices in *The Lyre of Orpheus* in much the same manner as "The Marriage at Cana" does in *What's Bred in the Bone*.

This is indicated by the way Arthur, Maria and Geraint are reconciled through the opera, in particular through Darcourt's libretto. Because of the way the two plots conjoin, one is given the impression that the successful resolution of the triangle the three find themselves in is dependent on the successful completion of the libretto by Darcourt. The opera is therefore an extremely strong framing device, explicating the novel in an obvious fashion. This has caused criticism in some reviews, notably from Kulyk-Keefer:

> How can we not know well before the characters do that Maria will be seduced by her Lancelot?... Davies seems to think that Maria's adultery and Arthur's infertility will strike the reader as enormous and persuasive surprises rather than wrenchings of the narrative to fit the overly schematic plot he's designed.[5]

However, it is this very artificiality that Davies is aiming for; he is encouraging the sort of reading Kulyk-Keefer favours.

The framing action of the tarot reading works in a different manner. In *The Castle of Crossed Destinies*, Italo Calvino uses a tarot deck to write stories. Exploiting the emblematic features of the cards, he develops storylines from the images evoked by the arbitrary placing of one card beside another. What emerges from this interplay is myth; Calvino conjures up the stories of Arthur, Roland, Faust, Don Juan, etc. This sort of mythmaking is what the tarot accomplishes in *The Lyre of Orpheus*. By "predicting" the destiny of characters, the tarot reading forces a formal structure onto the plots of those characters. Just as the arbitrary placing of one card beside the next seems to automatically engender myth, so do the "arbitrary" events of the characters' lives cohere to the mythic frame. A rather outdated expression which occurs several times in the novel is "according to Hoyle," meaning to play by the rules. The phrase refers to Hoyle's famous rules for card games, thus indicating the influence of cards upon the events of the novel. It is also significant that Hoyle is the last name of Zadok, who, as the unwitting father of Francis the First, initiates much of the action of *What's Bred in the Bone* (and therefore the whole trilogy).

Unlike the opera, which deals in specifics, the tarot reading frames the plot in a loose, thematic manner, including the opera itself within its scope of interpretation. Even those cards which are directly associated with characters are not restricted to the plots of those characters. Davies conceives of something larger and deeper for the tarot; he sees it as an emblem of the Collective Unconscious, replete with archetypes and Jungian symbolism, a representation of the deep well from which myths such as those of the opera can spring, much as Calvino uses the deck to create his myths.

It is apparent that the two framing devices, the opera and the tarot, do not separate the novel between them; their influence on the narrative overlaps. This is also true from a symbolic perspective: the two frames interconnect and synthesize at the level of myth. Jessie Weston, in *From Ritual to Romance*, suggests that the four suits of the tarot (cups, wands, swords and pentangles) are representations of the four life symbols (the cup, lance, sword and dish) which play an important part in the Grail legend.[6] There is a deeper significance to the symbolic aspect of the frames, however. The Grail or Arthurian legend itself, by Weston's analysis (which draws heavily on Frazer's *The Golden Bough*), derives from Mediterranean fertility rites of death and resurrection, one major example of which are the so-called Orphic mysteries; as Weston notes, "we can now prove by printed texts the parallels existing between each and every feature of the Grail story and the recorded symbolism of the Mystery cults."[7] This ties in wonderfully with the title of the novel, *The Lyre of Orpheus*, and the myth of Francis Cornish can at last be identified.

Francis is, in mythic terms, Orpheus. An artist of extraordinary gifts, late in his life he has a meaningful relationship with Aylwin Ross (his Eurydice), who dies through poison (albeit by his own hand). At the end of his own life, Francis descends to a supernatural place called "the Realm of the Mothers,"[8] a phrase whose connotations conjure up a sort of Jungian Avernus. Simon Darcourt then unearths "The Marriage at Cana," and discovers its significance by examining photographs of the people it depicts. In a literal sense of the word, Darcourt "dismembers" the painting; once unequivocally identified as Tancred Saraceni, for example, the red-haired figure in the painting can no longer be considered Judas. It is due to this analysis of the painting that Darcourt is able to set up the Francis Cornish Gallery and publish his biography. On a symbolic level, then, Darcourt rips apart Francis Cornish, and as a result immortalizes him, thereby completing his myth. I will return to discuss the highly ambiguous nature of this completion after an analysis of *The Rebel Angels*.

Turning now to the first novel in the trilogy, we find it is constructed in opposition to the highly schematic, heavily plotted *The Lyre of Orpheus*. *The Rebel Angels* is a narrative singularly lacking in plot. The novel has several main plot lines—Darcourt's love for

Maria, Maria's love for Hollier, Hollier's desire for the Gryphius MS, Parlabane's attempts to write a novel, etc.—but all these seem to lead nowhere. The infatuations fade or are resolved without ever reaching a real crisis; Hollier had the MS dropped in his lap unexpectedly, only to lose it; Parlabane, the brilliant philosopher, cannot write to save his life; and the two most interesting events of the novel, the murder of McVarish and the marriage of Arthur and Maria, seem quite startling and unexpected, even incongruous. The novel closes with a description of the work of Ozias Froats, whom any reader would have considered a minor figure up to this point, certainly not deserving of the concluding paragraphs.

Furthermore, *The Rebel Angels* lacks the all-encompassing frames encountered in the other two novels. Much as in the third novel, a tarot reading is performed in *The Rebel Angels*. However, whereas the result of the reading in *The Lyre of Orpheus* acts as a frame for the entire breadth of the narrative, this tarot reading only concerns itself with the last third of the novel and only has significance for Darcourt and Hollier. Furthermore, although the readings do encompass the events of the last third of the novel, the interpretation of several key Trumps *contradicts* the traditional meaning of the cards. In this way, Davies calls into question the tarot as a framing device. The crooked tarot reading makes us doubt the authority of such devices, makes us wary of the author as a charlatan.

There are many other incomplete frames in the novel, such as Darcourt's journal/narration, "The New Aubrey," Parlabane's novel, Rabelais' novel *Gargantua and Pantagruel*, *Paradise Lost* and even the apocryphal *Book of Enoch*, from which the novel's title is derived. However, none of these really works properly. There are too many elements of the novel that are excluded from one or another frame; no combination of devices can serve to draw the entire novel into a tidy little package as *The Lyre of Orpheus* appears to be. *The Rebel Angels* remains a rambling, loosely-stitched discourse, possessing none of the aesthetic clarity of *What's Bred in the Bone*.

What the novel does possess is a constellation of paired opposites, which have a dynamic tension but are unresolved. These oppositions proceed from the Gryphius MS, which has tucked into its back cover three letters written by Rabelais to Paracelsus, the alchemist and natural scientist. This pairing of writer and scientist immediately sets off oppositions between art and science, description and discovery, intuition and deduction, etc., which lead to further oppositions which are important in the novel: sex and religion, magic and realism, rebellion and authority, and creation and murder, for example. All these oppositions may be loosely categorized under the umbrella of root and crown, which the mad monk Parlabane uses to explain his philosophy:

> I recognize that a tree has a bottom as well as a top, a root as well as a crown. No splendid crown without the strong root that works in the dark.[9]

This opposition is presented structurally in the novel by the separate and alternating discourses of Maria and Darcourt. Each relates a view of life which contradicts the other, yet both are necessary and integral to the novel. It is the tension between the two which gives *The Rebel Angels* its energy.

This is an example of what Mikhail Bakhtin termed the dialogic functioning of the novel genre: "A language is revealed in all its distinctiveness only when it is brought into relationship with other languages…. Every language in the novel is a point of view, a socio-ideological, conceptual system of real social groups and their embodied representatives."[10] Barbara Godard, in her first Bakhtinian essay on Davies, uses the monologues of Maria and Darcourt as the central tropes for the double voicing of the novel:

> Davies' use of intercutting limited points of view gives perspective and objectivity while remaining myopic and self-centred…. As the reader becomes aware when confronting their [Darcourt and Maria's] opposition,…the oppositions cancel each other out but the book contains them both.[11]

Davies further undercuts the possible authority of either perspective by making each proponent dissatisfied with their role. Maria, the Gypsy girl, wants desperately to be a learned academic, while Darcourt, the refined Anglican priest, longs for some sort of emotional passion which would allow him to pursue his infatuation for Maria.

These oppositions often take the form of parody, with one trope used to displace or uncrown the authority of the other. Bakhtin called this attribute of the novel genre "carnivalization," and it is an important part of *The Rebel Angels* (and the rest of the trilogy). The carnival is exemplified by a world gone awry, a "topsy-turvydom," a reversal of traditional values and beliefs. As Bakhtin expresses it, "carnival celebrated temporary liberation from the prevailing truth and from the established order; it marked the suspension of all hierarchical rank, privileges, norms and prohibitions."[12] The Boxing Day dinner at Maria's mother's home, for example, is pure carnival. On Boxing Day, the servants traditionally exchanged roles with their masters, a remnant of the Roman festival. Thus the drinking, gorging, low humour and general bawdy revelry can be contrasted to the dinners held at the College on Guest Night, which, although hardly polite in character, nevertheless revolve around a certain number of polite rules and conventions, and at which the diners are identified by their academic titles. Carnivalesque elements are also evident in the figure of Ozias Froats, who at the end of the novel is rumoured to be a Nobel prize contender for his physiological analysis of human feces. This juxtaposition of excrement and scholarship relates strongly to the "root and crown" analogy.

*The Rebel Angels* can thus be described as an unravelling novel, denying precedence to either "reality" or myth. The title comes primarily from the biblical apocrypha, although there is mention of the rebel angels in the Bible (Genesis:6.2-4). Among its various meanings, the word "apocrypha" has that of a "hidden" text. The other two novels must now be examined from the dialogic perspective, revealing the hidden or implied text which contradicts the manifest, perfectly mythical text.

## II

I have already discussed how Darcourt completes the myth of Francis Cornish. Yet it is paradoxical that he can only complete this myth by destroying it. His tool for this destruction, or deconstruction, is the "Sun pictures," a set of photographs taken by Francis' grandfather in Blairlogie. In his essay, "The Rhetoric of the Image," Roland Barthes makes a distinction between the drawing and the photograph which is very useful here: "The photograph, message without a code, must thus be opposed to the drawing which is a coded message.... The denoted image naturalizes the symbolic message, it innocents the semantic artifice of connotation."[13] Here we have another oppo-

sition, one which follows the realism-mysticism axis already mentioned. The photograph denotes, the painting connotes, and each
presents a different perspective on the world.

However, Davies is not content to allow pure denotation to take
place. Barthes claims one of the distinctions between photograph and
painting is that "like all codes, drawing demands an apprenticeship."[14]
The "Sun pictures," however, are as apprenticed and as coded as "The
Marriage at Cana," for the Senator (Francis' grandfather) always
retouched his photos, altering the faces of his subjects as it suited him:

> The Senator never commented on these alterations to Francis, but
> he could be seen to smile as he brought them into being.... A
> portrait is, among other things, a statement of opinion by the artist,
> as well as a "likeness," which was what everyone wanted it to
> be.[15]

Davies permits no single version of reality in this novel, just as there
is no authoritative vision of truth.

In *The Lyre of Orpheus*, the "realistic"-mystic (or "denotative"-
connotative) opposition which runs through the trilogy figures prom-
inently through Davies' references to a book which doubtless is the
source of the alternating narrative structure of *The Rebel Angels*. This
book is *Kater Murr,* a fictional biography by Hoffmann of two of his
literary creations, Johannes Kriesler and Kater Murr. Kriesler is a
deeply romantic figure, full of tempestuous melancholy and metaphysical convictions, and can be considered autobiographical of
Hoffmann. Kater Murr, as the name suggests in German, is literally
a tomcat, who seeks nothing more out of life than comfort and
security. Gunilla Dahl-Soot, Hulda's doctoral advisor, explains the
genesis of the strange, pastiched biography:

> [Kriesler's] life has been written by a friend, and left on the desk;
> the tomcat Murr finds it and writes his own life on the back of the
> sheets. So off goes the copy to the printer, who stupidly prints the
> whole thing as a unity, Kriesler and Kater Murr all mixed up in
> one book. But Kater Murr is a deeply Philistine cat; he embodies
> in himself everything that Kriesler hates and that is hostile to
> Kriesler.[16]

Significantly, Hoffmann chose to express his life in an artistic
artifact, in much the same way as Francis Cornish did. If on a

symbolic level Francis Cornish equals "The Marriage at Cana," then we must also consider Hoffmann to be embodied in his work. Given this connection between the two artists, each of whom is "completed" through the articulation of their respective masterpieces, may it not be supposed that Limbo and the Realm of the Mothers have a similar address in the underworld? Although there seems to be little descriptive similarity between the two, the association of Francis and Hoffmann suggests some interesting questions about the function of Limbo in the novel.

In medieval cosmology, Limbo is the abode of those virtuous men who died before the birth of Christ and could not, therefore, ascend to heaven; their virtue was perfect but unfinished, lacking the spiritual completion made possible by the resurrection of Christ. Similarly, but within an artistic framework, Hoffmann describes Limbo as the home of those artists who died with their most important work incomplete. They are doomed there to remain until someone completes what they begin, in this case someone like Schnackenburg.[17] It is interesting that as it was the death of Christ which allowed the souls of men to reach Heaven, it is the death of Francis Cornish (otherwise Orpheus, who is often associated with Christ) which gives Hulda the financial freedom to write the opera, thus liberating Hoffmann. Limbo therefore represents the unfinished work of art, which leads us to speculate that Limbo could also be taken to be the trilogy itself, as an unfinished work of art requiring the imagination of the reader to complete it. Whether or not that completion is possible remains to be seen. For now it should simply be noted how even in the "overly schematic" third novel we find the tension between the two poles of interpretation of the world, each of which can only be read between the lines of the other. Structurally, as Barthes puts it, this "enables the text to operate like a game, each system referring to the other according to the requirements of a certain *illusion*."[18]

These conflicting illusions are evident in the many carnivalesque elements of the novel, where parody abounds, especially concerning itself with the toppling of the authority of the Arthurian myth. The mythically regal couple, *A*rthur and *M*aria *C*ornish, have their comical complement in the pathetic *A*l and *M*abel *C*rane, who are also expecting a baby and whose status as observers during the staging of the opera is somewhat similar to that of Arthur and Maria. Furthermore, the serious nature of the Grail quest as a framing device is satirized and undermined by continuous reference to "The Hunting of the Snark" by Lewis Carroll, a farcical quest which some of the characters suggest has a significant effect upon the events they experience.

A multiplying of readings is extremely important to Bakhtin's theory of the novel:

> Languages of heteroglossia, like mirrors that face each other, each reflecting in its own way a piece, a tiny corner of the world, force us to guess at and grasp for a world behind their mutually reflecting aspects that is broader, more multi-leveled, containing more and varied horizons than would be available to a single language or a single mirror.[19]

The Arthurian legend offers a perfect example of this multiplicity of vision. As Hollier remarks in an early discussion of the libretto:

> What attitude do we take to Arthur? Is he a sun-god embodied in legend by a people half-Christianized? Or is he simply the *dux bellorum*, the leader of his British people against the invading Saxons? Or do we choose the refinement of Marie de France and Chrétien de Troyes? Or do we assume that Geoffrey of Monmouth really knew what he was talking about, however improbable that may seem?[20]

On top of that crowd, the novel also alludes to the Arthur of Malory, Walter Scott, James Planche and Tennyson, before Darcourt finally discovers a source for his libretto.

Darcourt takes his unnamed source and manipulates and adds to it to fit the form of the opera, doing his best to make his restitchings unnoticeable. Thus he does for the libretto exactly what Hulda does for the opera itself, and what Saraceni and Francis spent their time doing at Düsterstein: embellishing, completing and imitating. As well as these associations, however, Darcourt's tinkering and reworking echoes words Maimas speaks about the life of Francis Cornish: "I am to be the grinder, the shaper, the refiner,"[21] which provides an interesting parallel.

Maimas interprets Francis' life, but to interpret is invariably to paraphrase, to distort, to place a formal construct upon the subject which is inevitably invalid but may precipitate some relative insight about the subject. To borrow a phrase from Derrida, Francis Cornish is the absent centre of the trilogy. The interpretation of his life presented by Maimas and Zadkiel is an interpretation without a subject, for we see that subject only through this interpretation; it has no separate reality. This is, of course, true of any fictional biography. However, Davies emphasizes the paradox by making Zadkiel's biography a completed piece of writing. Thus there is falsity within the frame of the novel, a falsity concerning the necessary but necessarily absent Francis Cornish. One must remember that the trilogy begins with the death of Francis Cornish (and the return, incidentally, of the carnivalizing figure of Parlabane), and that his death is necessary for the action of all three novels. Davies complicates this dynamic further by undermining the status of Maimas and Zadkiel as concrete characters by having them refer to themselves as "metaphors."[22] This not only brings into question their interpretive authority but furthermore collapses the supernatural device of the novel, producing a strange situation in which the framers inhabit their own picture and the frame of their story buckles and contorts, twisting its way into the dead centre of the trilogy as the metaphor bred into the bone of Francis Cornish.

## III

Through his use of framing devices in *What's Bred in the Bone,* Davies establishes the personal myth of Francis Cornish. That myth is simultaneously completed by *The Lyre of Orpheus* and unravelled by *The Rebel Angels.*

Another perspective on the trilogy is provided by Jacques Derrida's concept of supplementarity.[23] Derrida sees writing as a supplement to speech, as an addition to something which is apparently complete, but by the very existence of that addition cannot be. The supplement both completes and corrupts that to which it is added; it finishes the "original" and undercuts it at the same time. In the model of the trilogy and triptych, the side panels can be seen as supplements in the Derridean sense; while they appear to complete the myth of Francis Cornish, they also deconstruct it. Thus the conflated and inextricable energies of completion and unravelling are demonstrated.

Completion and unravelling are at the heart of this trilogy, and manifest themselves in a plenitude of dialogic pairings which illuminate each other through their unresolvable opposition. The quote from Keats which adorns the Cornish Gallery, "A Man's life of any worth is a *continual* allegory" (my emphasis), is appropriate to the trilogy, for it suggests patterning without closure. The trilogy seems complete, as does "The Marriage at Cana," because it is surrounded by a frame, an empirical border of enamelled wood or paper dust jacket. In fact, Francis begins his painting by cleaning the frame which will house it.[24] As in all dialogic texts, however, this frame is an illusion; it is an arbitrary closure which is undermined by the very structure of the trilogy. As Bakhtin wrote, "[carnival] does not acknowledge any distinction between actors and spectators"[25]; the carnivalized text cannot be enclosed and completed.

This is demonstrated by the way completion and mastery are treated in the trilogy. Proceeding from the paradigm of Christ's first miracle, each of the novels has a main character who is attempting to complete a specific task which will demonstrate their fitness to take their place among the masters of their craft. In each instance, however, this rite of initiation is negated, undercut, or parodied. In *The Rebel Angels*, Maria never finishes her doctorate. Francis Cornish does finish "The Marriage at Cana," but its completion means the end of his career as a painter. Finally, Hulda Schnackenburg also finishes her doctorate, but is humorously declared a doctor of music as she speeds away from the concert hall in an ambulance, unconscious after a suicide attempt. Throughout the trilogy the completion implied by mastery is undermined and lampooned; the trilogy in fact is a subversion of that genre it seems to exemplify, the *bildungsroman* or "coming-of-age" novel. At all levels, the trilogy fights against what it appears to be. The implicit text always subverts the authority of the closed, manifest text, but without establishing its own authority; there is a plurality to the trilogy which cannot be synthesized or concluded.

Through their very use, Davies questions the validity of framing devices. This questioning transgresses the frame of the trilogy and concerns the intelligibility of life. Do the aesthetic frames we place upon our experiences mirror a deeper cosmos, or are they mere artifices, false and hollow and ultimately futile? In his critique of Calvino's *The Castle of Crossed Destinies,* John Updike comments: "Behind the artist's transformative sorcery lurks, like a sheepish apprentice, an irrational willingness to view the accidents of the actual as purposeful and the given as sacred."[26] This is the paradox employed by the trilogy; the more thoroughly the framing devices Davies employs explain the trilogy, the more they seem hollow and meaningless. Yet without these frames (for a narrative is a frame by definition) the unordered events of the un-trilogy would seem equally meaningless. Davies provides no easy solution to this paradox. He merely allows his trilogy to examine the uncertain balance these opposing principles hold in all life. The trilogy is a pattern which cannot be entirely completed, yet cannot be entirely unravelled either.

In her analysis of *The Lyre of Orpheus*, Kulyk-Keefer extracts only half the story of the trilogy; astutely picking up on the artificiality of the framing devices, she fails to realize the necessity of that artificiality. She attempts to place a finite meaning on the text. However, as Barthes explains it:

> Reading is not a parasitical act, the reactive complement of a writing which we endow with all the glamour of creation and anteriority. It is a form of work.... [It] does not consist in stopping the chain of systems, in establishing a truth, a legality of the text.... It consists in coupling these systems, not according to their finite quality, but according to their plurality.[27]

Hoffmann supposedly was able to leave Limbo after *Arthur of Britain* was completed, although we never see him go. However, the trilogy itself must always remain in the Limbo of indefinite meaning, of infinite interpretation. It is the "liar" of Orpheus: having promised an epic, mythical world, the text instead delivers a world where pattern is discernible but not complete, where meanings abound but do not adhere. In this way it resembles the song of Orpheus itself; its persuasive perfection contains elements which subtly undermine the work of art and lead to separation, fragmentation and a death of form. The flaw of Orpheus is common to all art, of course; as Updike says, "the combinations the human mind invents are relatively facile and unmagical compared to reality's dovetailed richness."[28] Davies has given us a work which makes us question the conventions of narrative throughout their skilful and subtle use, and which gives us a glimpse of that dovetailed richness of reality by undermining the assumptions on which his trilogy rests.

# Notes

1   Robertson Davies, *What's Bred in the Bone* (Toronto: Macmillan, 1985), p. 357. Hereafter cited as *Bred*.

2   Janice Kulyk-Keefer, "Consolation and Exaltation," *Books in Canada* (August-September 1988), p. 9.

3   David Lodge, "Hermits and Fools," *The New York Review of Books*, Vol. 36, No. 6 (Apr. 13 1989), p. 35.

4   *Bred*, p. 435.

5   Kulyk-Keefer, p. 11.

6   Jessie Weston, *From Ritual to Romance* (New York: Doubleday Anchor Books, 1957), pp. 79-80.

7   *Ibid.*, p. 5.

8   *Bred*, p. 434.

9   Davies, *The Rebel Angels*, (Markham: Penguin, 1983), p. 197.

10  Mikhail Bakhtin, *The Dialogic Imagination: Four Essays.* Trans. Caryl Emerson and Michael Holquist, ed. Michael Holquist (Austin: University of Texas Press, 1981), p. 411.

11  Barbara Godard, "Robertson Davies' Dialogic Imagination," *Essays on Canadian Writing* 34 (Spring 1987), p. 75.

12  Mikhail M. Bakhtin, *Rabelais and His World*. Trans. Helene Iswolsky (Bloomington: Indiana University Press, 1984), p. 10.

13  Roland Barthes, *Image-Music-Text*. Trans. and ed. Stephen Heath (London: Fontana, 1987), pp. 43 and 45.

14  *Ibid.*, p. 43.

15  *Bred*, p. 88.

16  Robertson Davies, *The Lyre of Orpheus* (Toronto: Macmillan, 1988), pp. 187-88. Hereafter cited as *Lyre*.

17  *Ibid.*, pp. 47-48.

18  Roland Barthes, *S/Z: An Essay*. Trans. Richard Miller (New York: Hill and Wang, 1987), p. 10.

19  Bakhtin, *Dialogic Imagination*, p. 415.

20  *Lyre*, p. 97.

21  *Bred*, p. 83.

22  *Bred*, p. 435.

23  Jacques Derrida, *Of Grammatology*. Trans. Gayatri C. Spivak (Baltimore: Johns Hopkins University Press, 1974), p. 145.

24  *Bred*, p. 357.

25  Bakhtin, *Rabelais and His World*, p. 7.

26  John Updike, *Hugging the Shore* (New York: Alfred A. Knopf, 1983), p. 469.

27  Barthes, *S/Z*, p. 11.

28  Updike, p. 469.

# Robertson Davies and the Doctrine of the Elite: An Ideological Critique of the Cornish Trilogy

*Linda Lamont-Stewart*

In the first volume of Robertson Davies' Cornish Trilogy, *The Rebel Angels*, the reprobate scholar/monk John Parlabane outlines for Professor the Reverend Simon Darcourt his grandiose literary ambitions:

> It's a really great book, and I expect that when it has made its first mark, people will read and reread, and discover new depths every time...a book in which really devoted and understanding readers will find themselves, and thus will find something of the essence of our times....[1]

Parlabane explains that his great book is meaningful on multiple levels. While it can be read at a literal level, "its real movement is dialectical and moral" (*Rebel*, p. 240). On the allegorical level, the protagonist is a "modern Everyman," whose "recovery, through imagination, of a unified view of life, of a synthesis of unconscious fantasy, scientific knowledge, moral mythology, and wisdom that meets in a religious reconciliation of the soul with reality through the acceptance of revealed truth" (*Rebel*, p. 241) is a model for the reader. On the level of morality, the book offers "a treatise on folly, error, frustration, and the exploration of the blind alleys and false theories about life as currently propagated and ineffectually practised" (*Rebel*, p. 241).

But the crown of the book is the *anagogical* level of meaning, suggesting the final revelation of the twofold nature of the world, the revelation of experience as the language of God and of life as the preliminary to a quest that cannot be described but only guessed at, because all things point beyond themselves to a glory which is greater than any of them. And thus the hero of the tale...will be found to have been preoccupied all his life with the quest for the Father Image and the Mother Idol to replace the real parents who in real life were inadequate surrogates of the Creator. The quest is never completed, but the preoccupation with Image and Idol gradually gives way to the conviction of the reality of the Reality which lies behind the shadows which constitute the actual moment as it rushes by (*Rebel*, pp. 239-42).

Parlabane's vaulting ambition is justly rebuked; his grandly conceived masterpiece turns out to be unpublishable, indeed unreadable. But despite the mockery heaped upon Parlabane's unwieldy manuscript in both *The Rebel Angels* and the final volume of the trilogy, *The Lyre of Orpheus*, the reader who is familiar with Davies' fiction cannot help noticing that Parlabane's Frygian conception of his *magnum opus* bears a striking resemblance to the pattern of Davies' own fiction. Unlike Parlabane's book, Davies' fictions are eminently readable. His three trilogies have been popular successes and, since the publication in 1970 of *Fifth Business*, his novels have received substantial critical attention. Because Davies' fictions present themselves as novels of ideas and are extremely didactic, it is important to consider critically the lessons that they teach. The three most recent Davies novels, collectively known as the Cornish Trilogy, provide ample material for analysis.

The Cornish Trilogy invites us to read it as a unit. *The Rebel Angels* (1981) establishes the trilogy's central themes and motifs, which are elaborated in the second and third volumes, *What's Bred in the Bone* (1985) and *The Lyre of Orpheus* (1988). The trilogy offers itself, in effect, as a religious treatise—"religious" as the term is defined by Simon Darcourt in *The Lyre of Orpheus*: "seeking to know, and to live, beneath the surfaces of life, and to be aware of the realities beneath the superficialities."[2] Religion, of course, implies doctrine: viewed as a whole, the Cornish Trilogy comprises a single text which articulates an ideology, an apparently coherent system of aesthetic, philosophical and political values. Doctrine requires authority to guarantee its validity, and authority, in turn, requires assent; Davies' texts require "devoted and understanding readers" who are willing to accept their "revealed truth," willing to be convinced by Davies' version of "the reality of the Reality." The success of Davies' didactic enterprise depends on his skill in manipulating narrative voice in such a way as to win his reader's assent to the doctrinal authority of his discourse.

In "Robertson Davies and the Ethics of Monologue," Stephen Bonnycastle examines the narrative strategy of the Deptford Trilogy, which he describes as "a series of monologues arranged in a hierarchical order, with an absolute authority...at the top."[3] Bonnycastle argues that the "principle of relational identity"[4] which is at the core of the texts' teaching is in conflict with this authoritarian narrative mode. He concludes that the trilogy "promotes a fierce aristocracy of the spirit" and argues that "What is repugnant about this view of the world is not that it claims to be a statement of the facts, but that the people on top gain their sense of being from their superiority to those at the bottom, and do their best to keep them in their place."[5] Bonnycastle suggests that preaching the doctrine that truth is variable, while simultaneously demonstrating that knowledge of the truth is the property of an elite few, the Deptford novels are deceptive. The chief instrument by which they deceive is their monologic narration: "form and content come together to suggest that monologue is the summit of human discourse."[6]

Bonnycastle's primary concern in his analysis of the Deptford Trilogy is moral and ethical. He poses the question: "Is the morality of *Fifth Business* a substantial contribution to the debate about cultural values, or an illusion...?" He concludes that it is the latter. I wish to apply a similar analysis to Davies' Cornish Trilogy, but to place the emphasis specifically on the political ideology that these works advocate. First, however, it is necessary to examine the radically different assessment of Davies' narrative strategy offered by Barbara Godard.

In "World of Wonders: Robertson Davies' Carnival," Godard asserts that "Davies' fiction is a dialogue of two or more voices."[7] Godard applies Mikhail Bakhtin's concepts of carnivalization and dialogism to Davies' fiction, arguing in "Robertson Davies' Dialogic Imagination" that in his works "there is no single authoritative vision of truth."[8] While Godard demonstrates convincingly the abundance of carnivalesque imagery throughout Davies' fiction, her argument that Davies' imagination and fiction are fundamentally dialogic is less convincing. She identifies an apparent paradox in Davies' treatment of the issue of authority:

> Davies is very much aware of the force of tradition and its authority, which make originality, the saying of something new, difficult. Drawing on writers of the past, he is engaged in an originating act of parricide, both killing them off, to make way for something new, *and* enthroning the figure of authority.[9]

I would argue that Davies is engaged not in killing off his predecessors but in attempting to resuscitate them, that his primary concern is to recover the values of an earlier age and to restore the figure of authority to its throne.

At first glance, there appears to be a variety of narrative voices telling the stories of the Cornish Trilogy. *The Rebel Angels* has two alternating first-person narrators, graduate student Maria Magdalena Theotoky and the academic priest Simon Darcourt. It should be noted, however, that large parts of Maria's sections of the text are taken up by monologues by other characters, particularly Parlabane and Maria's doctoral supervisor, Clement Hollier. In *What's Bred in the Bone*, the life story of the artist Francis Cornish is narrated by the Lesser Zadkiel, the Angel of Biography, with occasional commentary by the Daimon Maimas, who was responsible for shaping the destiny of the late Cornish. The biographical narrative of *What's Bred in the Bone* is framed by brief passages set in the present and narrated by a third-person omniscient voice. The third-person omniscient voice returns in *The Lyre of Orpheus*, although the predominant point of view in this final novel is that of Simon Darcourt. E.T.A. Hoffmann (ETAH) also comments on the narrative from time to time as he languishes in limbo waiting for the contemporary characters to complete his unfinished romantic opera, *Arthur of Britain, or the Magnanimous Cuckold*.

The diversity of these narrative voices is more apparent than real. Stylistically, the voices of Maria Theotoky and Simon Darcourt are virtually indistinguishable from each other and from the voices of the supernatural speakers and the third-person omniscient narrator. All speak in the style Robert Cluett describes in "Robertson Davies: the

Tory Mode": their language is "archaic, Romanesque, and formal," designed for the "affirmation of the values of the past."[10] They speak with a single, authoritative voice, the voice of Robertson Davies. In "Victoria Rediviva: Robertson Davies in the First Person," Cluett extends his analysis of Davies' conservative and backward-looking style. Cluett remarks:

> The overall effect of monologues delivered in a style with such Johnsonian and Arnoldian elements in it is sometimes Olympian, sometimes pontifical, occasionally no more than pompous. What we are confronted with in [Davies'] texts is a writer who in several ways is convinced that he is far far better than the bulk of his fellow members of the human race.

I suggested earlier that Davies' Cornish Trilogy invites us to read it as a "religious" text, in Darcourt's sense of the term "religious," but the fiction's religious teachings are part of a broader political agenda. Cluett emphasizes that Davies' use of his "Tory" style is deliberate and serves ideological purposes: "Davies...turns to England and to an earlier time with political, as well as other, ends in view."[11]

In constructing a Bakhtinian reading of Davies' work, Barbara Godard is arguing that his novels are radically subversive of authority. In Bakhtin's terms, the novel is, by definition, a subversive genre. In "Discourse and the Novel," Bakhtin argues that the defining characteristic of the novel is dialogism:

> Authorial speech, the speeches of narrators, inserted genres, the speech of characters are merely those fundamental compositional unities with whose help heteroglossia...can enter the novel; each of them permits a multiplicity of social voices and a wide variety of their links and interrelationships (always more or less dialogized). These distinctive links and interrelationships between utterances and languages, this movement of the theme through different languages and speech types, its dispersion into the rivulets and droplets of social heteroglossia, its dialogization—this is the basic distinguishing feature of the stylistics of the novel.[12]

In her analysis of Davies' fiction, Godard points to the multiplicity of discourses contained in his work. Davies "continually plays with the novel's possibilities for developing intersecting planes in the specialized languages of professions, occupations, and classes.... It is the richness and variety, the incongruities of the juxtapositions, that characterize the heterogeneity of Davies' novels."[13] It is true that Davies' fiction embraces a plethora of discourses; however, the various specialized languages he incorporates represent not "a multiplicity of social voices," but rather a single, authoritative voice which speaks through various authorized characters. The Cornish Trilogy deploys academic discourse; mythological discourse (classical and Celtic); the discourses of astrology, alchemy and the Tarot; the discourses of the high arts (literature, painting, opera); and, underwriting all of these, the discourses of Jungian psychoanalysis and Anglican theology. What unites these disparate discourses is symbolism: each of the discourses provides a symbolic language by which experience can be interpreted in a non-rational, or supra-rational, way by the initiated. The interplay of discourses in these fictions produces not heterogeneity but homogeneity.

Bonnycastle remarks that "*Fifth Business* is a novel about a continuing apprenticeship, and what Ramsay learns from his teachers can best be described as a language."[14] Throughout the Cornish Trilogy, the most frequently recurring type of interpersonal relationship is that between master and apprentice, and the languages that the masters impart to their apprentices, however varied, all provide entry into the realm of symbolic communication.

In *The Rebel Angels* Maria is ostensibly an apprentice to her thesis supervisor, Clement Hollier, a "paleo-psychologist" who investigates the modes of thought of earlier eras. Her true master, however, is the demonic Parlabane, whose wisdom is Jungian. He teaches Maria the importance of acknowledging the "shadow" side of one's self, using a metaphorical tree: "the root is the contrary of the crown—the crown upside down, in the dark instead of in the light, working toward the depths instead of straining upward to the heights" (*Rebel*, p. 203). Maria learns her lesson quickly and thoroughly, and is soon thinking in terms of roots and crowns. Near the end of the novel she explains to Simon Darcourt the importance of Parlabane's teaching. She has tried to deny her Gypsy heritage "till I met Parlabane, but his talk about the need to recognize your root and your crown as of equal importance has made me understand that my Gypsy part is inescapable" (*Rebel*, p. 310). The root and crown metaphor finds its way as well into Clement Hollier's toast to the bride at the wedding of Maria and Arthur Cornish. Although Hollier has been a master rather than an apprentice, he too has learned Parlabane's lesson, and wishes the newlyweds "long life and every joy that the union of root and crown can bring" (*Rebel*, p. 319).

Such Jungian discourse is dispersed among the various masters who populate the Cornish Trilogy, even though they are experts in a wide range of differing symbolic languages. In *What's Bred in the Bone*, Francis Cornish undergoes a Jungian apprenticeship in which he eventually comes to recognize that his boyhood dressing in female clothing and his attraction to his beautiful but treacherous cousin Ismay represented his desire for his anima figure, "as a completion of himself, as a desired, elusive dimension of his spirit." He recognizes as well that his grossly deformed and retarded older brother, "Francis the First, the Looner, [was] the shadow of his boyhood...the secret, the inadmissible element which, as he now understood, had played so great a part in making him an artist."[15] Francis' masterpiece, "The Marriage at Cana," figures forth his psychological integration, containing representations of the formative influences of his life, including Ismay and Francis the First. Francis' mentor, the brilliant art restorer and crook Tancred Saraceni, recognizes the picture's significance, telling Francis, "You have made up your soul in that picture." Although Saraceni speaks in the symbolic language of alchemy—"transformation of base elements and some sort of union of important elements has worked alchemically in your life"—his message is Jungian. Simon Darcourt, who identifies Cornish's masterpiece in *The Lyre of Orpheus*, correctly interprets its psychological significance, even using the same words as Saraceni: "In that picture Francis was making up his soul.... What you see in the picture is the whole matter of Francis, as he saw it himself" (*Lyre*, p. 339).

The reliance on symbolic discourse in Davies' fiction is part of the texts' profound and all-pervasive, anti-modernist bias. Repeatedly, characters in all three novels of the Cornish Trilogy prefer the language of the past to that of the present, as does Hollier, for example, in warning Maria to be wary of Parlabane: "In the light of the work you and I share I don't have to explain in modern terms; very old terms are quite sufficient and exact—Parlabane is an evil man" (*Rebel*, p. 77). Davies' preference for the language of the past, as Robert Cluett suggests, has distinct ideological implications.

In his essay, "Epic and Novel," Bakhtin argues that the novel as a genre is by definition modern, concerned with the fluctuating issues and values of contemporary society:

> The novel might wish to prophesize facts, to predict and influence the real future, the future of the author and his readers. But the novel has a new and quite specific problematicalness: characteristic for it is an eternal re-thinking and re-evaluating. That center of activity that ponders and justifies the past is transferred to the future.[16]

"This 'modernity' of the novel," Bakhtin asserts, "is indestructible." Parlabane expects his devoted and understanding readers to find in his masterwork "something of the essence of our times," and Davies' fictions may be assumed to share this didactic aim. Curiously, however, although Davies' stories have a contemporary setting, they seem far less interested in "our" times than in earlier eras—the Middle Ages, the Renaissance, the early Romantic period. The truth that Davies' fictions seek to reveal is not, it appears, to be found within the "modern" world.

Throughout the Cornish Trilogy all things modern are disparaged and dismissed. The adjective "modern" turns up with particular frequency in *The Rebel Angels*, and invariably, its connotations are negative. For example, Simon Darcourt, one of the two narrators of *The Rebel Angels*, laments the sterility of the modern university:

> We humanists are an endangered species. In Paracelsus' time the energy of universities resided in the conflict between humanism and theology; the energy of the modern university lives in the love-affair between government and science, and sometimes the two are so close it makes you shudder (*Rebel*, p. 113).

Various characters express contempt for "modern" attitudes, but the anti-modernist bias of the text is most evident in the anti-feminist representation of this novel's other narrator, Maria Theotoky. Darcourt admires Maria because her appearance and deportment are not modern:

> She was beyond doubt a great beauty, though it was beauty of a kind not everybody would notice, or like, and which I suspected did not appeal greatly to her contemporaries. A calm, transfixing

face, of the kind one sees in an ikon, or a mosaic portrait.... She had covered her head with a loose scarf, which most of the women in the chapel had not done, because they are modern, and set no store by St. Paul's admonition on that subject (*Rebel*, p. 15).

In her own sections of the narrative, Maria makes it clear that she recognizes her anachronism:

I must serve; I must let my love be seen in humility and sacrifice...
Can I be a modern girl, if I acknowledge such thoughts? I must be modern: I live now...when I most want to be contemporary the Past keeps pushing in, and when I long for the Past...the Present cannot be pushed away. When I hear girls I know longing to be what they call liberated and when I hear others rejoicing in what they think of as liberation, I feel a fool, because I simply do not know where I stand (*Rebel*, p. 124).

In her longing for the past, Maria devotes herself to the study of Rabelais and Paracelsus, and although she is presented as a brilliant graduate student in a contemporary university, she shares Darcourt's dissatisfaction with modern academe: "I wanted nothing less than Wisdom. In a modern university if you ask for knowledge they will provide it in almost any form.... But if you ask for Wisdom—God save us all!... Intelligence, yes, but of Wisdom not so much as the gleam of a single candle" (*Rebel*, p. 38). Maria is indeed an old-fashioned girl—beautiful, submissive and, as Parlabane remarks, "a great girl for silence" (*Rebel*, p. 71). At the end of *The Rebel Angels*, when Maria is married to Arthur Cornish, she insists, with Darcourt's approval, on traditional vows, including the vow to obey (*Rebel*, p. 311).

The anti-modernist theme so prominent in *The Rebel Angels* persists in *What's Bred in the Bone* and *The Lyre of Orpheus*. Francis Cornish, the protagonist of *What's Bred in the Bone*, is a gifted artist who cannot work in a modern style. He becomes a master of Renaissance painting technique and produces his single masterpiece in Renaissance style, for which he is praised by his teacher: "You have found a reality that is not part of the chronological present. Your here and now are not of our time. You seem not to be trapped, as most of us are, in the psychological world of today" (*Bred*, p. 434). In *The Lyre of Orpheus*, when Simon Darcourt has correctly identified and interpreted Cornish's "The Marriage at Cana" and it has been enshrined in the National Gallery of Canada, Cornish is described approvingly as a man who "had dared to be of a time not his own" (*Lyre*, p. 467). This final novel presents another gifted female graduate student, Hulda Schnakenburg, who, in sharp contrast to Maria, is very much a modern girl, and Davies denigrates her by describing her as slovenly, filthy and foul-mouthed. Nevertheless, and even though she is said to be skilled in avant-garde musical forms, "Schnak" chooses, as her dissertation project, to complete an unfinished opera by the nineteenth-century composer E.T.A. Hoffmann.

Throughout *What's Bred in the Bone* and *The Lyre of Orpheus*, as in *The Rebel Angels*, modern ideas and attitudes, modern art, modern modes of dress and speech are mocked and rejected. According to Bakhtin, in "Epic and Novel," the epic genre, which supports a traditional, hierarchical view of society, adopts towards the past "the reverent point of view of a descendant" (p. 13), whereas the novel operates on the "plane of comic (humorous) representation" where "the role of memory is minimal; in the comic world there is nothing for memory and tradition to do. One ridicules in order to forget."[17] Davies' fictions are quite unlike the novel as Bakhtin understands the genre; they revere the past and ridicule the present. As Godard points out, Davies' novels are replete with mocking laughter and Rabelaisian references, but whereas the carnivalized text as defined by Bakhtin mocks the institutions of traditional authority, Davies' mockery is directed at those forces which would challenge the authority of a cultural elite.

When, in *The Rebel Angels*, Maria first attempts to read Parlabane's novel, she wonders whether it is "really a modern novel or perhaps a novel at all" (*Rebel*, p. 274). One might ask the same question about Davies' Cornish Trilogy. Certainly Davies' books are not modernist or postmodernist novels; they are traditional and conservative in form. But they differ as well from the "realistic novel" of the eighteenth and nineteenth centuries in that they attack rather than support bourgeois values. Davies' characters are not ordinary, middle class people. They are extraordinary, aristocratic people. Some of Davies' characters are of the traditional European landed aristocracy, such as the English Cornishes and the German Ingelheims. Others are of the new-world aristocracy of wealth, such as the Canadian Cornishes. Still others are of what Bonnycastle calls the "aristocracy of the spirit," set apart from, and above, ordinary mortals by their brilliance, wit and erudition, and by their commitment to the life of the mind and spirit. In Bakhtin's terms, Davies' texts are closer to epic than to novel; however, their true genre would appear to be another venerable narrative form, the romance.

The romance-quest pattern shapes all three novels in the Cornish Trilogy. In *The Rebel Angels*, both Maria and Simon Darcourt are engaged in a quest for Wisdom. For a while, Simon mistakenly thinks he has found it in Maria itself, whom he loves as "Sophia." Francis Cornish, in *What's Bred in the Bone*, is strongly drawn to the myth of King Arthur, and he lives his life as a quest for psychological wholeness. In *The Lyre of Orpheus*, the plot revolves around the completion and production of Hoffmann's romantic opera, which dramatizes Arthurian romance. The romance of Arthur invades contemporary reality when Arthur Cornish is forced to play the "magnanimous cuckold," accepting with astonishing grace his wife's infidelity, his best friend's betrayal and a bastard child. Also, throughout this text, Simon Darcourt is engaged in a quest to uncover the story of Francis Cornish's life and to solve the mystery of his painting of "The Marriage at Cana." Elements of popular romance forms abound in all three texts. In *The Rebel Angels*, mystery surrounds the disappearance of a Rabelais manuscript, the murder of Professor Urquhart McVarish and the suicide of Parlabane. In *What's Bred in the Bone*, Francis Cornish is involved in espionage work during and after the Second World War.

Like his adoption of a deliberately old-fashioned literary style, Davies' use of a medieval genre has ideological implications. His fictions are motivated by a deep nostalgia for an idealized past, in which society is hierarchically organized and authority rests with a powerful elite, in which there is no question as to who are the masters and who are the inferiors.

The anti-modernist bias of the Cornish Trilogy is associated with an anti-rationalist theme that pervades the novels—the theme, in Parlabane's words, of "the over-developed mind and the under-developed heart" (*Rebel*, p. 63). Hollier's interest, and Maria's as his student, is "in the persistence of old wisdom and old belief in this modern world, which so terribly lacks that sort of wisdom" (*Rebel*, p. 131). Maria's and Darcourt's complaints about the modern university are rooted in a dislike of scientific rationality that is shared by

Parlabane, who explains to Maria, "Beyond this world of doubt and sorrow lies Truth, and the Faith points the way to it because it is based on the existence of something above human knowledge and experience" (*Rebel*, pp. 195-96). Anti-rationalist sentiments are expressed by various characters throughout the trilogy. For instance, Miss Nibsmith, the governess/historian in *What's Bred in the Bone*, explains to Francis Cornish her belief in astrology "as psychology" (*Bred*, p. 358), and Tancred Saraceni interprets for him the deficiency of modern art: contemporary artists lack "a coherent language of mythological or religious terms" and so must paint their "inner vision" in a language that is private and inaccessible (*Bred*, p. 401). He lectures Francis on the spiritual poverty of the present day:

> People speak of our age as materialistic, but they are wrong. Men do not believe in matter today any more than they believe in God; scientists have taught them not to believe in anything. Men of the Middle Ages, and most of them in the Renaissance, believed in God and the *things* God had made, and they were happier and more complete than we...modern man wants desperately to believe in something, to have some value that cannot be shaken (*Bred*, p. 403).

The attacks on rationalism throughout the Cornish Trilogy are presented as arguments for a more spiritual view of life; however, the ideology that underlies this view of life is highly authoritarian.

The primary voice of anti-rationalism in *The Lyre of Orpheus* is that of Simon Darcourt, the scholar/priest, who muses that "Souls are not fashionable, at present. People will listen with wondering acquiescence to scientific talk...but they shy away from talk of souls" (*Lyre*, p. 308). Talk of souls runs throughout the Cornish Trilogy, as does talk of magic, myth and the arcane "sciences" of an earlier time. These various symbolic languages, which complement and reinforce one another, are the property of various masters who impart them, through monologue, to their apprentices. The master/apprentice relationship is a crucial element in the ideology of these texts, and it is a relationship in which violence is implicit.

The violent nature of the master/apprentice relationship is starkly exposed in the portrayal of the unlovely Hulda Schnakenburg in *The Lyre of Orpheus*, who is an apprentice to the eccentric but brilliant composer Gunilla Dahl-Soot, and to a lesser extent, Simon Darcourt.

Although Schnak has access to the realm of symbolic communication through her innate musical genius, she has been spiritually stunted by an unloving and repressive religious upbringing. The immediately obvious emblem of her spiritual poverty—her dirty and unkempt appearance—is remedied quickly by Dahl-Soot, but Schnak's problems are more than skin deep. She will never be an attractive woman, but the world of the spirit is open to her if she can learn its language and its manners. With the exception of the venal Wally Crottel, who speaks ignorantly, threatens Maria and is conveniently disposed of before the end of the story, Schnak's voice is the only voice in the text which in any way disputes its discursive coherence. Unlike Darcourt, Maria, Parlabane, Hollier, Saraceni, Dahl-Soot—the characters who are authorized to speak monologues and who share Davies' "Tory" style—Schnak speaks Davies' version of the modern vernacular—her speech is ungrammatical, and to the extent possible, monosyllabic. She says "yeah" and "shit" a lot. Darcourt begins her initiation into proper discourse in their initial meeting, when he browbeats her into saying "please" (*Lyre*, p. 28), but it is Dahl-Soot who truly tames the beastly Schnak. First she reduces her to her proper status as apprentice. Schnak offers to cut her teacher's grass:

> A simple question, surely? Yet as Hulda Schnakenburg uttered it to Dr. Gunilla Dahl-Soot it was total surrender;...it was an act of vassalage (*Lyre*, p. 181).

Although Hulda does not realize it, such humbling is precisely what she needs:

> A teacher, then? A teacher whom Schnak could truly respect? She had not quite known that that was what she wanted more than anything else in the world, and she came to such self-knowledge with mulish resistance. Now, at the end of her sixth session, she offered to cut the Doctor's grass. Schnak had met her master (*Lyre*, p. 183).

Schnak is now prepared to begin her apprenticeship, which has as much to do with learning language as with learning musicology, as is indicated when, during a conversation about providing a libretto for Hoffmann's *Arthur of Britain*, she reveals that she has been learning German; she also attempts to speak in the language of the culturally literate, but she says "pistache" when she means "pastiche." Darcourt and Dahl-Soot subsequently discuss Schnak's linguistic poverty, Dahl-Soot remarking, "she cannot be an artist in music and a hooligan in speech" (*Lyre*, p. 236). Although Schnak's education is incomplete at the end of *The Lyre of Orpheus*, she has made great strides. When her opera is about to be performed, Darcourt initiates her in the art of the curtsey (*Lyre*, p. 422-24).

The portrayal of Schnak reveals an inconsistency in the ideological stance of the Cornish Trilogy. As a musical genius "in the great romantic tradition" (*Lyre*, p. 29), Schnak should automatically take her place within the "aristocracy of the spirit"; she should be able to transcend the limitations of her narrow-minded, spiritually arid background, as do Monica Gall in *A Mixture of Frailties* and Dunstan Ramsay in *Fifth Business*. Schnak, however, at the end of *The Lyre of Orpheus*, remains gauche, clumsy and linguistically inadequate. The reason that Schnak cannot be fully integrated into the aristocracy of the spirit is that part of her symbolic function in the novel is to represent everything that Davies most despises in "modern" youth. The Dean of the Faculty of Music describes her as "the squalidest, rudest, most offensive little brat I have ever met" (*Lyre*, p. 11).

While Schnak is at least potentially redeemable because of her artistic genius, two other characters in *The Lyre of Orpheus* represent modern youth in its most unregenerate form. They are Al Crane, an American graduate student who arrives to write a detailed account of the completion and production of *Arthur of Britain* as his doctoral dissertation, and his pregnant girlfriend Mabel, whom he calls "Sweetness." Their ineligibility for admission to the aristocracy of the spirit is immediately evident in their slovenly appearance. Al is an intellectual parasite, feeding off the work of others and getting in everyone's way. He is also, despite his status as a doctoral candidate, a cultural illiterate, and like Schnak, linguistically impoverished. Maria remarks, "in the modern lingo, Al lacks verbal skills" (*Lyre*, p. 334). Maria carries her pregnancy elegantly, wearing "becoming gowns in which she did not look pregnant, like the women Darcourt saw in the streets who wore slacks in which their distended bellies were forced upon the world" (*Lyre*, p. 309). Mabel, however, is "monstrously pregnant" (*Lyre*, p. 327), and Maria reacts to her as a disgusting self-parody, rejecting firmly Mabel's claim of sisterhood because of their common condition (*Lyre*, p. 334). The mockery of

Al, and especially of Mabel, is vicious, and Maria is startlingly cruel in her comments on the other woman. "Sweetness," Maria says, "is a zealot, and she's deep into the squalor of pregnancy" (*Lyre*, p. 344). When Darcourt inquires why the couple have not married, Maria responds, "Sweetness has a cliché for everything. They do not admit that their union would be hallowed more than it is, if some parson mumbled a few words over them" (*Lyre*, p. 345). This refusal to conform to traditional practice seems to be the epitome of Al and Mabel's spiritual delinquency. Maria, who is properly married and intends to have her child properly baptized, gives birth, as it were, off stage, and presumably effortlessly. In one chapter she is pregnant and, when she next appears, she is the serenely composed mother of a son. Mabel, however, endures a prolonged labour during which she is abandoned by Al. Her child is stillborn, apparently, the doctor explains, because "she seems not to have had any pre-natal advice whatever" (*Lyre*, p. 381)—odd behaviour in a woman who is a "zealot" about childbirth. Maria steps in to take care of Mabel until she can be sent home to her mother, and it is difficult to escape the conclusion that she is to be seen as deserving her miserable lot.

Davies' nostalgic portrayal of a world in which extraordinary people live their lives as romantic spiritual and aesthetic quests and indulge in carnivalesque banquets and witty repartee in luxurious surroundings, insulated from mundane concerns by abundant wealth, may appear benign. Its ideological implications, however, are disturbing. Through his manipulation of narrative voices, Davies adopts the role of master; we, his readers, are expected to adopt the role of apprentice. Throughout *The Lyre of Orpheus*, the audience's complicity in the creation of dramatic illusion is emphasized. Darcourt, for instance, recognizes that "a great theatrical moment is created by the audience itself." As he watches the performance of the finally completed *Arthur of Britain,* he enjoys "the extra pleasure of the man who knows how it has been done" (*Lyre*, p. 450). Through the monologues of the various masters he presents in his fictions, Davies offers his readers that extra pleasure—he offers to initiate us into the aristocracy of the spirit. Such an offer can be seductive. The values that Davies' texts endorse and attempt to instill in his readers, however, are thoroughly at odds with those of contemporary society. The ideology of Davies' fictional world is profoundly anti-democratic.

It is also racist, sexist and, despite the profusion in his texts of sexually unconventional characters, homophobic.

The elitist way of life that the Cornish Trilogy endorses is dependent on the possession of great wealth, specifically, inherited wealth. The making of money is presented in these texts as an honourable but not particularly interesting enterprise. Maria, who has inherited her father's fortune, remarks in passing: "How he made so much money, I do not know. Many people think that business and a fine concept of life cannot be reconciled, but I am not so sure" (*Rebel*, p. 127). Arthur Cornish has inherited his uncle's immense fortune, which itself was inherited from Francis Cornish's father and from his mentor, Tancred Saraceni, whose own fortune was built at least in part from the proceeds of criminal activity. Arthur is represented as a highly successful businessman, but it is as a patron of the arts that he is valued. In *The Rebel Angels*, Arthur explains to Maria his ambition to become "a patron on the grand scale," a role which requires him to act "the autocrat," and to possess "exceptional taste...the authoritative taste that artists recognize and want to please" (*Rebel*, p. 144). In *The Lyre of Orpheus* Arthur is in a position to behave as autocratically as he wishes in administering the funds of the Cornish Foundation, and insists on supporting the grand project of completing and producing Hoffmann's opera. He dismisses the mundane requests of those who want to write books, edit manuscripts, show their paintings or perform their music (*Lyre*, p. 14). Great wealth confers freedom and power. Maria is somewhat less free than her husband; she frets over her scholarly inactivity, but devotes her energies to her role as wife and mother. She is uninterested in the sort of volunteer work wives of wealthy men are expected to perform:

> There is the great Ladder of Compassion, on which the community arranges a variety of diseases in order of the social prestige they carry. The society woman slaves on behalf of the lame, the halt, and the blind, the cancerous, the paraplegic, those variously handicapped, and, of course, the great new enthusiasm, AIDS. There are also the sociologically pitiable: the battered wives, battered children, and the raped girls (*Lyre*, p. 16).

This dismissive catalogue trivializes serious social problems. Such trivialization underlines the degree to which the grand life of the spirit requires a social order that exempts the elite few from any social responsibility.

Davies' reliance on monologue contributes to his articulation of reactionary political views. He frequently places his conservative rhetoric in the mouths of characters one would expect to hold radically different views. Parlabane, who is homosexual, remarks, "The Gays make me laugh; they're so middle-class and political about the whole thing. They'll destroy it all with their clamour about Gay Lib...let my sin be Sin or it loses all stature" (*Rebel*, p. 67). Maria, who is acutely aware that her Gypsy background marks her as different, is nevertheless capable of singing loudly in public a bawdy song containing the word "nigger" and dismissing the ensuing uproar as comically trivial (*Rebel*, p. 75). Maria is also the primary voice of anti-feminist rhetoric in the trilogy. Often such rhetoric is disguised as natural, part of Maria's thought processes. For instance, at one point in *The Rebel Angels*, she describes her perfectly justified anger as "feminine fury" (*Rebel*, p. 25), and throughout this text she continually thinks of herself as a "girl" rather than as a woman. At another point she recognizes in herself the "Maenad...that spirit which any woman of any character keeps well suppressed, but shakes men badly when it is revealed." Here, as elsewhere, Maria's language becomes overtly anti-feminist: "But I don't want to join the Political Maenads, the Women's Lib sisterhood; I avoid them just as Parlabane said he avoided the Political Gays; they make a public cause of something too deep, too important, for political, group action" (*Rebel*, pp. 76-77). This rhetoric is escapist. Relegating ideologically constructed social inequities to the realm of private experience denies any possibility of eradicating injustices through political action and leaves the elite few free to ignore the human suffering that supports their privileged status.

In "A Cycle Completed: The Nine Novels of Robertson Davies," George Woodcock emphasizes the fundamental conservatism of Davies' fictions, and suggests that it is their conservatism that makes these works so popular. Woodcock suggests that readers disturbed by "the nihilism of much modern art and literature" find Davies' orderly fictional world comforting:

> They need reassurance, and the novels of Robertson Davies, which present no real formal challenges, and whose essential optimism is shown in upbeat endings, with quests completed, wishes ful-

filled, evil routed, and villains destroyed, are admirably suited for the calming and comforting of uneasy Canadians. They exist on the edge of popular fiction, where Pangloss reigns in the best of possible worlds.[18]

While Woodcock appears to find nothing disturbing about Davies' conservative texts, he does remark that some critics have found Davies' conservatism "offensive to their ideas of what Canadians should be expecting of their writers."[19] Woodcock acknowledges the ideological conservatism of Davies' fiction, but he focuses primarily on the novels' formal qualities. Much criticism of Davies' fiction, however, treats his texts as serious novels of ideas from which we have a great deal to learn. In "Davies, His Critics, and the Canadian Canon," Anthony B. Dawson suggests that critics have been seduced into over-valuing *Fifth Business*, which "has proved to be a mecca for critics. Canadian literature has at last been blessed with a puzzle, a seemingly unbounded web of magian intricacies and mythological allusions, which unwary critics have wandered into, like flies into the spider's parlour. And, of course, they (we) have done so in response to Davies' arachnidian invitation."[20] The Cornish Trilogy, like the Deptford books, offers the reader clues to complex puzzles which may deflect critical attention away from the texts' ideological implications. Instead of examining the ideas Davies presents, one is tempted, as Dawson says, to "pursue allusions and intricacies beyond the text or chase them around within it."[21] This narrative strategy of presenting puzzles and offering enticing clues to their solution is a way of imposing authority in Davies' work. As readers and critics we may choose to participate in the game Davies' novels construct for us or to resist his texts' blandishments.

The critical response to Davies' work has been largely positive, but some dissenting voices have made themselves heard. The extent to which critical views of Davies' fiction may vary is dramatically demonstrated by a comparison of two scholarly reviews of *The Rebel Angels*. Susan Stone-Blackburn, in "Robertson Davies, Rebel Angel," strongly endorses the message of this text:

> The growth of the inner man is the enrichment of the novelist, and *The Rebel Angels* contains the added depths of Davies' most mature insights into problems of human growth. Professors can be grateful that Davies did not write his university novel until his humanist's

perceptions became as compelling as his humourist's observations. This is a book we might well choose to present to our most pragmatic politicians; if there is any possibility at all of changing their views on universities, *The Rebel Angels* could be the means. If it is heresy—or just naiveté—to think of using such a work of literature as a social tool, then we can simply be grateful that Davies is a rebel angel whose ideal of vital richness and originality in individual life and in university life is expressed in a vitally rich and original novel.[22]

In contrast, Diana Brydon, whose review is entitled "A Dangerous Book," argues that *The Rebel Angels* is "insidiously dangerous...because it encourages complacency and snobbery, disguising them as wisdom." She remarks that "the 'wisdom' [Davies] advocates would return us to the values of the middle ages." She also comments on the serious issues the novel raises and their implications for the contemporary university:

> The novel pretends to engage problems of deep human significance. How may we learn from the past? What is the role of the university and its scholars in our society? What can repressed areas of experience teach us? How can we distinguish wisdom from knowledge? How should we live? Raising these questions might have been a service in itself if Davies were not so quick and pat with the answers. Because he is, some readers may leave *The Rebel Angels* satisfied. Not me.[23]

Unlike George Woodcock, I cannot regard the conservative message of Davies' work with equanimity. Certainly I can not join Susan Stone-Blackburn in embracing Davies' idea of wisdom or his view of the life of the university. Like Diana Brydon, I consider the "unified view of life" that Davies advocates in the Cornish Trilogy, and in his fiction as a whole, to be dangerous. These texts preach a doctrine of absolute acceptance of arbitrary authority. They carefully manipulate narrative voice and offer intriguing puzzles, clever witticisms and snippets of arcane information in order to engage us in constructing their meaning, and to win, through our participation in the narrative process, our assent to their elitist ideology. Such texts need to be read in a manner which resists their spurious invitation to be counted among the exclusive inner circle of the aristocracy of the spirit.

# Notes

1 Robertson Davies, *The Rebel Angels* (Markham: Penguin, 1983), pp. 239-40. All subsequent references to the text are to this edition.

2 Robertson Davies, *The Lyre of Orpheus* (Markham: Penguin, 1988), pp. 340-41. All subsequent references to the text are to this edition.

3 Stephen Bonnycastle, "Robertson Davies and the Ethics of Monologue," *Journal of Canadian Studies*, 12, No. 1 (1977), p. 34.

4 *Ibid.*, p. 20.

5 *Ibid.*, p. 38.

6 *Ibid.*, p. 39.

7 Barbara Godard, "World of Wonders: Robertson Davies' Carnival," *Essays on Canadian Writing*, 30 (Winter 1984-85), p. 241.

8 Barbara Godard, "Robertson Davies' Dialogic Imagination," *Essays on Canadian Writing*, 34 (Spring 1987), p. 75.

9 *Ibid.*, p. 70.

10 Robert Cluett, "Robertson Davies: The Tory Mode," *Journal of Canadian Studies*, 12, No. 1 (1977), p. 41-42.

11 Robert Cluett, "Victoria Rediviva: Robertson Davies in the First Person," *Canadian Literary Prose: A Preliminary Stylistic Analysis* (Toronto: ECW Press, 1990), pp. 109-10.

12 Mikhail M. Bakhtin, *The Dialogic Imagination: Four Essays*. Trans. Caryl Emerson and Michael Holquist, ed. Michael Holquist (Austin: University of Texas Press, 1981), p. 263.

13 Godard, "Robertson Davies' Dialogic Imagination," pp. 77-78.

14 Bonnycastle, p. 25.

15 Robertson Davies, *What's Bred in the Bone* (Markham: Penguin, 1985), p. 459. All subsequent references to the text are to this edition.

16 Bakhtin, p. 31.

17 *Ibid.*, p. 23.

18 George Woodcock, "A Cycle Completed: The Nine Levels of Robertson Davies," *Canadian Literature,* 126 (1990), p. 48.

19 *Ibid.*

20 Anthony B. Dawson, "Davies, His Critics, and the Canadian Canon," *Canadian Literature*, 92 (1982), p. 155.

21 *Ibid.*

22 Susan Stone-Blackburn, "Robertson Davies, Rebel Angel," *Essays on Canadian Writing*, 28 (1984), p. 100.

23 Diana Brydon, "A Dangerous Book," *Canadian Literature*, 97 (1983), pp. 116-18.

# Contributors

*Elisabeth Sifton* is now an editor with Alfred A. Knopf Inc. in New York.

*Timothy Findley*'s works of fiction include *The Wars*, *The Telling of Lies*, and *Dinner Along the Amazon*.

*John Kenneth Galbraith* has published over 20 books during the past 40 years, including *The Affluent Society*, *The New Industrial State* and *Economics in Perspective*.

*Herbert Whittaker* was for many years the drama critic at *The Globe and Mail* in Toronto.

*Martin Hunter*, a former Artistic Director at Hart House Theatre in Toronto, is the author of many plays and of a large body of journalism.

*Hugo McPherson*, a former Chairman of the National Film Board, has written extensively both as a journalist and as an academic.

*Gordon Roper*, a professor of English at Trent University in Peterborough, has written widely on Canadian literature.

*Wilfred Cude* has lectured and written widely on Canadian literature at several Canadian universities and currently teaches at St. Francis Xavier University; he is the author of *The PhD. Trap* and *A Due Sense of Differences*.

*Patricia Monk*, author of *Introducing Robertson Davies' Fifth Business*, is a professor of English at Dalhousie University in Halifax.

*James Neufeld*, professor of English and Vice President (University Services) at Trent University, has written extensively on Canadian literature.

*Stephen Bonnycastle*, a professor of English at the Royal Military College in Kingston, is the author of *In Search of Authority: An Introductory Guide to Literary Theory*.

*Joyce Carol Oates*, author of over 25 novels and collections of short stories (most recently *Because it is Bitter and Because it is My Heart*), currently teaches in the Creative Writing Program at Princeton University.

*Clara Thomas* is a professor in the English Department and a Canadian Studies Research Fellow at York University in Toronto; she is the author of several works on Canadian literature, including *The Manawaka World of Margaret Laurence*.

*W.J. Keith* has been for many years a professor in the English Department of the University of Toronto. His most recent book is *A Sense of Style: Studies in the Art of Fiction in English Canada*.

*Richard Plant* teaches at Queen's University in Kingston; he is the editor of *The Penguin Book of Modern Canadian Drama*.

*Barbara Godard*, a professor of English at York University, is the author of several works on Canadian literature, including *Audrey Thomas and Her Works*.

*Ian Munro* was an undergraduate student at the University of the British Columbia when he wrote the piece that appears in revised form in this book; since then he has been pursuing graduate study in Canadian and Commonwealth literature at Harvard University.

*Linda Lamont-Stewart*, a specialist in Canadian literature, teaches at York University in Toronto.

# Acknowledgements

**Interview with Robertson Davies** copyright © 1986 *The Paris Review*. Reprinted with permission.

**Robertson Davies** copyright © Timothy Findley.

**The World of Wonders of Robertson Davies** copyright © 1982 The New York Times Company. Reprinted by permission.

**Rob Davies: Pioneer Playwright** copyright © Herbert Whittaker. Reprinted by permission.

**Magister Ludi: The Mask of Robertson Davies** copyright © Martin Hunter. Reprinted by permission.

**The Mask of Satire: Character and Symbolic Pattern in Robertson Davies' Fiction** copyright © 1960 Hugo McPherson, first published in *Canadian Literature* (Spring, 1960). Reprinted by permission.

**Robertson Davies *Fifth Business* and "That Old Fantastical Duke of Dark Corners, C.G. Jung"** copyright © 1978 Gordon Roper. This version first published in *The Canadian Novel Here and Now: A Critical Anthology* edited by John Moss (Toronto: NC Press, 1978).

**Miracle and Art in *Fifth Business* or Who the Devil is Liselotte Vitzlipüzli?** copyright © 1977 *Journal of Canadian Studies*. Reprinted by permission.

**Confessions of a Sorcerer's Apprentice: *World of Wonders* and the Deptford Trilogy of Robertson Davies** copyright © 1976 Patricia Monk. Originally published in *Dalhousie Review* (Summer, 1976). Reprinted by permission of the author.

**Structural Unity in the Deptford Trilogy: Robertson Davies as Egoist** copyright © 1977 *Journal of Canadian Studies*. Reprinted by permission.

**Robertson Davies and the Ethics of Monologue** copyright © 1977 *Journal of Canadian Studies*. Reprinted by permission.

**One Half of Robertson Davies** by Robertson Davies copyright © 1978 Joyce Carol Oates. Originally published in *The New Republic* (April 15, 1978).

**The Two Voices of** *A Mixture of Frailties* copyright © 1977 *Journal of Canadian Studies*. Reprinted by permission.

*A Mixture of Frailties* **and "Romance"** copyright © 1990 W.J. Keith. Reprinted by permission.

**Cultural Redemption in the Work of Robertson Davies** copyright © 1981 Richard Plant. Originally published in *Canadian Drama*, 1981. Reprinted by permission of the author.

**Writing Paradox, the Paradox of Writing: Robertson Davies** originally published in *Essays on Canadian Writing* as "World of Wonders: Robertson Davies' Carnival" (Winter 1984/85) and "Robertson Davies' Dialogic Imagination" (Spring 1987). Reprinted by permission of the Canadian Literary Research Foundation.

**The Liar of Orpheus: Framing Devices and Narrative Structure in Robertson D** ... © 1991 Ian Munro. Reprinted by

**Robertson Davi** ... itique of the Corn ... ewart. Reprinted by